THE REICH
INTRUDERS

Other books by Martin W. Bowman:

Fields of Little America
The Encyclopaedia of American Military Aircraft
The B-24 Liberator 1939–45
Castles in the Air
Home by Christmas?
The Bedford Triangle
Wellington: The Geodetic Giant
The World's Fastest Aircraft
Famous Bombers
Classic Fighter Aircraft
Modern Military Aircraft
Flying to Glory
Spirits in the Sky (with Patrick Bunce)
Four Miles High
Great American Air Battles 1942–1992
Eighth Air Force at War
Thunder in the Heavens (with Patrick Bunce)
The Men who Flew the Mosquito
The USAF at War
Low Level from Swanton
Confounding the Reich (with Tom Cushing)
Raiders of the Reich (with Theo Boiten)
The Royal Air Force at War
The USAAF Handbook 1939–45
Stearman: An Illustrated History (with Jim Avis)

As part of our ongoing market research, we are always pleased to receive comments about our books, suggestions for new titles, or requests for catalogues. Please write to: The Editorial Director, Patrick Stephens Limited, Sparkford, near Yeovil, Somerset BA22 7JJ.

THE REICH INTRUDERS

Dramatic RAF medium bomber raids over Europe in World War 2

MARTIN W BOWMAN

Patrick Stephens Limited

First published in 1997

British Library Cataloguing-in-Publication Data

A catalogue record for this book is available
from the British Library

ISBN 1 85260 539 1

Library of Congress catalog card no. 97-70204

Haynes Publications Inc.,
861 Lawrence Drive, Newbury Park,
California 91320, USA.

Patrick Stephens Limited is an imprint of
Haynes Publishing, Sparkford, Nr Yeovil,
Somerset BA22 7JJ.

Designed & typeset by
G&M, Raunds, Northamptonshire
Printed and bound in Great Britain by
Butler & Tanner Ltd, London and Frome

Contents

Acknowledgements

I must first single out Jim 'Dinty' Moore and John Bateman, both RAF Retd, both of whom graciously made available their precious squadron albums and photos on more than one occasion; Mike Bailey, for his guidance, proofing and loan of photos and reference books; Bob Collis, for his invaluable input of research material and advice; Paul McCue, England, Dr Theo Boiten, Holland, and Eric Mombeek, Belgium, Les Bulmer, RAF Retd; Jan Kloos in Switzerland; Julian Horn and Paul Lincoln of the Wartime Watton Museum; Ole Rønnest in Denmark; and last but by no means least, Sister Laurence Mary; all of whom filled many gaps with valuable photos and material.

All pictures are captioned from the left unless otherwise stated.

I am no less indebted to the following: Steve Adams; Arthur Asker; Eric Atkins DFC* Krzyz Walecznych*, Chairman, Mosquito Aircrew Assoc; Gerald Baker; Jack Bartley; the late Gordon Bell-Irving; The Rt Hon Tony Benn MP; Philip J. Birtles, Chairman, Mosquito Museum; Leslie Bond; Roy J. A. Brookes JP, Chairman, 88 Sqdn Assoc; Nigel Buswell; Arthur Butterworth; S/L Ray Chance; Wilf Clutton; W. G. 'Bill' Cooper, 137/139 All Ranks Assoc; Bill Corfield; Tom Cushing; S/L Mike Daniels RAF Retd; Rene Deeks; Reg Everson; John Foreman; Bob Gallup; Rev Nigel L. Gilson; Ken Godfrey; Ted Gorman; Peter B. Gunn; Hans de Haan; Nicholas Heffer; Carl Heinz Jeissman; Bernard M. Job; Jack Lub; Jock MacDonald; Peter Mallinson; S/L Hugh Milroy RAF; Norma Moore; W. J. Morris; Aubrey Niner; Simon Parry; Jack and Freddie Peppiatt; Chief Tech Steve Pope RAF; Tony Rudd; Peter Saunders; Steve Snelling, EDP, Norwich; Jerry Scutts; Mrs Vera Sherring; A. M. J. Smith; Steve Smith; Adam Szajdzicki; Herbert E. Tappin; G/C Bill Taylor; Andy Thomas; 'Slim' Trew; Colin 'Ginger' Walsh; Colin Waugh; and Tony Wilson.

Finally, my thanks to Graham Holmes for his excellent design, and to the PSL editorial team for their patience and professionalism.

Martin Bowman
Norwich, 1997

Primary sources:

Aalborg 13 August 1940 by Ole Rønnest

The Aalborg Attack, Paul Lincoln (After the Battle, No 72)

A-20 Boston At War, William N. Hess (Ian Allan Ltd, 1979)

A War Record, John Bateman (unpublished)

Air Gunner, Mike Henry DFC (G. T. Foulis & Co Ltd, 1964)

Bomber Squadrons of the RAF & Their Aircraft, Philip Moyes (MacDonald, 1964)

Bombers of WW2, Vol 2, Philip J. R. Moyes (Hylton Lacy, 1968)

Churchill's Light Cavalry (2 Vols), Jim Moore (unpublished)

Defending The Reich: The History of JG1, Eric Mombeek (JAC Publications, 1992)

Dunsfold: Surrey's Most Secret Airfield, Paul McCue (Air Research Publications, 1992)

Fighter Squadrons of the RAF & Their Aircraft, John D. R. Rawlings (MacDonald, 1969)

Lorraine Squadron, Paul Lambermont (Cassell & Co Ltd, 1956)

Low Level From Swanton, Martin W. Bowman (Air Research Publications, 1995)

Mosquito, C. Martin Sharp & Michael J. F. Bowyer (Faber & Faber, 1967)

Mosquito Squadrons of the Royal Air Force, Chaz Bowyer (Ian Allan Ltd, 1984)

2 Group RAF: A Complete History 1936–1945, Michael J. F. Bowyer (Faber & Faber, 1974)

2nd Tactical Air Force, Christopher F. Shores (Osprey, 1970)

The Men who Flew the Mosquito, Martin W. Bowman (PSL, 1995)

RAF Great Massingham:A Norfolk Airfield at War 1940–1945, Peter B. Gunn (1990)

320 Squadron RAF Memorial 1940–1945, Jan P. Kloos (1987)

RAF Marham, Ken Delve (PSL, 1995)

We Shall Be There: A History of 107 Squadron, 1918–1963, Arthur Butterworth (1990)

Sgt Peter K. Eames, WOP/AG; P/O Donald M. Wellings, pilot, and Sgt Don A. W. McFarlane, observer, are all smiles for the camera in front of UX-N of 'B' Flight, 82 Squadron at Bodney, satellite of RAF Watton, Norfolk, in the summer of 1940. The crew were plucked from the jaws of death on 13 August, when, at the 11th hour, they were pulled out of the 12-ship formation while taxiing out, to be told that they were posted. P/O E. R. Hale, Sgt R. G. Oliver and Sgt A. E. Boland, who took their place, were one of the 11 crews who failed to return from the catastrophic operation to Aalborg, Denmark. F/Sgt Eames DFM was KIA, 26.4.41 and P/O Wellings DFC was killed in 1944. F/L McFarlane DFM retired from the RAF in 1947. (via Theo Boiten)

Glossary

AC2	Aircraftsman 2nd Class	
AI	Airborne Interception (radar)	
AM	Air Marshal	
AOC	Air Officer Commanding	
ASH	AI Mk XV radar	
ASR	Air Sea Rescue	
AVM	Air Vice Marshal	
Bordfunker	German wireless operator	
Circus	Usually a formation of medium bombers heavily escorted by fighters with the primary object of drawing the enemy fighters into combat	
DFC	Distinguished Flying Cross	
DFM	Distinguished Flying Medal	
Diver	V1 operation	
Düppel	German code name for *Window*	
DSO	Distinguished Service Order	
F/L	Flight Lieutenant	
F/O	Flying Officer	
F/Sgt	Flight Sergeant	
Fähnrich	(Fhr) Flight Sergeant	
Feldwebel	(Fw) Sergeant	
Flower	British low-level night intruder patrol of German airfields	
Freelance	Patrol with the object of picking up a chance contact or visual of the enemy	
Freshman	1st operation by new crew	
G/C	Group Captain	
Gee	British navigational device	
Hauptmann	Flight Lieutenant	
H2S	British 10 cm experimental radar	
IFF	Identification Friend or Foe	
Instep	Patrol seeking enemy air activity in Bay of Biscay	
Intruder	Offensive operation to fixed point or specified target	
JG	Jagdgeschwader	
LAC	Leading Aircraftsman	
Leutnant	(Lt) Pilot Officer	
Mahmoud	High-level bomber support sortie	
Major	(German) Squadron Leader	
Oberfaehnrich	Warrant Officer	
Oberfeldwebel	(Ofw) Flight Sergeant	
Oberleutnant	(Oblt) Flying Officer	
Oberst	(Obst) Group Captain	
Oberstleutnant	(Obstlt) Wing Commander	
Oboe	British ground controlled radar system of blind bombing	
Op	Operation	
OTU	Operational Training Unit	
Outstep	Patrol seeking enemy air activity off Norway	
P/O	Pilot Officer	
R/T	Radio Telephony	
Ramrod	*Circus* but with US aircraft also involved	
Ranger	Operation to engage air and ground targets within a wide but specified area	
Rhubarb	Low-level daylight fighter sweep	
S/L	Squadron Leader	
Unteroffizier	(Uffz) Corporal	
Vic	Formation of three aircraft	
W/C	Wing Commander	
W/O	Warrant Officer	
WOP/AG	Wireless Operator/Air Gunner	
W/T	Wireless telegraphy	

Chapter One

Full Cry

'Out of England, over France,
Three by three, in swift advance,
Eager as at the first cock-crow,
Let the hunting Blenheims go!'

'Full Cry' by F/L Anthony Richardson RAFVR, Adjutant, 107 Squadron

'There is quite a panic on here. We are going away today to WATTON. About 20 miles from Norwich. The reports of the place are not so hot. Will write soon as we get settled down now. Cheerio. We are off in about 1 hour. With love . . .'

So wrote 18-year-old LAC Freddie Thripp, of 82 Squadron, in an urgent postcard home in August 1939. His squadron was one of ten in 2 (Bomber) Group, which had been formed on 20 March 1936. Now, in August 1939, war with Germany, which had been avoided at Munich in 1938, loomed large and 2 Group would be in the front line, long before a large part of the rest of Britain's armed forces.

With headquarters at Wyton, Cambridgeshire, 2 Group numbered five wings, with 70 Wing at Upper Heyford controlling 18 and 57 Squadrons; 79 Wing at Watton, 21 and 82 Squadrons; 81 Wing at West Raynham, Norfolk, 90 and 101 Squadrons; 82 Wing at Wyton, 114 and 139 Squadrons; and 83 Wing at Wattisham, 107 and 110 Squadrons. All 2 Group squadrons were

Blenheim I aircraft of 21 Squadron at RAF Watton in June 1939. (Wartime Watton Museum)

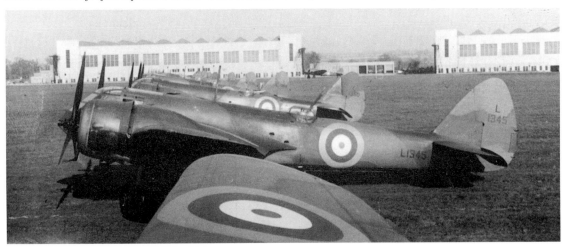

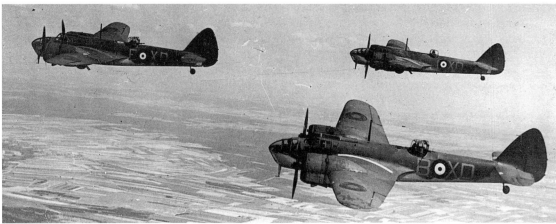

Top *A 139 Squadron Blenheim IV during the Battle of France, 1940.* (IWM)

Above *139 Squadron Blenheim IVs over France in 1940.* (IWM)

Below *Blenheim IV YH-D of 21 Squadron pictured at Watton at the outbreak of war.* (Wartime Watton Museum)

equipped with the twin-engined Bristol Blenheim I or IV (21, 18 and 57 Squadrons were still in the process of converting to the IV). Britain and her Allies were, however, ill-equipped to prevent a repetition of the fate that had already befallen Poland.

Nos 79, 81, 82 and 83 Wings formed the 2nd echelon of the Advanced Air Striking Force, and 70 Wing was earmarked for service in France supporting the BEF along with squadrons of obsolete single-engined Fairey Battles. The Battle and Blenheim monoplane bombers were a vast improvement on the Hind biplane bombers that had equipped 2 Group in the mid-1930s, but the Air Ministry seemed to have little conception of modern fighter tactics.

A Blenheim cost £20,000 and, sadly, was about to be exposed as an expensive machine, in terms of lives spent for little offensive reward (it could only carry 1,000 lb bombs internally). Apart from a fixed forward firing gun in the wing operated by the pilot, and another under the nose, there was a rather ancient Vickers Gas Operated .303 machine gun in a dorsal turret, which was fed from circular ammunition pans, each of which contained 100 rounds. Spare pans were clipped on to the side of the turret. The crew of three comprised pilot (an Officer or F/Sgt), observer (normally a senior NCO), and upper gunner, (usually an Aircraftsman 1st or 2nd Class, Leading Aircraftsman or Corporal). Blenheim gunner AC1 Jack Bartley recalls:

'The pilot, navigator and the air-gunner lived in three entirely separate social worlds. The only time the SNCOs and the officers met was once a month on invitation to the opposite mess. The airmen only met the officers at the annual airmen's Xmas dinner when the officers traditionally served the meal. The SNCOs and officers enjoyed a high standard of living in their respective messes, while the Wireless Operators/Air Gunners lived in barrack rooms together with the lowest ACHs who might have cleaned the toilets. Even when waiting for take-off during a stand-by we would be in separate crew rooms in the hangar.

Prior to June 1940 (when all operational aircrew below the rank were promoted to Sergeant), WOP/AGs were "other ranks" (AC2, AC1, LAC and Corporal) and as such were subject to normal station duties including guards, which could mean you were flying by day sitting behind a machine gun, and slinging a rifle for 4-hour spells patrolling the dispersed aircraft through the icy nights that the 1939/40 winter produced. The one privilege we

The early Blenheims carried a rather ancient Vickers Gas Operated .303 machine gun in a dorsal turret, which was fed from circular ammunition pans, each of which contained 100 rounds. Spare pans were clipped on to the side of the turret. Initially the upper gunner was usually a lowly Aircraftsman 1st or 2nd Class, Leading Aircraftsman or Corporal. The rank depended on his trade rank as a wireless operator. (IWM)

A Blenheim IV of 82 Squadron at RAF Watton, Norfolk, in the winter of 1939–40. (Wartime Watton Museum)

enjoyed apart from the princely sum of an additional shilling per day flying pay plus sixpence a day for the Flying Bullet Air Gunner badge, was a monthly two-day leave pass.'

New recruits were blissfully unaware of all this. On Monday 28 August 1939, having been advised to report to the Recruiting Depot at Bradford, Yorkshire, 19-year-old Jim Moore caught the train from his home in Hawes at the head of Wensleydale and set off on the first leg of a journey that would last six years and five months. During the summer of 1939 he had been accepted as a wireless operator. AC2 Moore's

Pilots of 21 Squadron pose for the camera in Hangar No 1 at RAF Watton. Seventh from the right is P/O Ian Stapledon, KIA 6 April 1940. (Wartime Watton Museum)

feelings were a mixture of excitement and apprehension, and he certainly had no idea that within 12 months he would be flying over Western Europe as a member of the crew of a Bristol Blenheim. He was at Padgate, a training establishment on the outskirts of Warrington, when on Sunday morning, 3 September, the radio in his hut was switched on and instead of the normal programmes serious music was being played. 'Dinty' Moore recalls:

'It was then solemnly announced that the nation was to be addressed by the Prime Minister, Neville Chamberlain. His address began, "This morning the British Ambassador to Berlin handed the German Government a final note saying that unless we hear from them by 11 o'clock that they were prepared, at once, to withdraw their troops from Poland, a state of war would exist between us. I have to tell you that no such undertaking had been received and that, consequently, this country is at war with Germany".

The remainder of his speech was drowned by cheers and excited conversation for, it must be remembered, we were all youngsters who were actually excited at the prospect of being at war with our old enemy. Considering that the last war, the war to end all wars, had ended only 20 years earlier with an appalling loss of life, we should have had a clearer idea of the reality of war. I suppose those who were actually involved were reluctant to talk of their experiences, and our attitude had been influenced by books recording the heroics.'

At the time of Chamberlain's historic broadcast, a Blenheim IV of 139 Squadron, piloted by F/O Andrew McPherson (KIA 12 May 1940), was preparing to take off from Wyton. His crew was Commander Thompson RN, acting as observer, and his WOP/AG Cpl V. Arrowsmith (KIA 24 Sept 1940). A minute later they were airborne heading out over the North Sea to reconnoitre the German Battle Fleet at Wilhelmshaven. As they gradually gained height through haze and a freezing mist, which caused the camera and the radio to freeze up, they must have had doubts as to whether they would be able to see their objectives. On reaching 24,000 feet they flew on to Wilhelmshaven, where Commander Thompson was able to sketch details of the location of the enemy fleet. Finally, after the first operational flight of the war, which had lasted 5

hours 50 minutes, they landed safely back at Wyton.

The following day, 4 September, despite appalling weather conditions, McPherson and his crew again took off to repeat their recce mission. On this occasion, due to the weather, he was forced to fly under the cloud at a height of about 250 feet. This time the camera was operational and they returned, after a flight of some 4 hours, with the desired photographs.

Awaiting McPherson's return were 15 Blenheim crews, five each from 107, 110 and 139 Squadrons, and ten Wellingtons. They had been briefed to attack ships of the German fleet in the Schillig Roads and nothing else. Further, their approach to the target must be made from over the land in order to avoid the possibility of any civilian casualties.

Without waiting for the result of McPherson's second reconnaissance to be evaluated, the three formations of five aircraft took off independently on the first bombing raid of the war. They flew across the North Sea through blinding rainstorms but, miraculously, the Blenheims of 110 Squadron, led by F/L Kenneth Doran, made their intended landfall at Heligoland before changing course for their target. On approaching their quarry the cloud base had lifted to some 500 feet when a cargo ship came into view and just beyond it the battleship *Admiral Scheer*. The Kriegsmarine was obviously quite unprepared for the assault – the aircrews reported seeing washing hung out to dry – so Doran led his formation straight into the attack. Three hits were claimed on the battleship, although it is now known that they failed to explode. Their attack brought no reaction and they flew off unscathed, although one Blenheim failed to return to base, becoming the first RAF casualties of the war.

The five aircraft of 107 Squadron, led by F/L W. F. Barton, arrived over the target some 10 minutes later to find the enemy very much alert, their gunners throwing up a murderous curtain of flak through which the Blenheims had to fly. One Blenheim crashed on to the cruiser *Emden*, causing some damage but losing its entire crew, while another three Blenheims were shot down, the only survivors being F/O W. J. Stephens and his crew, who became lost in the low cloud and rain, and never found the target. Some bombs bounced off the armour plating, while others exploded on the ships, and may have accounted for the loss of at least one of the Blenheims. First-hand information on the raid was later learned by an escaping PoW in a train compartment in northern Italy, who overheard a sailor talking to his companion, remarking on the gallantry of the aircraft crews and impressed by the close attack of the aircraft. He also told how he saw one of the aircraft blown to pieces by the blast of a bomb burst.

Only one crew of the Blenheims shot down lived to tell the tale, although the pilot, Sgt A. S. Prince of 107 Squadron, died from his wounds five days later. The observer, Sgt George Booth, and the WOP/AG, AC2 Larrie Slattery, had the dubious distinction of becoming the first prisoners of war in this conflict.

The third squadron, 139, perhaps fortuitously but understandably in view of the weather conditions, failed to find the target and returned home carrying their bombs. This was indeed a disastrous start to the war, with the loss of five of the ten aircraft that had found and attacked the target.

W/C Haylock, who had taken over command of 107 Squadron in April 1939, was posted within a few days, and there arrived at Wattisham on 15 September W/C Basil E. Embry DSO AFC. He was described by aircrew as a 'little ball of fire', just the type of leader who was needed to instill urgency into what so far was almost a non-event, with neither side anxious to provoke the other. As far as the Germans were concerned, these conditions suited them, as they were content to carry on preparing and planning for the Blitzkrieg that they were now about to unleash with such staggering success. The Allies, on the other hand, would not allow themselves to believe that the war would ever really start in earnest. Leaders like Chamberlain seemed to believe that his appeals to the German people for peace would be accepted. The period became known as the 'Phoney War', when little aggressive action was taken by either side in the conflict.

AC1 D. M. Merrett, an armourer in 107 Squadron at the time, wrote:

'For us the "Phoney War" never existed, due in large part to Embry's terrific drive. He realised right from the start that the war would have to be pursued relentlessly, and within his powers as a squadron commander he ensured that this was done. "Battle Orders" were issued almost daily, and the squadron was constantly on operations, although this did not invariably result in bombs being dropped, because targets were not always reached or located. This increased the armourer's work, for aircraft returning with bombs had to be de-bombed, and there was considerable changing of bomb loads as different targets were selected by 2 Group.

The meagre armament of the Blenheim left a large blind spot when attacked from below and astern. Embry demanded a quick remedy of his Engineer Officer, F/O Edwards. Working together, Maintenance Flight and Armament Section provided a solution. Aft of each engine in the nacelle was found sufficient space to accommodate a rearward-firing .303-inch Browning gun and ammunition box. Each gun protruded through a hole cut in the nacelle, and was fired by a fantastic length of Bowden cable, leading to a huge firing lever mounted in the dorsal gun turret.

In addition, a Vickers Gas Operated (VGO) gun was inverted and fitted into the stern frame aft of the tail wheel, with a further Bowden cable running up to the fuselage lever. This gun was very exposed, and immediately before take-off the armourer would secure a magazine to it. As this was in the pre-runway era, when conditions were wet the tail wheel lathered the gun and magazine with mud during take-off, to the detriment of both, so the scheme, though welcome, was not an unqualified success. The Brownings were successful, however, and may have saved several aircraft, but it was never possible to equip the whole squadron.

Increasing armament did not rest there, for the same team perfected a twin .303-inch Browning gun installation to replace the single VGO in the turret, and this was officially adapted for all Blenheim IVs. Forward of the nose, the escape hatch position was used to add first a single then twin underslung rearward-firing .303-inch Brownings, fired by the observer, and jettisoned if use of the escape hatch became necessary. The bomb doors were not hydraulically operated – they merely flew open when the weight of a bomb fell on them and were returned to the closed position by bungy cords. When 4 lb incendiaries were required, the doors were removed altogether.

Of Embry, well, he expected everyone to match his

Blenheim IVs of 82 Squadron at RAF Watton photographed by Sgt 'Bish' Bareham from the Watton Watch office. P6915 UX-A (which has one of the first rearward-firing nose guns) was shot down on 7 June 1940. Note the asphalt applied to the grass behind the Blenheims to simulate hedges. (Wartime Watton Museum)

own fierce energy and enthusiasm, a tall order. He commanded the greatest respect and admiration, but not, in my view at least, affection.'

Embry led 12 Blenheims on 27 March, when he sighted a German cruiser and four destroyers about 70 miles NNW of the Hrons Reef in the Heligoland Bight. The formation followed the ships, and 4 minutes later sighted most of the German Fleet on its way to support the invasion of Norway. An attack was made out of the sun, engaging the *Scharnhorst* and *Gneisenau*, and a message was sent giving the position and course of the Fleet. Because of poor communications, this information only reached the authorities when the aircraft landed back at Wattisham some hours later.

On 9 April Norway was invaded by the Germans, and on the 14th, in response to a request from the Norwegian Government for military assistance, an advance party of an Allied Expeditionary force was landed at Narvik in north-western Norway. The problems facing the bombers of the RAF in giving much-needed support were to an extent overcome by placing two Blenheim squadrons, 110 and 107, on temporary detachment to RAF Lossiemouth, from where they could attack shipping and the German-held airfield at Stavanger in southern Norway. On 17 April Stavanger was attacked from low level by 12 of 107 Squadron's Blenheims, their bombs causing a great deal of damage to enemy aircraft on the ground. A fierce firefight developed when they were attacked by a number of German fighters, a combat that lasted for some 65 minutes and from which two Blenheims and their crews failed to return.

Another of these sorties took place in the late afternoon of 30 April when six Blenheims of 110 Squadron led by Kenneth Doran, now a S/L, attacked enemy shipping. They, in their turn, were descended upon by a host of Bf 109s, which shot down two of the Blenheims. One of those lost was piloted by F/Sgt R. Abbott, while the other was flown by Doran, who became a PoW. During this short campaign seven Blenheims and their crews were lost before the two squadrons returned to their bases in East Anglia.

On 10 May the 'Phoney War' ended. In the early hours German troops crossed the frontiers of Holland and Belgium in force, supported by paratroops, glider-borne troops and hordes of bombers and fighters. Everyone listened anxiously to the radio to try and keep in touch with events, which were to change with astonishing rapidity. Reserves were posted to France to reinforce the squadrons; the medium bomber squadrons there comprised six squadrons of Blenheim IVs and eight squadrons of Fairey Battles, supported by seven Blenheim squadrons, 40, 15, 82, 21, 101, 107 and 110, in East Anglia.

The Battles went into action within an hour of being given authority to do so by the French High Command, but their losses were high (23 Battles were shot down during the day) and would remain so throughout the short campaign. Meanwhile, at 0905 hours on the morning of 10 May the first of several operations was carried out by two Blenheims of 40 Squadron at Wyton, with S/L Paddon and F/O Burns reconnoitring the Dutch German border. Burns crash-landed after being hit by flak, and he and his crew were made PoW. Paddon's aircraft, while damaged, made it back to Wyton with one engine smoking. At noon nine Blenheims of 15 Squadron, also from Wyton, bombed Waalhaven amid heavy flak, and while several Blenheims were damaged, they all returned safely.

During the afternoon 40 Squadron sent 12 crews to attack Wypenburg airfield near The Hague. F/L R. H. Batt (KIA 9 July 1940) led the first of the attacks and dropped his bombs without reply, but once the defences were alerted the other vics did not fare so well. Three Blenheims were shot down by flak and F/L Smeddie's machine returned badly damaged and with the crew suffering injuries.

The next day, 11 May, German armour and motorised infantry were pouring across the River Meuse at Maastricht, where the bridges over the Albert Canal were still intact. The Belgian High Command considered the destruction of these bridges to be vital and at first light Blenheims of 114 Squadron based at Conde Vraux near

Soissons were briefed to bomb them. The aircraft were lined up on the airfield and the crews were ready to take off when nine Dornier 17s surprised them, making first a bombing then a strafing run, destroying the squadron in 45 seconds flat. After the Fairey Battles and the Armée de l'Air had failed to destroy the bridges, one further attack was carried out that evening by 12 Blenheims of 21 Squadron from Wyton. They approached the target at 3,000 feet in the face of a tremendous flak barrage and heavy fighter opposition. Four Blenheims were shot down and the rest were damaged.

On 12 May nine Blenheims of 139 Squadron at Plivot tried once more to destroy the bridges, but they were attacked en route to the target by 50 Bf 109s, which shot down seven of the bombers. Meanwhile 12 Blenheims of 107 Squadron led by W/C Embry took off from Wattisham at 0810 hours and headed for the bridges, which would be bombed from 6,000 feet, a height that Embry considered would be the most effective. Fifteen miles before the target the Blenheims too were fired at by anti-aircraft fire, which continued all the way to the target. However, despite this they flew on and dropped their bombs. One of the bridges was damaged, but the Blenheim piloted by P/O S. G. Thornton was shot down and every other aircraft was damaged during the run-in. Then the Bf 109s attacked, shooting down three of the remaining Blenheims; the eight survivors, though severely damaged, managed to make it back to Wattisham.

An attack by six Fairey Battles of 12 Squadron later that morning resulted in all the attacking aircraft being shot down, and 12 Blenheims of 15 Squadron at Alconbury, which had been standing by since 0530 hours, lost six of their number before the survivors, all badly damaged, limped back across the Channel towards England. Twelve Blenheims of 110 Squadron reached the bridges and 11 claimed to have hit their targets, but one aircraft was shot down and another crash-landed in Belgium after being attacked by Bf 109s. Blenheims of 82 Squadron, meanwhile, which had been standing by at Watton since 0730 hours, took off at 1930 for an attack on the Albert Canal near Hasselt. The raid was successful and all the crews returned safely. Finally, the last operation of the day was flown by nine

Blenheims of 21 Squadron, also from Watton. Their target was a road at Tongres, which they bombed at 2040 hours from 7,000 feet. At least two of the Blenheims were damaged by flak, but they were able to take advantage of cloud cover for their withdrawal, all of them returning safely.

On 13 May the losses had been such that only one daylight raid by the RAF was possible, an operation flown by only a few Battles of 226 Squadron. On the afternoon of 14 May 71 Battles, every aircraft that was fit to fly in 12, 88, 103, 114, 142, 218, 226, 105 and 150 Squadrons, flew an operation against pontoon bridges across the Meuse; no fewer than 40 were shot down, though six crews did manage to evade capture and return to their lines. Then it was the turn, in the late afternoon, of the Blenheim squadrons in East Anglia.

AC1 Jack Bartley, in 21 Squadron at Watton, wrote:

'On the morning of 14 May we looked up at the clear blue sky with not a little apprehension. We all knew the Germans were advancing with amazing rapidity through the Low Countries, and we also knew that, cloud cover or no cloud cover, we should be required to attack and bomb some sector of the enemy columns that day in an attempt to stem their advance at that point. Throughout the morning we were standing by while our sister squadron [82] made a short 2-hour trip to attack the victorious Panzers in Northern Holland, carrying out the raid without loss to themselves.

At last the long-awaited summons to the Ops Room was announced, and received with the quickening of the pulse that it never failed to effect in me, and sighs of genuine relief from all in the crew room. We had been "standing by" since 4 am and activity of any sort was infinitely preferable to that tedious occupation.

With assumed nonchalance we trooped into the crew room to receive the "gen". Our target, as it had been at Maastricht on the 10th and Tongres on the 11th, was the advancing mechanised columns, with the additional attraction of an important crossroads at Sedan, near the Luxembourg frontier. We were to make a dive attack for accuracy, but to repair quickly to formation after the attack for protection against the Jerry fighters, whose presence was regarded as inevitable. Take-off was at 4 pm, and at that hour 12 sleek and shining Blenheims were lined up on the 'drome awaiting the order to start engines.

I was to be found standing near my machine, a little nervously, laughing with the ground crew who had been mercilessly ragging me the night before to the effect that it was my "turn" – as it undoubtedly was if the previous alphabetical sequence of losses of air gunners was to be adhered to. 'Tich' Birch had never returned from a Heligoland "recco" – Johnny Ball had been killed in action a fortnight back – Paddy B had died on landing from the Maastricht raid after getting the only bullet that hit his aircraft through his lung – and 'Butch' Burgess had piled straight in from 15,000 feet over Tongres the day after when his machine received a direct hit from flak. I had been flying No 3 to his leader at the time, and after seeing pieces of his tailplane flying past my turret, had watched as if hypnotised the crippled machine's devastating plunge down on to the target culminating in a terrific

Sgt D. R. C. 'Jock' MacLagan, a WOP/AG in 21 Squadron, has his photo taken in the pilot's seat of his Blenheim at Watton. Prior to take-off on 8 June 1940 Jock shook hands with a member of the ground crew to say goodbye. He had a feeling he would not be coming back. His premonition came true. (Wartime Watton Museum)

explosion. I was the only remaining "B", so I was forced to agree that it was my turn, though privately I had other views on the subject.

The signal to run up was given and the engines roared into life, when down the line of machines came the CO's car. Stopping at our machine he yelled out that a fighter escort of 30 Dewoitine machines had been arranged to patrol the target area from 6 to 6.30. I have often wondered since if that information was for the benefit of our morale, or indeed if the French even possessed 30 Dewoitine fighters. The fact remains that rendezvous was destined never to take place.

We took off just after 4 pm in a cloud of dust, and as I saw the faces of my friends amongst the ground crews rapidly receding I began to wonder – but I'd had those doubts before and returned safely, so I fought down that feeling of over-excitement mixed with a little fear that seems to bring your heart into your mouth and keep it there. My services weren't needed for a little while, so I rested my forehead on the chin-rest of the gun mounting and closed my eyes to allow the excitement to die off, and to get my thoughts into order for the approaching zero hour.

When I again looked up we were just about to cross the coast and I watched the chalk cliffs slowly grow indistinct in the summer haze. I'd often had the experience before, yet never before had I felt quite so wistful towards them, or realised more fully how much they really meant to me as on that lovely still afternoon in May.

Followed the boring flight over the Channel, the monotonous ripples broken only at one spot by the ugly hull of a merchant vessel that reared almost vertically out of the water, presumably the victim of an enemy bomb or mine. We at times came across mines on the return trip when pilots would put machines' noses down to nought feet and cut the wave crests with spinning "props", giving one a most exhilarating sensation of speed that was not entirely without foundation. I often thought the trips well worth while if only for that exultant flight home, careering over the wave tops.

The French coastline appeared out of the haze (it might have been Holland – discipline would not allow the pilot or sergeant navigator to discuss where they were with the AG!) and our presence sent a small convoy of merchantmen zig-zagging frantically. We had climbed to 12,000 feet so perhaps there was some excuse for their failing to identify us, but the same cannot be said of the AA gunners at different points along the whole of our journey across France, whose fire, though sparse and rather inaccurate, was at the same time infuriatingly misdirected. However, it served considerably to relieve the monotony of that seemingly endless flight across France, for we kept to 15,000 feet, and could not improve our knowledge of the countryside from that height.

At long last Johnny, my pilot, yelled out that we were approaching the target area, whereupon I gave the magazine of "ammo" on the gun a reassuring slap to ascertain its being properly fixed, and forsaking my comfortable pose for a more alert attitude, kept my eyes skinned. I set the turret buzzing around and looked ahead, but could make out no sign of activity. It was 6 o'clock and we had 5 minutes before being due over the target. We flew on. I began to have misgivings about our fighter escort, which were by no means decreased when I caught sight of two machines 2,000 feet or so above and flying across our track, their square wing-tips almost spelling out the word Messerschmitt. Holding myself in readiness, and watching them like a hawk, I wondered why they made no attempt to attack us, when suddenly the reason was forming all about us in the shape of hundreds of black puffs, and we were going down in a dive.

For a moment I thought we had been hit, but a glance showed me that the rest of the squadron were with us in our descent, though the formation was loosened to go through the flak. Ack-ack fire is always rather awe-inspiring, especially when you know you are the object of its attention. Big black blobs appear all over the sky with not a sound to announce their arrival, or so it seems after one's helmeted ears have listened to the roar of the engines for an hour or so, and even those that burst close enough to set the machine staggering drunkenly appear to make as much noise as a penny demon on 5 November, though there is more significance in the sharp report of shrapnel piercing the metal fuselage.

We straightened out at about 8,000 feet, leaving behind us the large artificial black cloud that was ack-ack. A jubilant shout through the phones compelled me to lower my eyes and see that Sgt B. had landed his bombs smack on the crossroads. Looking around for the remainder of the squadron, my eyes were arrested by the sight of a Blenheim in flames about 2,000 feet below, and going down, but before there was time to watch for the crew's escape my attention was riveted on a 109 fighter approaching from above and on the port quarter. Yelling out the "gen" to

Johnny, I saw that one of the Jerries had singled me out for attention, and swiftly got him in my sights, until at 200 yards he started firing, giving the appearance of blowing smoke rings from his leading edges. Tracers were zipping a little over my head and I gave a short burst in reply to see where my tracer was going. He closed in further and I held on until I really had the weight of him, as he evidently had of me, for I felt a couple of slaps on my legs and holes were appearing in the fuselage around my turret. Then I gave him all I had as he neared 50 yards range, keeping my trigger depressed and seeing my tracers going firstly into his port wing and then raking his fuselage, as clearly as I saw his streams of tracers coming straight at me and seeming to veer off at the last moment.

Unwaveringly he kept on until at 30 yards it seemed he was intent on ramming us, when suddenly his nose dropped and he was gone. The unorthodoxy of the dive led me to believe I had him, and I was leaning out to watch some glimpse of him when I felt a terrible pain in my back as if a red hot poker had been thrust into it, and turned to see a second ME about to break off his attack, made from the opposite beam simultaneously with the first machine.

Immobilised with pain for a second or two, I recovered too late to get a smack at him. In any case my "ammo" was expended, so with a twist of my turret control I lowered myself into the fuselage, hurriedly removed the empty pan and reloaded before elevating myself again, to be greeted with the sight of a fighter dead astern at 400 yards. Jagged holes appeared in the tailplane while I manipulated foot and hand levers till the gun was in position for shooting alongside fin and rudder. He closed in until his machine guns sounded like a much accentuated typewriter tapping in my ears above the engine noises and in between my own bursts of fire.

Attempting to follow him down after his break away, my heart missed a beat or two when I found that my turret would no longer respond to pressure on the hand bar – the hydraulics were evidently severed. Desperately I grasped the pillars of the turret and shoved, but to no avail; the turret just would not budge. I was, in effect, disarmed. Fortunately at this juncture there was a lapse in the attack. Placing my hand to my aching back I brought it away covered with blood, and a feeling of nausea swept over me. Blood was also streaming from a wound in my thigh, so I decided to leave the cordite-reeking atmosphere of the useless turret and have my wounds attended to,

pressing the emergency lever that would lower my seat and allow my exit.

To my horror I felt no lowering of my seat in answer to pressure there, and realised that I was virtually trapped in my turret. I doubled my body down in an effort to slip off my seat and fall into the fuselage, and was rewarded only by a shower of petrol in my face as it came below the level of the fuselage; it must have been leaking in through the wing roots from the severed feed pipes. I became aware that we were diving steeply and for the first time in the action I had time to be frightened. Feverishly I relieved myself of my parachute harness, tore at the strings of my Mae West and fumbled with the Irvin zip until with a manoeuvre worthy of a contortionist, I at last managed to extricate myself.

With the machine still roaring earthwards I donned my harness, this time with parachute attached in readiness, replugged my phones in the midships socket and, wondering if Johnny had given the order to jump, or indeed if he were still alive, yelled down the mike, "I'm out of action, Sarge, I'm out of action, Sarge!"

There was no reply, but my increasing fears were allayed by the gradual straightening out of the machine, and through the camera hatch I saw that we were flashing over forest land, barely clearing the tree tops.

Then my hopes of survival recently cherished were dashed to the ground as more jagged rips appeared in the already riddled fuselage, bullets whipped inside the machine, clanging against metal, and above it all, nearer and nearer, the terrifying tapping of those lethal typewriters. A couple of bullets smacked into the parachute fastened to my chest, and deciding that I had not much longer to live, the mortal fear I had of being wounded in the stomach forced me to double up and point my head towards the tail, resignedly hoping for a mercifully quick end. The fact that I presented a small target in that position was purely incidental, though it was probably responsible for saving my life, for though I received two ricocheting splinters in my side during the next few seconds, live through the inferno I did, much to my surprise, though the ache from my wounds and the infuriation at my inability to retaliate knew no bounds.

The firing stopped as suddenly as it had begun and all went comparatively quiet. I fervently hoped that was the last of the fighters to pay us its unwelcome attentions. My wishes in this respect were borne out, though we were still not out of the wood, as, wriggling over the bomb well and peeping over the pilot's seat, I could see that Johnny was having one royal time endeavouring to keep the machine on some sort of course and to check her pitching, the difficulty arising, we afterwards found, from the fact that half the tailplane was non-existent and that the rudder resembled a tattered rag, fluttering in the breeze. I managed to attract my observer's attention and he placed a shell dressing over the worst gash in my back from which blood still oozed in a steady stream.

Johnny yelled out that he would have to lob her before the remaining fuel supply gave out, and after flying over seemingly endless forests covering the slopes of the Ardennes we perceived through the cabin perspex, which had not escaped the onslaught unscathed, a comparatively flat stretch of grassland. Banking steeply, Johnny prepared to put her down, and, realising that even if the attempt were successful the landing would be a very bumpy affair owing to the unserviceability of the undercarriage from both tactical and practical points of view, I rolled myself up in the bomb well, the strongest part of the aircraft, and gripped the nearest fuselage rib as if my very life depended on it.

I saw the ground approaching through the rips in the metal fuselage, heard the swish of air as the flaps lowered, and a crash that shook every bone in my body as I was torn from my grip of the rib, dashed against the ceiling of the fuselage and down again two or three times, until with a scraping and rending the battered machine came to a halt, and all was curiously quiet.

Here let me pay tribute to Johnny's grand show in landing that crippled machine on that rough and steeply sloping grassy stretch in the Ardennes without so much as scraping a wing tip, though of course the propeller tips and bomb doors were buckled.

The possibility of the kite firing spurred me in my opening the hatch and scrambling on to terra firma, over which I stumbled for 20 yards or so, followed by Johnny and Sergeant B. until my injured leg refused to carry me any further and buckled beneath me, and I fell to the ground, weak, sick and exhausted, but with that triumphant feeling of exhilaration that only those who have passed through the Valley of Death and survived can ever know.'

First to attack had been six Blenheims of 107 Squadron, supported by strong fighter support. They were peppered with flak but none were shot down. Behind them came 12 Blenheims of 110 Squadron, but five of their number were shot down by Bf 109s. The last to bomb were 10 Blenheims of 21 Squadron, two of which were lost and the remainder suffered severe battle damage.

On 15 May three Blenheims of 40 Squadron piloted by W/C Barlow, F/O J. E. Edwards and Sgt Higgins bombed a bridge at Dinant and were then attacked by Bf 109s, which broke up their formation. Barlow's gunners fought off the fighters but Edwards's and Higgins's crews were never seen again. 15 Squadron Blenheims also bombed the bridge, approaching from 10,000 feet and diving to 5,000 feet before releasing their bombs. P/O Harrison's Blenheim was hit by flak and he was forced to crash-land in Belgium.

At 0400 hours on the morning of 17 May 12 crews of 82 Squadron gathered in the briefing room at Watton to be told to attack an enemy column near Gembloux. Their expected fighter escort did not materialise and they ran into a severe flak barrage, which split up the formation, allowing the Bf 109s to attack with great effect. Only one Blenheim, flown by Jock Morrison on one engine, managed to get back to Watton, the rest being shot down.

82 Squadron was now non-operational, but the CO, W/C the Earl of Bandon, made sure the Squadron was reformed and it resumed operations just three days later. Also on the 17th, three out of six Blenheims of 15 Squadron were lost during an attack on German troop concentrations, and two were damaged beyond repair. By the end of this, the eighth day of the campaign, the RAF had lost 170 medium bombers.

On 18 May four Blenheim squadrons, 15, 21, 40 and 110, dispatched aircrews to attack enemy troops approaching Le Cateaux. One squadron quickly lost three Blenheims, while two aircraft were so badly damaged that they had to be written off. Next day the remnants of the RAF squadrons flew back to England, the remaining surviving personnel following by boat. On arrival at Watton, three crews from 18 Squadron volunteered to fly with 82 Squadron in a raid on a Panzer division. One of the 18 Squadron crews, captained by P/O C. Light, was mistaken for a Ju 88 and shot down by a Hurricane. On 22 May W/C Embry led 107 Squadron in an afternoon attack on troops closing in on Boulogne, hitting

The rear fuselage section of Sgt A. F. 'Jock' Morrison's Blenheim IV L8858 of 82 Squadron, which was peppered with 279 holes on the low-level operation to Gembloux, Belgium, on 17 May 1940, when this aircraft was the only one of the 12 to return. Back at Watton Sgt Mike Cleary, who was awarded the DFM for shooting down one of the attacking fighters, showed his pilot the damage and Morrison promptly collapsed! (Mike Cleary via Wartime Watton Museum)

vehicles in the fields. The Squadron mounted a second attack that day in the same area, and Embry led a third with 110 Squadron, making a dual attack on a German HQ at Ribeaucourt. With darkness and fog at Wattisham, landings were made at Manston in Kent.

On 26 May it was decided to evacuate as many troops as possible from Dunkirk, so operations were directed to support the beleaguered BEF forces around the town. On 27 May, during one of these raids, by 12 Blenheims of 107 Squadron led by the dynamic W/C Embry, they flew into the expected curtain of flak. Embry's Blenheim was severely damaged and his WOP/AG killed;

Embry and his observer bailed out. His loss was a shattering blow to everyone on the Group, but Embry, three times captured but never made a PoW (the second time, unarmed, he fought his way out, then, with a 'borrowed' German rifle, killed three Germans) eventually returned to England by way of the Pyrenees, Spain and Gibraltar. He landed at Plymouth on 2 October after this epic journey and returned to his squadron.

On the last day of May, as the evacuation from Dunkirk reached its climax, the Blenheims in East Anglia flew by far the greatest number of operations on any one day during the campaign. These missions were directed at enemy troops massing for an all-out attack on the evacuation area and it was largely due to their efforts, and those of RAF fighter pilots, that this attack was halted and the BEF was able to be evacuated so successfully.

AC2 Jim Moore had listened to the accounts of the 'Miracle of Dunkirk', during which the remnants of the British Army had been rescued from the French beaches.

'We had also been told of the magnificent efforts of the RAF in covering the withdrawal. It was, therefore, a sobering experience when on the train to Upwood I met some of the survivors from the Dunkirk beaches who made some very uncomplimentary remarks about the lack of air support they had received. Neither they nor I had any idea how few operational aircraft were available to the RAF at that time.'

Freddie Thripp, by then promoted to Sergeant in 82 Squadron, tried to explain it all in a letter home on 3 June.

'Here we are all safe and sound. Boy, what a week I have had. From last weekend, I made 8 raids in 9 days, then a little rest, and 3 times in 24 hours, and they say that we have been harassing the movements of the enemy, but believe me, they want 3 RAFs to stop that mob. My one fear is having to swim the Channel, as it is quite a way, and there is rather a lot of dirty-looking oil floating about – it is a change to see the sea. It is all very well saying that the BEF are a fine lot of blokes, but I should think they should know a Blenheim when they see one. They shot one of the other squadron's down, then apologised, after killing the observer; the other two are back now. We have one of our operators back and his observer, and the pilot of my pal. He says that he did not feel much, as he was dead before the machine fell to pieces. And two officers have returned a while before, and one observer. It is nothing unusual now to hear guns blazing away on the coast. If only you knew what the Gerrys [sic] have been doing round this district in the flat parts for quite a while before war started, and the AM has only just realised it, and what panic it would cause if released . . .'

By now the overall losses of Blenheims totalled at least 150 aircraft, the rough equivalent of *nine* fully established squadrons. They had been thrown into the Battle for France without any

LAC Freddie Thripp, F/O Harries and Sgt Harold J. W. 'Bish' Bareham, observer, of 82 Squadron early in 1940. During the 'Phoney War' Bareham volunteered to go on the first aircrew decompression tests at Farnborough and during his three-day absence from Watton F/O Harries was detailed to carry out a raid against flak ships in the Heligoland Bight. Sgt H. H. Kelleway took his place (KIA) and his regular WOP/AG accompanied them. They did not return. Freddie Thripp was KIA flying from Malta on 18 July, aged 20, when his Blenheim was shot down by an Italian fighter after an attack on a power station at Tripoli. (Wartime Watton Museum)

clear idea on how to conduct their operations, and experienced many bitter lessons from which they had learned a great deal. Now they maintained better formations, operated at more appropriate heights, either from low level or at heights that made the task of the AA gunners more difficult, and were afforded more fighter support. On 5 June, for example, enemy supply columns were bombed by 24 Blenheims of 107 and 110 Squadrons, followed the next day by 15 and 21 Squadrons, which with fighter escort bombed four railway bridges over the River Seine without loss.

On 9 June, however, 18 Blenheims of 107 and 110 Squadrons, with fighter escort, bombed enemy troops in the Forest of Boray near Poix for the loss of two to flak. Twelve Blenheims were lost over three days in support of the beleaguered 51st Highland Division aiming for the sea at St Valery-en-Caux. Battles flew their last major daylight op on 13 June, when 48 bombed German troop concentrations for the loss of six bombers.

Then during June Blenheims began a new phase of operations by bombing Luftwaffe airfields, and losses began to rise again. In July the 12 Blenheim squadrons of 2 Group lost 31 aircraft in action, and amongst the aircrew losses were three wing commanders. It was therefore decided to withdraw most of the Blenheims from daylight operations and to employ them in night attacks, initially on the Channel ports, in support of the Hampdens, Whitleys and Wellingtons of Bomber Command.

After brushing up their gunnery skills at Squires Gate aerodrome near Blackpool, on 12 August Jim 'Dinty' Moore, now a Sergeant, was posted with his crew, Sgt Roger Speedy, 'a very competent pilot who came from Worcester' and Sgt Bob Weston, from Coventry, 'an extremely good navigator', to 18 Squadron at RAF West Raynham in Norfolk. S/L Deacon, a rather reserved, fatherly figure, was in charge of 'A' Flight to which the crew were allocated. 18 Squadron, like every other, had been badly mauled in France, losing nine aircraft and their crews during the month of May. Personnel had arrived in England in just the clothes they stood up in and, with only three Blenheims left, they had finally decamped to West Raynham in June, where the

Top *Shirt-sleeved fitters carry out a double engine change to a Blenheim IV at Bodney on a warm summer day in 1940.* (Wartime Watton Museum)

Above *Blenheim IV UX-Z R3800 of 82 Squadron hidden beneath the trees at Great Wood, Bodney, during the summer of 1940. This aircraft failed to return from the Aalborg raid on 13 August 1940 when it was flown by F/L Syms.* (Wartime Watton Museum)

Below *Blenheim IV UX-T R2772 of 82 Squadron lies wrecked in the sea off Aalborg on 13 August following the disastrous operation that cost 11 of the 12 Blenheims dispatched from England. Incredibly, Sgt W. Greenwood, WOP/AG, and Sgt D. Blair, pilot, were only slightly injured.* (Wartime Watton Museum)

After the crash, Sgt W. J. Q. 'Bill' Magrath, observer aboard UX-T R2772, found himself partly unconscious floating on his back held up by his Mae West. Magrath spent a year in hospital before he escaped from a PoW camp at Rouen late in 1941 and, after crossing the Pyrenees in the depths of winter in January 1942, he eventually reached England and was awarded the Military Medal. Magrath lost his flying pay (which he would have kept had he remained in PoW camp) when he failed a medical! (Wartime Watton Museum)

painful task of rebuilding the squadron was taking place. Jim Moore and his crew were unaware of the appalling losses being suffered by the Blenheim squadrons (2 Group had lost no fewer than 31 aircraft in July, with three written off because of battle damage, and four in accidents; three wing commanders, 15 other officers and 40 sergeants had also been killed). They also had no idea that the 'powers that be' had decided that most of the squadrons in 2 Group were to go over to night operations, although 'Dinty' was acutely aware that he had

Blenheim IV UX-L T1889 lies wrecked in a field after the belly-landing by Sgt John A. Oates (who lies badly injured in the foreground with a fractured skull, a broken back and both legs paralysed). P/O R. M. N. Biden, observer, and Sgt T. Graham, gunner, both survived. (Wartime Watton Museum)

Blenheim IV R3800 UX-Z, hit by flak, falls blazing into Limfjord, 50 yards offshore by Aalborg See, the Luftwaffe seaplane base at Aalborg. F/L Syms and Sgt Wright baled out, but Sgt E. V. Turner was killed. (Wartime Watton Museum)

just 56 hours by day and just 3 hours 50 minutes at night under his belt.

In anticipation of the expected invasion of England by the Germans, the following Battle order was issued: 'Attacks will be pressed home regardless of cost. Each aircraft should aim to hit one vessel with one bomb and machine gun the enemy whenever possible. Squadrons equipped with gas spray are to be ready to operate with this at the shortest possible notice, but it will only be used as a retaliatory measure.'

Until the threat of invasion receded, as soon as an aircraft returned from an operation, it was immediately re-armed and re-fuelled ready for take-off. Ground crews were also immediately available, some staying near the aircraft for 24 hours a day, while aircrew were kept on stand-by.

At Watton on Tuesday 13 August, a bright clear day, 12 crews from 82 Squadron were briefed to attack Aalborg airfield in Denmark,

Sgt Wright in the custody of German personnel. (Wartime Watton Museum)

Luftwaffe ground crew replenish ammunition at Rørdal airfield following the successful action by eight Bf109Es of 5.Staffel/JG 77 which shot down five of the 11 82 Squadron Blenheims lost in the operation to Aalborg airfield, Denmark, on 13 August 1940. Only one Blenheim returned to Watton. (Ole Rønnest via Jørn Junker)

occupied by Major Fritz Doensch's Ju 88s of I./JG30, which were making sporadic raids on Scotland and northern England. The Luftwaffe would fly 1,485 sorties on a day that would go down in their history as *Adler Tag* ('Eagle Day'), while the Blenheims were to be used as bait to stop fighter gruppen moving westwards to join the mass attacks on 11 Group's already beleaguered airfields, and also to forestall raids by Luftflotte 5 on the northern sector stations.

82 Squadron was under no illusions: it would be a one-way trip. The target was at the extreme limit of the Blenheim's range and pilots were told that if they used their 9 lb of boost to evade fighters, the best they could hope for was to head for Newcastle and put down as near as possible to the coast.

At 0845 W/C E. C. de Virac Lart DSO led 'A' Flight off from Watton, while 'B' Flight took off from the Bodney satellite field. P/O Donald M. Wellings' crew gained an 11th hour reprieve when, taxiing out, they were recalled because their posting had just come through! P/O Hales' crew took their place. They would not return. Over the North Sea the two formations veered slightly off course, taking them many miles south of their intended landfall. At this point Sgt Baron decided that he would run short of fuel if he continued, and he aborted (he was subsequently court-martialled but found not

guilty). Unfortunately the formation had been identified and its intent correctly deduced. Flak batteries were alerted and eight Bf 109Es of 5./JG77 from Stavanger-Sola, which had just flown an escort mission, landed at Aalborg, re-fuelled and were in the air again as the Blenheims approached. Five Blenheims were shot down by flak, then, led by Oblt Friedrich, the Bf 109Es attacked the survivors, shooting down five of them between Kaas and Pandrup.

Sgt John Oates survived but was hopelessly low on fuel and badly damaged, so he turned around and crash-landed in a field. Oates, P/O R. M. N. Biden, observer, and Sgt T. Graham, gunner, survived, though Oates had a fractured skull, a broken back and both his legs were paralysed. In all, 20 of the 33 Blenheim crewmen (including Lart) were killed, and were later buried in the cemetery at Vadum with full military honours.

Despite the Blenheim crews' best efforts, three days later, on 15 August, 50 Ju 88s of KG30 from Aalborg attacked Driffield, Yorkshire, and, from 25 August, I./JG77 formed the nucleus of the IV Gruppe, JG51, being redeployed to St Omer in the Pas de Calais. In 2 Group over the next two years there would be many more brave, yet futile, ventures like the attack on Aalborg, and often the sacrifices made by Blenheim crews would be just as great.

Chapter Two

The Night was Evil

'The night when you went in low, the moon was grey,
Like an old nun's face a-dying,
And the wind was high and shrilling
Calling for the day,
Moaning for the day, because the night was evil
And intent for killing.'

'Derek' by F/L Anthony Richardson RAFVR

On 16 August 1940 Jim 'Dinty' Moore in 18 Squadron at West Raynham looked at the Battle Order.

'There were our names at the top of the list of six crews detailed to fly on operations that night. I don't know about Roger and Bob, but I do know my feelings were a strange mixture of excitement and apprehension. This was it, this was what we had been preparing for, and above all there was a feeling of expectancy. Time almost seemed to stand still, though eventually we were called to the Operations Room where there was a buzz of conversation as we awaited our briefing. Behind a raised dais was a curtain, which was unveiled after the CO took his place to reveal, not surprisingly, a map of Western Europe indicating that our target was the Luftwaffe aerodrome at De Kooy in Holland.

After the CO's opening address, the "Met" Officer gave us his weather forecast including details of the winds we could expect, which were so important to the observer. It was then the turn of the Intelligence Officer to advise us about known anti-aircraft concentrations and so on. The actual course to and from the target was left to the individual crew, as we shared the skies over Western Europe throughout that winter with a limited number of Wellingtons, Whitleys and Hampdens which represented the heavy bombers of the RAF. Those of us who had the privilege of flying in the Blenheim developed a real affection for these machines.

Jim 'Dinty' Moore. (Jim Moore collection)

This was the first time the squadron had operated at night, so it was a new experience for all concerned. We were due to take off at 9 pm, so during the evening we got our flying gear together, emptied our pockets of any item that might be of interest to the enemy and, as we would be flying at heights of up to 10,000 feet, put on sufficient clothing to keep warm.

The minutes ticked slowly by until the flight truck was ready to take us out to the dispersal point where our aircraft 'L-Leather' was waiting for us. She was still painted with daylight camouflage, though the underside of the wings were later painted a non-reflective black. The ground crew fussed around, making sure everything was in order, while we climbed in, Bob and I stowing our parachutes and settling into our positions. I switched on the radio and we conversed on the intercom to make sure it was working.

Roger started up the engines in turn, revving them up to a healthy roar, to make sure they were in order. At a signal from him, one of the ground crew removed the chocks from the front of the landing wheels. We then taxied out to the boundary fence, turning into wind to await our signal to take off. On seeing the signal from our flight controller, Roger revved up the engines again before releasing the brakes, when we started to move, gaining speed as we headed across the field until we lifted off over the far hedge. Roger flew back over the aerodrome before turning on to the first course Bob had given him, gaining height as we flew towards the coast.

It was still daylight, and looking down at the fields, houses and villages, they seemed to assume a special significance. I still felt the thrill of flying but this was something new, an adventure that for us was into the unknown. What exactly was waiting for us on the other side of the North Sea? As I looked back at the coast of Norfolk I couldn't help wondering if I would ever see it again.

We droned on over the sea, gradually gaining height on the course dictated by Bob as the daylight faded. My responsibilities were to search the sky for enemy night fighters and to listen out on the radio in case there were any messages for us. I had, after checking with Roger, fired a short burst from my machine gun, once we were over the sea, to make sure it was working satisfactorily. In due course I heard Bob say that we could see the Dutch coast and we were making our correct landfall. Turning the turret around to look ahead I could clearly see the coastline in the moonlight just as if I were looking at a large map.

Our arrival had not gone unnoticed and soon we could see the beams of searchlights probing the sky looking for us accompanied by bursts of inaccurate flak. The light flak was multi-coloured, rather like some of the rockets on Bonfire Night, whereas the heavy flak bursts left ominous-looking small black clouds.

Bob had given Roger a new course in crossing the coast, so we were now heading for the target, where we hoped to dish out treatment to the Luftwaffe, in the same way they had been bombing our aerodromes in East Anglia. On the final run up to the target Roger kept the aircraft in a straight run responding to Bob's instructions: "Steady – steady – left – steady" and so forth – until I heard him say, "Bombs Gone!"

Our aircraft lifted, relieved of the weight of our four 250 lb bombs. It had been, as it always would be, an uncomfortable few minutes on the bombing run, as there was no question of taking evasive action to avoid the flak and we were at our most vulnerable. Having delivered our bombs, feeling very relieved, we turned on to another course for home.

We had turned on to this course when, to my surprise, I saw the silhouette of a single-engined fighter in the moonlight behind and slightly above us. It was the accepted policy to avoid combat with fighters if possible, so, resisting the natural temptation to open fire, I gave Roger directions to take evasive action and we soon lost him. This brief encounter made me appreciate how absolutely vital it was for me never to relax and to keep searching the sky.

We crossed the Dutch coast, heading for home, when Bob asked me to get a radio fix. In order to do this I contacted the wireless station at Bircham Newton, near Hunstanton, requesting a fix. On receiving an acknowledgement, I was required to press my Morse key for a few seconds, during which time two ground stations took bearings on our position. Where these two bearings crossed fixed our position on the map and these details were supplied to me by the operator sitting comfortably on the ground. I passed on this information to Bob, who could then check if we were on course or whether we needed to make any correction. Soon I heard Bob say that he could see the coast of Norfolk and shortly afterwards he asked me to contact the operator at West Raynham to get a bearing, which would give us the course that would take us home. I must confess to feeling rather pleased with myself for getting the necessary information of my radio on this, our first operational flight.

Sgt Sid Merrett (air gunner), P/O Frank Metcalfe (pilot) and George Martin (observer) of Blenheim IV 'The Cracked Jerry' in 82 Squadron pose cheerfully for the camera at Bodney in September 1940. On the night of 10/11 November, while returning from a bombing raid, the crew ditched in the North Sea after running low on fuel in a gale. Merrett perished but Martin managed to pull the badly injured Metcalfe into a life-raft and they were picked up by HMS Vega, a Navy minesweeper, which then hit a mine and sank. An ASR craft from Felixstowe picked them up and Metcalfe survived, spending several weeks in hospital. Sent home on R&R by train, the train crashed, killing 16 people! (Wartime Watton Museum)

Finally, we could see our aerodrome identification letters being flashed in Morse Code from the beacon near the field and on the ground the lights of the kerosene lamps that had been lit on the edge of the runway to guide us in. Roger made a perfect landing, taxying to our dispersal point where our ground crew were anxiously waiting to greet us. It was a marvellous feeling to climb out of the kite, feeling stiff, after a flight of 3 hours and 15 minutes, but we had really made it; we were now an operational crew.

No sooner had we left the aircraft than the ground crew were re-fuelling and bombing it up again, a practice that was to continue until the threat of invasion faded. We were looking forward eagerly to our first operational breakfast of bacon and eggs in the Sergeants' Mess, which no doubt would be accompanied by a great deal of excited conversation going on over the events of the night, but first we had to attend de-briefing. We gave the Intelligence Officer details of the operation. He was particularly interested in the fighter I had seen. We then discovered that we were the only aircraft that had been on operations, as the trip for the other five crews on the Battle Order had been cancelled after we became airborne!'

During August 2 Group lost 28 Blenheims and eight were damaged beyond repair. 'Dinty' adds:

'The squadron dispatched 62 aircraft on operations, losing four aircraft and their crews, none of whom we had the opportunity to really get to know. During the latter part of the month we moved our squadron's aircraft to a temporary aerodrome at Great Massingham, some 3 miles from West Raynham. The object of the exercise was to spread our aircraft on the ground to minimise the damage that could be caused by attacks from enemy bombers. Apart from the landing field, there were none of the buildings one found on a permanent 'drome, only a few Nissen huts. It was necessary, therefore, to find accommodation for us in the lovely little villages of Great Massingham and Little Massingham, which adjoined the airfield.

They were so close, in fact, that the roofs of one row of cottages were damaged, from time to time, by the trailing aerials of Blenheims when the WOP/AG had forgotten to wind them in as, of course, he should have done before coming in to land.

The larger village of Great Massingham was built around two large ponds and a village green and had two or three public houses, which were to be popular with one and all. The problem of accommodation was solved by literally taking over both villages, the Sergeants' Mess being housed in a rather dismal, rambling old vicarage in Little Massingham. Another building was taken over as a theatre, dance hall or church as required, another as our Operations Room, and so on. On 9 September, leaving 101 Squadron to the delights of West Raynham, all of us, both air and ground crews, followed our aircraft and moved into whatever accommodation had been found for us.

On 1 September, on attending our briefing, we were informed that we were to make our first visit to the Ruhr, the industrial heart of Germany. The "Met" Officer advised us that the weather would be clear all the way to and from the target. At 2130 hours we took off, as planned, climbing steadily to our operational height of between 10,000 and 12,000 feet, droning steadily along the North Sea. On arrival at the Dutch coast we found that we were flying over a pretty solid bank of cloud, which rendered their searchlights useless, although some bursts of flak lit up the sky.

Roger flew on in the faint hope of finding a gap in the cloud through which Bob could identify our target. We stooged around for ages, without any luck, before turning for home. Finally, in the region of Schiphol in Holland, we at last found a gap in the cloud through which a bunch of searchlights did their best to latch on to us. Not wishing to take our bombs home Bob lined up the aircraft on to the source of this nuisance and dropped our full load on them.

By this time our true position had, due to the cloud over which we were again flying, become a matter of guesswork, so the radio fix I was able to obtain from Bircham Newton was particularly helpful. We found our way back over the North Sea, looking forward to touching down at Massingham, when I received a signal informing us that due to the weather this was not practicable. We were directed to Honington, not far from Massingham, the home of a Wellington squadron where we were thankful to land after being in the air for 4 hours 40 minutes. We were made very welcome, being able to get a little sleep before flying home.

Within a few days of the fall of France, the Germans started moving hundreds of barges, each 300 feet long, along the canals of Western Europe towards the North Sea and the Channel ports. These enormous barges were essential to the invasion force that they intended to land on the shores of our embattled island. These concentrations of barges were to be the focus of the attention of all the squadrons in Bomber Command during September. As a nation we were preparing, within our limited resources, to prepare a welcome for these unwanted visitors. On the squadron we were briefed as to the type of attacks we would be required to make on German naval vessels and troop-carrying craft. We were also advised that, should the invasion take place, we would be moving to an aerodrome near Exeter.

The Germans had either installed or seized from the French some heavy naval guns at Cap Gris Nez on the French coast, which had developed the unpleasant habit of shelling shipping passing through the Straits of Dover and the town of Dover itself. In August/September we made three trips to bomb these guns and followed with attacks on barge concentrations in the ports of Dunkirk, which we visited three times, Flushing, Boulogne, Ostend and Calais. On these trips, which took approximately 3 hours, the defences were very alert with large concentrations of searchlights and pretty spectacular displays of anti-aircraft fire. We only trusted that we were doing the maximum amount of damage to these barges, which represented such a threat to our island.

On one of these trips it was still daylight when we clambered into our aircraft to prepare for take-off. Roger hadn't started the engines when the anti-aircraft gunners on the 'drome opened fire at some low-flying Junkers 88 medium bombers which were paying us a visit. Roger and Bob shot out of their hatch like corks out of a bottle while I, hampered by heavy clothing, followed a poor third to take refuge under a heavy log. Not very heroic, though with the engines switched off my turret couldn't be operated, so I was unable to fire at the intruders who flew on to West Raynham where they dropped their bombs, inflicting little damage. During the month the squadron flew 127 sorties with, thankfully, the loss of only one aircraft and crew.

At the beginning of October the weather was less kind to us and a number of operations had to be cancelled. In fact, the squadron was only able to fly 51 sorties. Roger, Bob and I did, however, make another visit to Cap Gris Nez on the 9th, followed by an attack on the docks at Boulogne on the 13th. By now the Battle of Britain was over and the immediate threat of invasion had receded, at least for the winter, so the efforts of Bomber Command could be directed at targets of industrial importance in Germany. Without wishing to take anything away from the heroic efforts of our fighter pilots during the Battle of Britain, one should not disregard the efforts of the crews of Bomber Command as a whole, in bombing the ports and concentrations of barges, as a persuasive argument to the German High Command to postpone their plans to invade the United Kingdom.

We now had more spare time, and while Fakenham and King's Lynn were within easy reach, the most popular venue was the beautiful city of Norwich, some 30 miles away. A number of us would share a taxi to spend the evening doing what came naturally. Norwich had already been the subject of attacks by German bombers both by day and by night, though at that time it was still relatively undamaged. After one such low-level attack carried out in daylight, Lord Haw Haw, in his English broadcast from Berlin, informed us that the crews involved in this raid had reported that the clock on the city hall was slow.

At 2240 hours on 24 October, in accordance with the Command's new policy, we took off for an attack on the railway yards at Haltern in the heart of the Ruhr. It was a trip that lasted for 4 hours and 5 minutes, and we found that the Germans had been very busy improving their defences. The concentration of flak was not only heavy over the target area but also at intervals all the way from the Dutch coast. Nevertheless, we were able to deliver our bomb load on schedule – everything, including the weather report, going according to schedule. We had been warned that our bombers were being attacked as they were coming into land after operations by German intruders. It was, therefore, evident that the WOP/AG could never afford to relax from searching the sky at any time during an operation. The only time I wasn't doing so was when it was imperative to use the radio to get a fix or a bearing.'

Three days later, on 27 October, Massingham and West Raynham were indeed raided by German intruders. Three aircraft, thought to be Ju 88s, attacked three times, dropping ten bombs that destroyed one Blenheim and damaged 11 others, although these were soon repaired. Four personnel were killed and seven injured, three seriously.

Roger Speedy's crew's next operation was on 29 October. 'Dinty' Moore recalls:

'On this occasion our target was another railway yard, this time at Krefeld in the Ruhr, or, as it was popularly known, the "Happy Valley". It was identical to our attack on Haltern and we returned "in one piece" after a flight lasting 3 hours and 50 minutes. Many aircrew returning from operations over western Europe were forced to ditch in the North Sea, where some of the more fortunate ones were able to get out alive and climb into their inflatable dinghies. On the 31st we were briefed to fly at low level over the North Sea in daylight, searching for any aircrew who had managed to survive in this way and were awaiting rescue. We took off at 1055 flying to within sight of the Dutch coast, feeling very much alone, searching the area that had been allocated to us. It seemed strange to be operating in daylight, over a sea that looked both cold and cruel, without, sadly, having any success. We landed back at Massingham after a flight that had taken us 3 hours and 20 minutes. It was at least comforting to know that should the same fate befall us we would not be forgotten and there was a chance of us being rescued. There can be no figures to say how many aircraft and their crews were lost due to faulty

A dramatic wartime print featured in Aeroplane *magazine showing a devastating raid by Blenheims and entitled 'Britain's Strength in the Skies', which no doubt boosted the morale of the British public.* (Aeroplane)

weather forecasts, but there must have been many of them.

The first three operations in November took place in weather that, much to our surprise, was as predicted by our "Met" Officer, and we were able to identify and bomb the targets allocated to us. On the 5th our target was the oil works at Antwerp, on the 7th the Krupps armament factory at Essen, and on the 10th the docks at Le Havre. As the weather became colder the "boffins" came up with a variety of bright ideas to make life easier for we aircrew. One, which applied to all of us, was what we would call "Wakey Wakey" tablets. We took one tablet before take-off and another in flight, and these were supposed to help us stay alert. This was fine, except on occasions when, having taken the first tablet, the operation was cancelled and you were unable to go to sleep. Another idea was a tot of rum on returning from an operation to "help the circulation". We were also encouraged to eat plenty of carrots, which were supposed to improve our night vision, and to take a variety of capsules for the same reason. We were also issued with flight rations, of which barley sugar was the most popular.

The WOP/AG had the coldest position in the aircraft, with temperatures down to 10 degrees below zero, so they devised a woollen-lined leather suit, with electrically heated gloves and boots. They worked very well, though they were so cumbersome you felt as if you were dressed for deep-sea diving, and they made it especially difficult to operate a wireless set. Whenever possible, rather than wear this outfit we wore three pairs of gloves, the first silk, the second wool, and the third leather, with thick woollen underwear, flying suit and boots with thick woollen stockings.

On 13 November we were briefed for another trip to the Ruhr, so at 0210 we took off and headed for the Continent following our usual plan in climbing steadily as we crossed the North Sea. On our arrival over the Dutch coast we encountered dense cloud, over which Roger managed to climb, keeping to the course Bob had worked out for us. We flew on and on, searching in vain for a gap in the clouds through which we could identify the target. Finally we did find a small gap in the clouds through which we could see some searchlights, on which we dropped our bombs, though where exactly these were is doubtful. We finally turned for home, flying over mountains of enormous white clouds, passing between some of them as if we were flying through a valley and watching the sun rise, which was truly beautiful.

Wandering about over western Europe in daylight was not to be recommended, and we watched the sky anxiously in case any Luftwaffe fighters had managed to find their way up through the cloud. We were beginning to wonder where the cloud would end when, well out over the North Sea, on our way home, we left it behind. Once again I was able to raise the wireless station at Bircham Newton where the operator was able to provide us with a fix for which Bob was more than usually thankful. Arriving over the Norfolk coast I contacted West Raynham and obtained the necessary bearing to get us home.

By the time we were coming in to land, having been in the air for 5 hours 45 minutes, Roger would have been so very weary that he must have allowed his concentration to lapse, the result being that we landed very heavily. The undercarriage collapsed under this treatment and we skated merrily across the airfield before coming to a stop. There is always a risk of fire in these circumstances, although we cannot have had much fuel left, so we wasted no time in getting out, feeling more than thankful that we had dropped our bombs somewhere over Germany. The fire tender and sundry ground crew were quickly on the scene and seemed rather frustrated to find us all in one piece. Thankfully there was no fire and the aircraft was soon repaired and back in action.

Sitting in one position, in cramped conditions, subjected to the severe cold, the contrasting noise and smell of the engines, never able to relax and ever conscious of the dangers of flak and enemy fighters, made great physical demands on all three of us, but this was especially true of the pilot. There was no automatic pilot, so there was no opportunity for him to relax. We managed to get some sleep before spending an hour carrying out some take-offs and landings, which was the usual practice after this kind of incident. Despite this bumpy landing Bob and I had complete faith in Roger and would not have wanted to fly with anyone else.'

In the early afternoon of 14 November crews in 105 Squadron at Swanton Morley, in 101 Squadron at West Raynham, and 110 at Horsham St Faith, were briefed for a night raid on enemy air fields. Meanwhile, across the North Sea, Luftwaffe crews prepared to raid Coventry. Altogether 20 Blenheims from 105 Squadron, using Wattisham as their base, were involved. The RAF bombers attacked airfields at Amiens, Etaples, Knocke and Rennes. Sgt E. A. Costello-

Bowen had an engagement with a Heinkel 111 and returned safely.

That night the Luftwaffe devastated the city centre of Coventry. Plans of the large-scale attack were known in advance because of *Ultra* intelligence, but the knowledge had to be kept secret from the Germans, so no additional measures were taken to repel the raid. However, squadrons from 2 Group were directed to attack aerodromes from which the enemy bombers were operating to cause as much disruption as possible. 'Dinty' Moore again:

'At our briefing we were instructed to attack the aerodromes at Flers and Lesquin, spending some time over their airspace to deter them from using their landing lights. At 1910 hours it was our turn to take off. We were soon climbing away from the airstrip and turning on to course. On this occasion the weather was exactly as predicted, so, despite the attention of the anti-aircraft gunners and searchlight operators, we were able to find both aerodromes. We stooged around for a while without seeing any signs of activity, before dropping our bombs and turning for home. We certainly hoped we had been able to dissuade some of the bombers from taking off to deliver their bombs over our country.

In a similar attack, during November, on the Luftwaffe base at Melun, our P/O, Reg Buskell, made two attacks from a relatively low level, causing a great deal of damage. He was awarded the DFC, the first

"gong" to be given to a member of the squadron since our arrival. This attack is another illustration of how the route to and from the target and the manner of attack were, at this stage of the war, generally left to the individual crew.'

On the afternoon of 15 November nine 105 Squadron crews were briefed to attack returning German night bombers over their airfields at Antwerp and Brussels, but bad weather prevented all but five from taking off. Four Blenheims attacked Dieghem airfield. F/O D. Murray DFC and Sergeants C. D. Gavin and T. Robson were killed when their Blenheim was downed by intense flak and the aircraft exploded in a fireball. This crew had returned from a raid on Etaples on 25 October in T1890 on one engine after the propeller and reduction gear on the starboard engine fell away over the French coast. On that occasion Murray had managed to land safely at Deboler.

As 'Dinty' Moore remembers:

'The attack on Coventry seemed to me to bring about a change of policy for the bombers of the RAF, which up to that point had generally been instructed to aim for targets of industrial or military importance. In our case, at our briefing on 16 November, we were initially briefed to bomb the docks at Hamburg. Later we were recalled to the briefing room to be directed to drop our bombs on the city itself. War in the air is

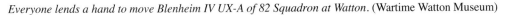

Everyone lends a hand to move Blenheim IV UX-A of 82 Squadron at Watton. (Wartime Watton Museum)

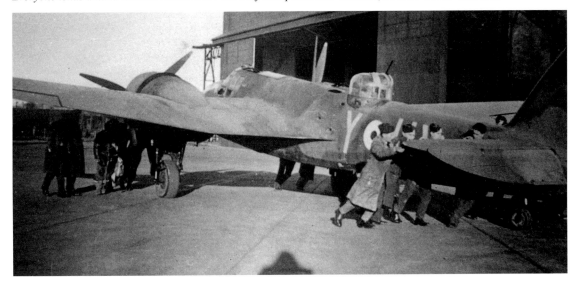

impersonal, but in the case of Bob and others who were from Coventry, or other English towns that had been bombed, they may well have felt differently as their families and friends were likely to be killed. In their case could you blame them if they felt that this was an act of retaliation, though to be fair to Bob, he never spoke about it in this way.

At 1905 hours we took off on this operation, which was to last for 4 hours 25 minutes, against a target that was particularly well defended. The city, being on an estuary, was relatively easy to find, although the reception we received by way of flak and searchlights was pretty impressive. Bob picked up the target, on to which he directed Roger, the seconds ticking away like hours as we flew straight on the bomb run, before those magic words "Bombs Gone!" and we were able to take some evasive action. Following this operation we were granted leave. My brother Peter was still at home, though he was eagerly waiting his call-up into the RAF as an electrician.'

On 26 November eight crews of 105 Squadron were dispatched to Cologne, together with a *Freshman* flight to Boulogne. However, the weather deteriorated before all the crews could bomb and the aircraft returned. After receiving clearance to land, P/O L. T. J. Ryan RNZAF flew off towards the beacon, but crashed into Foxley Wood near the airfield. Ryan and Sergeants S. W. Slade and R. Meikle were killed. Sgt Costello-Bowen, meanwhile, was above dense cloud and completely unable to find his base. Looking for a gap in the cloud, he finished up near Liverpool, 200 miles away! He flew around desperately calling for help until there was no fuel left. Finally he, Sgt Tommy Broom and Cameron bailed out at Harrup Edge near Stockport while the Blenheim flew on to crash at Mottram, in Longendale on the eastern outskirts of Manchester.

During December operations were again curtailed by the weather. The targets, both airfields and industrial, were often blanketed by low cloud. 'Dinty' Moore takes up the story:

'On return to Massingham we were soon in action again, our first operation being on 6 December when we took off at 2325 to attack and disrupt the Luftwaffe aerodromes at Harkamp and Rotterdam. Apart from dropping our bombs, we loitered around over these aerodromes for some time in order to prevent their use. We landed back after a flight lasting 3 hours 40 minutes, hoping that we had caused the German bombers as much discomfort as possible.

Two days later it was back to the "Happy Valley" with an attack on Düsseldorf, where we found the

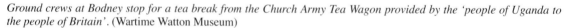

Ground crews at Bodney stop for a tea break from the Church Army Tea Wagon provided by the 'people of Uganda to the people of Britain'. (Wartime Watton Museum)

defences had been greatly improved, as they had at all targets in Germany. At one stage we were caught by the searchlights, which is a terrifying experience, feeling like a fly caught in a spider's web. Roger, by changing height and direction, was able to shake them off and we were able to bomb the target. On our way back to Massingham Bob asked me to get the usual fix, but when I went to let out the trailing aerial I found that it was missing. Thankfully the weather was being kind to us and Bob was pretty confident of our position so he was able to manage with the assistance of some bearings I was able to get from the wireless station at West Raynham. As always we were thankful to touch down at Massingham after a flight that, on this occasion, had lasted 4 hours 25 minutes.

During our flights to targets in Germany the Intelligence "boffins" at Air Ministry had found us an additional pastime. This was to act as "litter louts", scattering propaganda leaflets across the countryside, advising the Germans that they ought to make peace. In order to drop these leaflets it was necessary to open the escape hatch, and some of my friends hit on the idea of dropping empty beer bottles at the same time. On the 11th, as a spot of light relief, we made yet another trip to bomb our old friends, the heavy naval guns at Cap Gris Nez, an operation that went off without incident.'

On 11/12 December F/O P. R. Richardson and crew of 105 Squadron were killed when they were shot down at Zedelgem near Bruges. On Christmas Eve the CO of the squadron had to hand over command to Acting W/C Arnold L. Christian (a relative of Fletcher Christian of 'Mutiny on the Bounty' fame), after fighting against a persistent recurrence of an old illness. The new CO had very little luck with the weather during his first month in office. Although operations were briefed every day, only 14 sorties, six on the 3rd, six on the 9th and two on the 22nd, were mounted.

On 21 December 'Dinty' Moore found that his target was to be an oil refinery at Gelsenkirchen.

'A tour of operations was 30 trips; this was our 27th together, so we were looking forward to a rest. Nevertheless, having got this far, you began to feel rather anxious, hoping your good luck would continue. At 0320 hours the following morning, when all good people should be in bed, we took off and headed once again for the Ruhr. We need not have

worried for everything worked perfectly; we were able to bomb, return and land at Massingham at 0730, as it was becoming light.

On 22 December we attended what was to be our last briefing together, although we were not to know this at the time. We found that our target was to be the railway yard at Wiesbach. Again we took off at 0315 hours for an operation that was to last for 5 1/2 hours. There were the usual searchlights probing the sky and the bursts of light and heavy flak along our route and especially over the target, but our luck was in, and having bombed the target we flew back over the Dutch coast unscathed. Returning over the North Sea it was becoming daylight, and we felt very exposed although no enemy fighter appeared on the scene.

During our partnership we had flown nearly 100 hours in completing our 28 operations. During that time we had suffered no battle damage, had always dropped our bombs, and had found our way back to base even though, on one occasion, we were directed to land elsewhere. Many were less fortunate, some suffering from inaccurate weather forecasts; for example, one crew were so far off course that they landed at Acklington, north of Newcastle, instead of East Anglia. Another crew, having flown over continuous banks of cloud across the North Sea, first saw land over Norfolk, but the observer believed he was still over Holland. Further, he would not accept the wireless bearings obtained by his WOP/AG as being correct until they found themselves over the Irish Sea. Being concerned, those of us who had already landed were in the wireless station at West Raynham listening to the exchange of signals. They finally landed at an airport near Liverpool, with about enough fuel left in the tanks to fill a cigarette lighter. This crew were taken off operational flying, the only member to come out of the incident with any credit being the WOP/AG. These are just two of the many examples of the problems that faced Bomber Command during the winter.

On the 28th we were briefed for another operation and I duly put on my flying suit in readiness for take-off, though I was feeling far from well, going alternately hot and cold. Thankfully the operation was cancelled and the next morning my friends sent for the Squadron Medical Officer. He diagnosed pneumonia and I was duly dispatched by ambulance to the RAF hospital at Ely. I felt terrible and had hardly any recollection of the journey or of my first few days in the hospital.

In my absence Roger and Bob, without flying on

Blenheim IV 'W', a replacement for Sgt A. F. 'Jock' Morrison's Blenheim in 82 Squadron at Watton. (Wartime Watton Museum)

any further operations, were told that their first tour was over and they were to be posted "on rest". This was the term used to describe the periods between operational tours, which normally would be duty as an instructor. However, in their case they were to go to Takoradi in West Africa where they were to fly Blenheims, guiding Hurricanes as they were delivered by sea, across the African continent to our forces in Egypt. Apart from being an unpleasant place to fly from, it was a really hazardous duty as it meant flying over wild and uncivilised country where they could ill afford to force-land. We had no opportunity to say goodbye nor have I met them since, but I sincerely hope that they both survived the war. Roger was a truly competent pilot, ideally suited for the type of operations in which we had been engaged, while Bob was a first-class observer and I was truly sorry we had to part company. However, while I hardly enjoyed my period in hospital, someone up there spared me from this distinctly unpleasant duty in Africa.'

During January/February 1941 the Blenheim squadrons continued flying night operations. On 10/11 February the largest raid yet mounted by 2 Group took place when 221 bombers, including 40 Blenheims of 18, 21, 105, 107 and 110 Squadrons, took off to attack U-boat factories at Hanover. F/L Peter Simmons DFC of 107 Squadron became completely lost when his W/T failed after flying for $6^{1}/_{2}$ hours, and he had to crash-land.

Meanwhile German intruders were active over eastern England. S/L J. S. Sabine, for example, was coming into land, his mission completed, when he was attacked by an intruder and forced to crash-land. At Bodney, Sgt A. Chatterway was circling the aerodrome awaiting his turn to land when his aircraft was shot down, killing him, seriously wounding his observer, P/O Cherval, and wounding his WOP/AG, Sgt Burch, in the leg. On 15 February 2 Group participated in the Main Force attacks on an oil refinery at Homberg and at Cologne; 26 of the 35 aircraft dispatched by Nos 18, 101, 105 and 107 Squadrons to Homberg claimed to have bombed, while 12 of 16 aircraft attacked Cologne.

At the beginning of March 'Dinty' Moore returned to Massingham after recuperation, having been declared fit for flying.

'During my absence 18 Squadron had suffered from bad weather, which had limited them to 29 operational sorties in January, and 40 in February (compared with the 127 we had flown the previous September). During March the situation was not much better, 33 sorties having been flown, with, sadly, the loss of one crew. Not being part of a crew, I felt very much the odd man out, even though there were a number of new faces. Then for some reason a WOP/AG in one of the crews was taken off operational flying and I was elected to take his place. I could not have been more fortunate because the pilot, Sgt George Milsom, who hailed from Coningsby in Lincolnshire, had a natural flair for flying, coupled with courage and the ability to be decisive in combat. His observer, Sgt Ron Miller, a New Zealander, turned out to be very competent and both of them were easy to get along with. They had joined the squadron shortly before I was admitted to hospital and had, so far, flown six night operational flights. We became known as "The Three Ms" (Milsom, Millar and Moore). I was now about to share in what, I believe, was the most exciting period in the life of the aircrews of 2 Group.'

Chapter Three

Ramrods and Circuses

'The high sky was the amphitheatre, in the arena were the Blenheims;
all around them were the Gladiators – British and German fighters.'

Eric Atkins DFC* Krzyz Walecznych* (Cross of Valour)

On 6 March 1941 Churchill made a decision that was to have a far-reaching effect on the lives of the crews of the Blenheims based in the UK. The battle of the Atlantic was causing a great deal of concern, with the U-boats taking a heavy toll of Allied shipping, so Bomber Command was now to concentrate on naval targets. The role of the Blenheims of 2 Group, and the Beauforts, Lockheed Hudsons and Blenheims of Coastal Command, was to harass, damage and as far as possible destroy communications between East to West by sea in daylight. Although naval patrol boats were out every night looking for enemy shipping, the Navy could hardly undertake this task in daylight without running an excessive risk from aerial bombardment. German shipping habitually sailed close to the enemy coastline where the Luftwaffe could readily bomb any ships or submarines that attacked its convoys, as they had already demonstrated.

The AOC 2 Group, AVM 'Butcher' Stevenson, was ordered to see that any enemy ship putting to sea between the Brittany Peninsula and the coast of Norway should be sunk irrespective of the cost. The cost proved to be considerable. The manner in which the campaign was to be carried out was to break down the whole length of the enemy coast into 'beats'. The formation of

The only way a Blenheim crew could successfully attack a ship was to approach from wave-top height, lift to clear the masts of the ship, and either land the bomb on the ship or skim it along the surface of the sea to explode against the side of the ship. The attack would last for a matter of seconds, but, all too frequently, with fatal results for the bomber crew. (Wartime Watton Museum)

A Blenheim IV of 21 Squadron making a low-level attack on enemy shipping, captured on film by the WOP/AG 'Steve' Stephens. Operations against shipping opened on 12 March 1941 but the Blenheim had hardly been designed for anti-shipping strikes, and losses on these operations were high. (Wartime Watton Museum)

Blenheims would fly at wave-top height to the 'start line', which would be approximately 30 miles from the coast, from where they would fly towards the coast at specified distances apart, dependent on the weather conditions. On reaching a point 3 miles from the coastline they would turn at right-angles and fly for 3 minutes parallel to the coast before turning for home. The order was to sink the first ship sighted, or indeed any ship in the 'beat' area.

The Blenheim had hardly been designed for this type of operation, for the only way it could successfully attack a ship was to approach from wave-top height, lift to clear the masts of the ship, and either land the bomb on the ship or skim it along the surface of the sea to explode against the vessel's side. Within weeks of the opening of this campaign, enemy convoys were always escorted by heavily armed motor patrol boats, so, with the combined anti-aircraft armament of all the ships in the convoy, the bombers had to fly through an enormous concentration of fire. The attack would only last for a matter of seconds, but all too frequently with fatal results for the bomber crew.

Low-level flying is always a risky pastime, demanding absolute concentration on the part of the pilot, while over the sea this becomes even more hazardous in hazy conditions when it is very difficult to judge height above the water. Because low-level flying was to become a major feature of the life of Blenheim crews during that summer, over land it meant keeping as low as the contours of the ground would allow, having to lift *over* trees, telegraph wires, electricity pylons and so on.

These new operations against shipping opened on 12 March 1941 when five Blenheims of 139 Squadron attacked a convoy of four ships, losing one aircraft. Two days later W/C W. E. Cameron of 107 Squadron was more fortunate in bombing and sinking a 2,000-ton ship off Norway (Cameron and his crew were lost off the coast of Norway on 6 April). On the 23rd it was the turn of 82 Squadron; they found a convoy of five ships, including a destroyer, off the Ems estuary, which they attacked and claimed to have damaged. The squadron carried out its second shipping sweep the next day when, in attacking another convoy, it lost its first crew in this campaign. These sweeps continued daily. On the

Low-level flying was to become a major feature of the life of Blenheim crews during the summer of 1941. Always a risky pastime, demanding absolute concentration on the part of the pilot, this became even more hazardous while over the sea in hazy conditions when it was very difficult to judge height above the water. (RAF)

29th, during an attack on a 5,000-ton tanker off Flushing, which was surrounded by six patrol boats, the Blenheim flown by W/C Bartlett was very badly damaged. Bartlett, showing great skill and determination, managed to bring the aircraft home on one engine. On 31 March the crews of 82 Squadron reported a very successful attack on a convoy of six ships off Le Havre, during which they left a 3,000-ton tanker ablaze.

At this stage a new operation, known as the 'Fringe Attack', was introduced. Fighters were given 'Fringe Targets' if no enemy aircraft came up. They were split roughly into three sections: 'Close Encounter', to protect the Blenheims, 'High Wave', to mass for attack at 20,000 feet, and 'Withdrawal', to protect the Blenheims on return. Military targets could be found a few miles inland from the enemy coast, which was very convenient, though they were also in the most heavily defended areas. It was now decreed that 'in order to cause alarm and to embarrass the enemy air defence system' transport columns, vehicles, troops, guns, searchlight emplacements and so on should be attacked from low level.

These operations could be either the objective or, having flown a shipping 'beat' and finding nothing to attack, the crews would be directed to cross the coast to bomb any suitable target.

Operations at this time were described by Sgt Freddie Thripp of 82 Squadron, who was by now fast approaching 50 operations, in a letter home on 19 March:

'We have been leading the attacks on those fire blitzes, and what a time too! One night we got down low to miss the fighters, then we got a bit off course, and found ourselves in the centre of Antwerp, then a few hectic moments, a wide circuit, then we found ourselves below the roofs of Brussels, after that Ghent, eventually coming out in the Channel, with somebody jamming our D/F station, but we got back OK.

We got back into camp yesterday, and in the evening we were away again, and as usual first on one of their northern ports, and what a do. We have been there before, so we knew the easiest way in, but after watching a nice, or a lucky, shot in amongst the buildings around the docks, one of their searchlights

If during shipping 'beats' Blenheim crews found nothing to attack, they were expected to make 'Fringe Attacks' on military targets a few miles inland from the enemy coast 'in order to cause alarm and to embarrass the enemy air defence system'. This target is burning after a Blenheim attack on 16 April 1941. (Wartime Watton Museum)

got us then about a dozen lit us, then hell was let loose, and so were we. We were at 12,000 feet, then when the machine gun stuff started coming up, my driver just managed to find our altimeter, and pulled out at about 4,000 feet, and just about shook them off, and was I glad . . .'

On 31 March, in accordance with 2 Group's new shipping 'beat' decree, S/L 'Atty' Atkinson led eight crews of 21 Squadron, having been briefed to attack ships off the Dutch Frisian Islands and to open the campaign against 'Fringe Targets'. Atkinson proved to be one of the most courageous and resourceful leaders in 2 Group. They certainly had beginners' luck for it proved to be a most successful foray over enemy territory. First of all they found two destroyers, which they bombed, one being hit on the stern, whereupon a black column of smoke belched forth. Not content with this success, they flew on over the islands, skimming over the ground and disrupting a parade of German troops, which they sprayed with machine gun fire. Still they flew on, shooting up guns, more troops, pill-boxes and a radio station, before Atkinson

decided to lead his troops home. Their visit had not gone unnoticed, for their presence had attracted a great deal of flak, which, not too surprisingly, accounted for two of the Blenheims.

On 3 April W/C C. G. Hill DFC took command of 18 Squadron in place of W/C A. C. H. Sharpe (who took up a position at the Air Ministry) and moved it to Oulton, near the market town of Aylsham. 'Dinty' Moore recalls:

'Our accommodation could not have been less like that which we had enjoyed at Massingham, for we now found ourselves living in the beautiful Blickling Hall, the home of landed gentry since the time of the Domesday Book. The last owner, Lord Lothian, who had been our ambassador to the USA until his death in 1940, had left the house and grounds to the National Trust. However, before the National Trust could claim its inheritance, the Air Ministry commandeered the property with 114 Squadron being the first occupants. This Squadron had been posted to RAF Leuchars in Scotland to make way for us. We occupied about two-thirds of the house and most of the buildings in the grounds, with access to the acres of grounds and the lake in which we were able to swim despite the presence of a large swan who appeared to resent our presence. The estate even had its own church and a small public house.

The Wing Commander had a very grand room, which, it was said, had been occupied by Anne Boleyn, overlooking the park and the lake. Many of the estate employees still lived in their cottages and must have found our presence somewhat different from anything to which they had become accustomed. On one memorable occasion one of our colleagues, having spent the evening in Norwich, imbibing more than his share of the local ale, took a fancy to one of those large yellow balls on the top of a pedestrian crossing sign. He purloined this, bringing it back joyfully to the hall, where he deposited it in the garden. The following morning the head gardener

emerged from his cottage and, having heard warnings of explosive devices being dropped by the Luftwaffe, hurriedly alerted the bomb squad. On their arrival these gentlemen were not impressed and their comments are unprintable!

One major improvement that had been carried out to the Blenheims during the winter was the removal of the single Vickers Gas Operated machine gun in the turret, which was replaced by two Browning .303 machine guns. These guns were fed not by pans of ammunition, but by belts.

My return to the squadron had coincided with a decision by Bomber Command that No 2 Group must adopt a much more aggressive role and there were to be no more night operations. On 11 April 1941 Blenheims of 105 Squadron flew the last 2 Group

Two views of Blenheim 'Q for Queenie' of 18 Squadron at Great Massingham early in 1941 with the observer, P/O C. C. Sherring, standing by the wing. Note the twin Browning .303 machine gun installation in the turret, which had replaced the single VGO in the winter of 1941. (Mrs Vera Sherring)

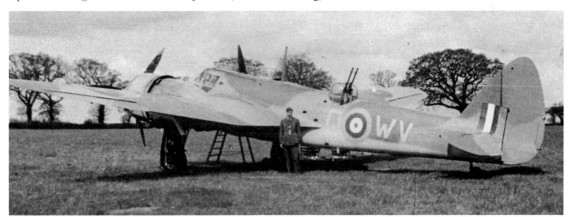

night operation, bombing targets at Cologne, Bremerhaven and Brest. Instead, we were to operate in daylight on tasks that came roughly under two headings, which are as follows:

1. Attacks at low level on enemy shipping close to the enemy coast, these shipping lanes from Norway to the Bay of Biscay being split into "beats". We would either be detailed to look exclusively for shipping or, on occasions, when no shipping was sighted, to cross the coast to look for and bomb suitable targets.
2. Low-level attacks on industrial or military targets on the Continent, sometimes using cloud for cover.

Later (during May) we were allocated a further task, to operate in formation at heights of about 10,000 feet with fighter escort. These operations, known as Circuses, were to be flown with the primary objective

In May 1941 Blenheims began Circus *operations at 10,000 feet with fighter escort in an effort to entice German fighters into action.* (Truett Woodall)

of persuading the fighters of the Luftwaffe to attack us so that they could be engaged and destroyed by our escorting fighters. Similar operations, known as *Ramrods*, were also to be flown where the target, rather than ourselves, acting as the "sacrificial lamb", was the primary objective.'

The year 1941 would become known as 'the year of the *Circus*'. It was the aim to entice enemy fighters into the air and destroy them over France – perhaps with as few as a 'box' of six Blenheims (the bait) and 103 British fighters from as many as nine squadrons (the hunters). The Blenheims were not only bait as they also had a bombing target in the range of the fighter cover. The campaign actually began on 12 March, when one of the other squadrons in the Group patrolling a shipping 'beat' along the Dutch coast, sighted a ship of about 1,000 tons, which they bombed.

The *Circus* operation was not without some problems: a tight formation with no straggling; straight and level bombing on the leader; fighters and bombers being exactly at the right spot on the right time; and sorting out friendly fighters from enemy aircraft. Flying at 10,000 feet in broad daylight and attracting heavy flak, the Blenheims were wallowing around in the thinner air, far short of their best performance, wanting the enemy to come and attack but dependent on friendly fighters, which had limited range, to stop them.

By 12 April the Blenheims had flown 315 sorties and 121 ships had been attacked, of which six were believed to have been sunk and eight damaged, with the loss of nine aircraft and their crews. On 19 April three crews of 18 Squadron, led by S/L H. J. N. Lindsaye, found a 7,000-ton freighter with a destroyer escort that was belching out what must have seemed to the attackers to be an impenetrable wall of flak. Undeterred, they ploughed in, delivering their attack from mast height and gaining hits on the freighter, which was soon listing and was firmly believed to have been sunk. On 15 April W/C C. G. Hill and his crew were lost without trace during another shipping strike. W/C G. C. O. Key took over command of 18 Squadron on the 23rd.

On 24 April a new and, if possible, even more dangerous tactic was introduced for the crews of

2 Group, known officially as 'Channel Stop', although those involved gave it a less complimentary title. The object of this particular exercise was to close the Straits of Dover to enemy shipping during daylight, leaving the motor torpedo boats of the Royal Navy to carry out the same exercise at night. The Blenheim squadrons would, in turn, be based at RAF Manston; as soon as shipping was sighted they would take off and attack, accompanied by an escort of Spitfires or Hurricanes.

The first aircraft to be committed to this task was a flight of 101 Squadron, which waited at Manston for a report on shipping movements. This information was supplied by fighters patrolling the Straits, who became known as 'Jim Crows'. On 28 April word came that there were some enemy trawlers off Calais, and three of the Blenheims set off in pursuit with their escort. During the attack one of the Blenheims was shot down by the frightening firepower from the ship, though their escort drove off an enemy fighter that tried to intervene. The crews of 101 Squadron continued their role with varying degrees of success and casualties; for example, on 3 May, while attacking a small convoy off Boulogne, two of the three crews were lost to flak. On 9 May, no doubt to the relief of those who had survived, the crews flew their Blenheims back to their base at West Raynham, 'Channel Stop' being postponed, but only for a while.

Not content with the variety of tasks to which the Blenheim squadrons had been committed, on 26 April six crews from 21 Squadron, led by the indomitable S/L Atkinson, flew out to Malta to study the feasibility of operating from that beleaguered island. The previous day was momentous for the crews of 18 Squadron, one of the crews finding a large merchant ship of at least 7,000 tons with an escort of motor patrol boats. A hit was scored on the ship, which caused an enormous explosion, while two of the escort vessels were bombed, a hit being claimed on one of them.

'Dinty' Moore takes up the story:

'Having been involved in night operations, our squadron began a period of low-level flying exercises across the East Anglian countryside, preparing to make our contribution to this campaign. Flying low meant literally skimming over hedgerows, with telegraph and electrical wires proving to be quite a hazard, while flocks of birds were the cause of many accidents; collecting twigs and assorted greenery on the leading edges of the wings was commonplace. Compared with flying at medium or high level, when you were not conscious of the speed at which you were travelling, flying at low level was truly exciting and exhilarating, requiring total concentration by the pilot who could ill afford even to sneeze. Over the sea it was even more difficult, the sea and sky seeming to merge, especially if it was at all hazy. We also dropped practice bombs on the wreck of a ship lying just off the cliffs at Trimingham.

Our aircraft were now fitted with twin .303 Browning machine guns in the turret, fed by belts of ammunition. We WOP/AGs now felt we had something worthwhile to fight back with, and we were to be given the opportunity to make full use of them. The black paint had been removed from the underside of the wings and replaced by a light blue to make us more difficult to find.

There were said to be five good reasons for us to fly at low level:

1. It was well nigh impossible for us to be picked up by German radar.
2. We presented a fast-moving target for German anti-aircraft gunners who would only have us in their sights for moments.
3. Enemy fighters could not attack us from below where we were most vulnerable.
4. Our camouflage was excellent, making it difficult for patrolling enemy fighters to see us from above.
5. We obviously had the opportunity to drop our bombs on the target with greater accuracy.

We were declared operational shortly after our move to Oulton and dispatched crews on the shipping patrols, though 'The Three Ms' had to wait. On 15 April our new CO, who had been with the squadron less than a month, with his crew, was shot down attacking one of the first convoys sighted. Flying at 200 mph, skimming the waves, there was little hope of survival if the aircraft or the pilot was hit by flak. The casualties among the senior officers in the Group were to prove to be exorbitantly high.

On 25 April, a very pleasant spring day, we caught the flight truck up to the airstrip as usual, but this was to be a day different from any that had gone before. We were called to the briefing room where we were briefed for a solo 'fringe beat' off the Dutch coast near

Flushing; if we failed to sight any shipping, we could fly inland to search for a suitable target on which to unload our four 250 lb bombs, which had been fitted with 11-second delay fuses. Once again there was that same mixture of excitement and apprehension I had experienced on the occasion of my very first operation in August 1940.

The minutes seemed to stand still as we waited our time for take-off, but finally it arrived and we taxied out and took off at 1848 hours, climbing to about 1,000 feet before setting course for the Norfolk coast where, as soon as we were over the sea, George brought the aircraft down to nought feet, our slipstream making a wake in the sea behind us. We flew on alone until the flat Dutch coast came into view, then turned north and flew parallel to the coast, searching in vain for any sign of enemy shipping.

At the end of our area of search George turned the aircraft and headed for the land, where I felt the aircraft lift as we went over the sea wall like a steeplechaser. The countryside was very flat, not unlike parts of East Anglia, and an old man on his bicycle looked up and gave us a cheery wave. We flew on undisturbed until we found ourselves on the outskirts of Flushing, where, having found no other suitable target, my colleagues decided to drop our bombs on the docks, but just as Ron was pressing the bomb switch, George had to lift a wing to miss a derrick, and the bombs fell on the railway line. This aggressive act was the signal for German anti-aircraft gunners to open fire with great enthusiasm to indicate their disapproval of our disturbing their evening schnapps or whatever.

They must have been pretty accurate, as they managed to knock two sizeable holes in our tail unit. George responded by "putting his foot down", still keeping at nought feet, and dropping down over a sea wall into an estuary that led to the sea. At one stage, as we were flying along the estuary, I was actually looking up at a German gun emplacement, which must have been infuriating for the gunners, who couldn't depress their guns sufficiently to fire at us whereas I was able to fire at them.

We headed out to sea expecting, but not receiving, the attention of the Luftwaffe, landing at Oulton after a flight lasting 2 hours 20 minutes feeling very pleased with ourselves. It had been a fairly exhilarating experience in which thrill had taken the place of fear – certainly an operation I will never forget. As well as being able to see what we were actually bombing and, in the case of the gun emplacement, to see the face of the enemy, gave a whole new meaning to the task in which we were engaged, and was such a marvellous contrast to the night operations on which we had flown the previous autumn and winter.'

The following day it was the turn of six crews from 21 Squadron to find a convoy of three 4,000-tonners, eight smaller ships and three flak ships, which between them were able to put up a murderous hail of flak. W/C G. A. Bartlett DFC, leading the attack, was fatally hit, crashing into the sea. He was followed almost immediately by the aircraft piloted by Sgt C. F. Spouge, both crews being killed. The same day 12 Blenheims from 82 Squadron carried out a sweep off Norway, where they attacked three cargo ships, while other crews were flying 'fringe beats' with varying degrees of success. P/O R. E. Tallis and his crew bombed and machine gunned five Bf 110s on an airfield west of Sand, destroying one and damaging the others. He was joined by Sgt Inman and his crew, and together they successfully survived a 16-minute battle with three 109s. (F/L Tallis DFC was lost on 29 April when 82 Squadron dispatched 15 aircraft in a sweep off Norway. P/O D. White also failed to return.)

'Dinty' Moore recalls:

'On the morning of 27 April we flew south to Chivenor in North Devon to re-fuel and to patrol a shipping beat off the French coast. At 1320 hours we took off again with five other Blenheims heading south until we reached a point 30 miles from the enemy coast, where we split up into three pairs to sweep a larger area. We and our partner flew on until we were close to the coast, when we saw the telltale smoke of a small convoy of two merchant ships escorted by a patrol boat. There was no hesitation as we headed for our target, each aircraft heading for a different ship, George jinking our kite to present a more difficult target. We remained at nought feet until at the last moment George hauled us up just over the masts of our target while Ron dropped our bombs. As we hurtled over the top of the mast I found that I was looking up at the belly of the other Blenheim that had just bombed, but fortunately we did not collide.

We returned to nought feet immediately and I was able to fire several bursts at the unfortunate seamen who, together with the patrol boat, had sent up a terrific concentration of flak, through which we had to pass, without managing to hit us. As we flew away, looking back, I'm afraid I was unable to report any dramatic hits on our targets, though it must be remembered that the fuses on our bombs had an 11-second delay. We called in at Chivenor to re-fuel, after a flight that had taken 3 hours 50 minutes, stopping about an hour before flying back to Oulton.

During the month one particularly successful shipping strike was carried out by the Commander of 'B' Flight, S/L Lindsaye, who found and attacked a 7,000-ton enemy vessel, gaining a direct hit and leaving it with a 35-degree list. Sadly, a few days later, on the 30th, he was flying a Blenheim locally on a test flight when the aircraft crashed, killing him and F/O Frank Holmes. While we were saddened by the losses

The grave in the churchyard of St Andrew, Little Massingham, of S/L Hugh J. N. Lindsaye, 18 Squadron, killed on 30 April 1941 while piloting Blenheim IV V6389 in an accident during a drogue-towing practice. The Blenheim dived into a field at Hillington, killing all three crew including Sgt A. E. Stone, observer, and F/O F. Holmes, air gunner. (Author)

on operations, the impact was even greater when they died as the result of an accident.'

On 3 May 18 Squadron moved, temporarily, to a new airstrip at Portreath near Redruth on the north coast of Cornwall. On the 5th 17 Blenheims of 105 Squadron left for Lossiemouth on detachment to attack shipping off the coast of Norway, where supplies of iron ore were being convoyed to Germany. On the 7th 'Dinty' Moore's crew carried out a shipping patrol, within sight of the French coast, without seeing signs of any shipping. However, at the same time, in an attack on an enemy convoy, S/L Robert Bramston 'Binks' Barker (who had replaced Lindsaye) was shot down and killed. His observer, Sgt Norman H. Meanwell, was a very good friend of 'Dinty', who had taken him

S/L Robert Bramston 'Binks' Barker, 18 Squadron, the pilot of R3741 WV-X, which was shot down on 7 May 1941 after an attack on a cargo vessel. Barker, Sgt N. H. Meanwell, observer, and Sgt V. Hughes, WOP/AG, were killed. (Mrs Vera Sherring)

to his home at Great Yarmouth to meet his wife Margaret and their baby daughter.

On 8 May six Blenheims, operating in pairs, made the first successful attack when the first pair, flown by W/C Arnold L. Christian and P/O J. Buckley, found 20 ships forming up at the entrance to Hvs Fiord. During a low-level dive on a steamer, Christian's Blenheim was hit by flak and he was last seen 2 miles off the Norwegian coast with the port engine burning furiously. F/Sgt H. F. Hancock, his observer, and Sgt G. Wade, the WOP/AG, also perished. Buckley probably destroyed a merchant ship, and managed to return to Lossiemouth. The other pairs returned without sighting any ships. The loss of Christian, his skill, sense of fun, dry

Hughie Edwards, who assumed command of 105 Squadron after the loss of W/C Arnold Christian during a shipping strike off Norway on 8 May 1941. (RAAF Point Cook)

humour and superb airmanship, was a huge blow to the squadron that he had rapidly transformed to efficient daylight low-level operations. Just two days later, 26-year-old W/C Hughie Idwal Edwards, an Australian of Welsh ancestry, replaced him.

At Horsham St Faith W/C Edmund Nelson, on taking command of 139 Squadron, with no experience of operational flying, found that the squadron had suffered from the losses of aircrew and had few experienced crews. However, there was one Sergeant pilot who had almost completed his operational tour, so it was from this lowly officer that Nelson obtained most of his knowledge for his new command.

On 9 May 'Dinty' Moore's crew were more successful.

'Patrolling off Brest we saw smoke on the horizon, and as we approached we found a small convoy with the usual escorting patrol boat. We flew straight into the attack, following the same pattern as before, George doing his best to drop our bombs down the funnels of the merchantman. Quickly returning to sea level after the attack, I was again able to machine gun the decks of this ship and the patrol boat. Sadly we were unable to claim any direct hits, though we didn't hang around to find out. The concentration of flak was just as impressive but "lady luck" was with us and we emerged unscathed. On our way back to Portreath, where we landed after a flight lasting 3 hours 35 minutes, we flew over the Scilly Isles, which, as we had climbed to a reasonable height, looked very small indeed.

The same afternoon, in attacking another convoy, we lost one of the original pilots of the squadron, who had been a member at the outbreak of the war, F/L R. Langebear and his crew, F/Sgt A. K. Newberry and Sgt J. R. Stone. On the 12th those of us who had an aircraft that had not been damaged in the raid by the Luftwaffe flew away from sunny Cornwall to the grey skies of Oulton and the comfort of Blickling Hall.

The following day, in company with other members of the squadron, we took off to fly another shipping "beat", but finding the weather most unfriendly we were back on the ground within 1 1/4 hours. We were quickly re-fuelled and back in the air in a quarter of an hour to complete the patrol, without sighting any shipping, on a flight that lasted 3 1/2 hours. On the 17th we took off at 1010 hours to fly another shipping "beat", being in the air for 3¹/₂ hours, doing our best to find a target, but without success.'

On 11 May 107 Squadron, commanded by W/C Laurence V. E. Petley, a square-jawed, pensive and unassuming man known as 'Petters', arrived at Great Massingham from Leuchars, Scotland, where they had been based temporarily since March, attached to Coastal Command flying shipping sorties. Although they had attacked two U-boats during April and had distinguished themselves in several shipping strikes and convoy escorts, the squadron had lost two COs, W/Cs J. W. Duggan, on 21 January 1941, and W. E. Cameron, on 6 April.

No sooner had the Blenheim crews touched down and found their billets, in houses and country homes in the village, than they were on their way again, this time on a shipping strike off Heligoland on 13 May. Twelve aircraft were detailed to attack, and they flew across the North Sea in line abreast, led superbly by leading navigator Sgt J. C. 'Polly' Wilson RNZAF. Two Blenheims returned early with mechanical problems, but the remaining aircraft went in at 200–400 feet and dropped almost 4 tons of bombs smack on the target. The attack was achieved with complete surprise and the Blenheims were safely away before the Luftwaffe could intervene. A congratulatory telegram arrived the same day from the AOC: 'Well done 107 Squadron – Stevenson'.

On 21 May 107 Squadron once more went after shipping at Heligoland. The Blenheims roared in at 50 feet, the prevailing good visibility unfortunately ensuring that there could be no element of surprise. As the formation drew level with the coast the gunners opened up in an

Officers of 18 Squadron in front of the Old Rectory at Massingham in March 1941. Back row: P/O R. Daniel (KIA 22.3.41); P/O Gibbs; P/O Gilbert; P/O O'Brien; P/O W. J. Fenton (KIA 3.4.41); P/O C. C. Sherring; P/O G. H. Cowings (KIA 22.3.41); P/O Duffell. Front row: F/O Frank Holmes (KIA 30.4.41); F/O R. F. Tapp (KIA 13.4.41); F/L P. H. M. Clark (KIA 5.11.41); S/L D. Addenbrooke (W/C, 101 Sqn, KIA 3.4.41) ; W/C A. C. H. Sharpe; S/L Clayton (Admin); F/L J. F. G. 'Jenks' Jenkins (W/C, DSO DFC, 114 Sqn, KIA 27.3.42); F/L Dick O'Farrell; F/O Navin (Doctor). (Mrs Vera Sherring)

Officers and wives of 18 Squadron pictured in the lounge of the Dixon-Spains' house which served as an officers' mess for 18 and 107 Squadrons at Massingham for a time. Back row: S/L Deacon; F/L P. H. M. Clarke (KIA 5.11.41); F/O Nairn; Vera Sherring; Mrs Sharpe; W/C A. C. H. Sharpe; F/O R. F. Tapp (KIA 13.4.41); S/O Joan Forbes WAAF; F/O Frank Holmes (killed 30.4.41); 'Jenks' Jenkins; Mrs Yvonne Lindsaye; P/O G. H. Cowings (KIA 22.3.41) (behind); S/L Hugh J. N. Lindsaye (who with Frank Holmes was killed in a Blenheim accident during a drogue-towing practice on 30.4.41 when the drogue separated from the cable and fouled the port tailplane); Michael Dixon-Spain RNVR (behind, with glass raised). Seated: Paul Brancker, Jenkins's observer, and (behind bottle) Nora Clayton. The house is now a religious retreat. (Mrs Vera Sherring)

attempt to swamp the enemy defences, but they were immediately enveloped by bursts of heavy flak. F/Sgt Kenneth Wolstenholme's Blenheim was hit and he left the scene as fast as he could with one engine on fire and 'Polly' Wilson dead at his position. Another Blenheim was forced to ditch and would almost certainly have been picked up by the Germans if Sgt Roy Ralston, the pilot of another Blenheim, had not turned back, climbed to 1,500 feet and sent out a distress signal in plain language, giving the position of the ditched crew who by now had taken to their dinghy (except F/Sgt D. J. R. Craig, who drowned). They were rescued by ASR and Ralston was awarded the DFM for his action. Wolstenholme (who became famous after the war as a BBC sports commentator) made it back to Massingham, where 'Polly' Wilson was

laid to rest in the lovely country churchyard close by the airfield.

Shipping sweeps continued on 22 May, but 105 Squadron made only one attack, in poor visibility, on a 1,000-tonner, without results. However, a sweep on the 25th proved more rewarding. Three aircraft attacked two 6,000-ton and one 4,000-ton merchant ships, and hits were observed on all three. Twenty miles away, and only 3 minutes later, another 4,000-tonner was attacked by another crew, but without visible result. Intense light flak was met during all attacks, and north of Texel P/O G. E. J. Rushbrooke's Blenheim was hit. Although apparently undamaged, they were last seen flying toward Ameland.

Eight aircraft had been briefed for the shipping attacks and a further three joined five of 18

Squadron in an attack on Nordeney. The formation was met by intense heavy and light flak when within 3 miles of the town, and the leader turned away to assess the situation, only to be set upon by two Bf 109s. One aircraft lost an engine and dropped behind, but the attacks were beaten off successfully. Later three more 109s appeared, but the formation held close together and only one Blenheim, of 18 Squadron, was lost, the gunner of another being killed. One of the 109s was damaged.

'Dinty' Moore describes these operations:

'On each shipping patrol you took off with your desire to find a convoy to attack, which you knew would be defended by a murderous curtain of flak, fighting with your natural desire to stay alive. You would fly alone or in company mile after mile over an empty cruel-looking sea searching continuously for an elusive target. If your search was successful, or unsuccessful, dependent on your point of view, the whole action would be over in a matter of moments. I submit that the manner in which this campaign was carried out, in aircraft ill-suited for the task, showed a high degree of courage and determination on the part of the crews involved. Such attacks were later made by cannon-firing fighters and Beaufighter strike wings, some carrying torpedoes and others fitted with cannon, both of which were extremely successful.

On 25 May, a beautiful Sunday afternoon, we were briefed to carry out a low-level attack on a seaplane base on the island of Nordeney in the Frisian Islands off the north-west coast of Germany. The raid was to be carried out by eight Blenheims, five from our squadron and three from another in the Group. The raid was to be led by S/L Johnny Munro, a man for whom we had the highest regard. On the ground he had a slight speech impediment, whereas in the air he was articulate, decisive and a born leader. The plan was to fly to a point north of Nordeney and to approach the target from that direction with the intention of confusing the defenders.

We taxied out and took off at 1355 hours, one behind the other, forming up into three vic formations with ourselves as No 2 to Munro. We crossed the Norfolk coast before coming down to sea level, settling down on to a course that would take us to the point where we would turn for our run into the island. It was a beautiful sunny day with excellent visibility and one couldn't help wondering what the folk at home would be doing on this Sunday afternoon.

The grave in the churchyard of St Andrew, Little Massingham, of Sgt J. C. 'Polly' Wilson RNZAF, 107 Squadron observer, who was killed by flak on an operation to Heligoland on 21 May 1941 in a Blenheim piloted by F/Sgt Kenneth Wolstenholme, the famous post-war sports commentator. (Author)

We knew it was to be a long flight, during which we would be constantly on the alert, searching for any sign of either ships or enemy aircraft. During operational flights we were required to keep radio silence so as not to give our position away to the enemy, so when we changed course to head for Nordeney, we could only make frantic signals to our leader to indicate that I had seen the smoke of a convoy on the horizon. On this occasion the land target was our main priority so, although there was the risk of an alert wireless operator on the convoy notifying the defenders on Nordeney of our approach, there was little choice but to carry on. Finally the island came into view, with a heavily armoured German patrol boat directly in our path, which we could have avoided. However, as if that wasn't enough, patrolling over the island were five Me 109F fighters who were obviously a welcoming committee we could have done without.

It is stating the obvious to say that "our cover was blown", so our fears of an alert wireless operator reporting our approach were justified. Whatever Munro might have decided as to whether or not to carry on with the raid, the matter was decided for him as the three aircraft from the other squadron turned inside us and headed west with the rest of us in hot pursuit. We kept close together for our joint protection, jettisoning the bombs, giving the engines full boost and keeping as low as possible. The fighters wasted no time in mounting an attack and the sea bubbled and foamed as bullets and cannon shells churned up the water. There was no time for fear as we fought back, firing as the fighters came into range. There was the stench of cordite from my guns, then a perspex panel in my turret blew out so I felt as if I was sitting in a hurricane. I could see that the WOP/AG in the aircraft next to us had been hit and there was blood all over the back of his turret. One of our formation, obviously hit, crashed into the sea and disintegrated, but this success did not satisfy the enemy, who still came in to attack, though one of the fighters, obviously damaged, with its undercarriage hanging down, finally withdrew. After what had seemed like an eternity, the others flew off, either due to lack of ammunition or fuel. I found I had no ammunition left for one gun and only ten rounds for the other.

At the conclusion of the engagement one Blenheim, piloted by "Tich" Thorne, who had joined the squadron with me, had been very badly damaged, to such an extent that I doubted if he would make it back to base. We were unable to stay with him as we had to limp home with damage to both wings and the tail. We landed at our parent 'drome, Horsham St Faith, after an operation that had lasted 4 hours.

We had not been on the ground for many minutes when we saw another Blenheim, which was obviously in some difficulties, coming in to land. The pilot successfully landed and as the aircraft taxied towards us we could see that it was so badly damaged it looked like a sieve. Miraculously it was "Tich" Thorne and his crew, none of whom, despite the enormity of the damage, had received a scratch.

We now made enquiries to find out "who had got the chop" and were told that they were F/Sgt D. G. Keane, pilot, Sgt G. M. 'Jock' Duffus, observer, and Sgt L. E. Crow, WOP/AG. The dead WOP/AG was Sgt E. A. Lloyd, who had flown with P/O Watson, pilot, and P/O E. K. Aires, observer. This had been a bad day for the squadron as 'B' Flight had lost another Blenheim crew that morning in attacking a ship: Sgts F. Wood, pilot, E. G. Baker, observer, and C. N. Harris, WOP/AG. It is difficult to describe one's feelings after the loss of so many friends, for while we mourned their loss, we could not suppress a sense of elation at having survived. The only way you could carry on and retain your sanity was believing, no matter what, you would be the one to get back.'

Chapter Four

Churchill's Light Cavalry

*And you who trod the clouds – Oh! great of heart! –
And you who laughed beneath the shadow of death –
And you who toiled that other men might live –
Oh! getting on in years and short of breath!*

'Recompense' by F/L Anthony Richardson RAFVR

June 1941 saw the continuation of the search for shipping, 'fringe attacks', *Circuses* and deeper penetration of enemy territory using cloud cover when it was available. Thursday 6 June was an important day in the lives of everyone in 2 Group when the Prime Minister, Winston Churchill, visited them. Jim 'Dinty' Moore, now a F/Sgt, remembers the occasion:

'During the day aircraft were lined up for inspection by the great man and two crews of each of the squadrons in the Group arrived to take part in this special occasion. In addition to the Bristol Blenheims there were Short Stirling, Handley Page Halifax and Flying Fortress I aircraft, and the twin-engined Avro Manchester. These aircraft, with wing spans of nearly 100 feet, looked enormous beside the Blenheim with its wing span a mere 56 feet.

"Winnie", as he was popularly known, appeared, accompanied by members of the Government, and sundry senior officers. He mounted some steps used for the inspection of aircraft engines and invited us to gather round him. We did, with alacrity. During his speech he referred to 2 Group as his "light cavalry", and in his address he began by reminding us that 43,000 civilians had been killed in air raids on Britain in the previous 12 months and that his promise that the RAF would retaliate by day and by night had not yet been fulfilled. He had come personally, he said, to

explain the importance of the special tasks we would be undertaking in the next few weeks, when our operations were likely to have a major impact on the course of the war.

He then gave us some more unpalatable facts.

Prime Minister Winston Churchill, flanked by AVM Sir Richard Peirse, C-in-C Bomber Command (right) and G/C Paddy Bandon, Station Commander (left), visits West Raynham on 6 June 1941. AVM Stevenson is second from left, while behind Churchill (left to right) are ACM Sir Charles Portal, Prof Lindemann and Clement Atlee, deputy PM. (Mrs Vera Sherring collection)

German intervention in the Middle East was turning the war against us in that theatre. "Germany must be forced to move her fighters westwards," he told us. So, escorted by large numbers of fighters, we would attack targets in the West that Germany would have to defend. Our purpose was to relieve pressure on other fronts and to ease the stranglehold on our life lines. "I am relying on you," were his closing words. There is little doubt that the personal visit of this determined individual with his magnetic personality was greatly appreciated by all of us who were present. He made us feel that the operations in which we were involved were well worthwhile. The great man made a second visit to the Group shortly after Germany attacked Russia on 22 June. On this occasion he reiterated his determination to carry the war to our enemy in every possible way in order to assist our new Allies.'

Churchill's visit was a morale boost, and crews badly needed one. Losses had got so bad that the mood among them, while determined, became grim, so much so that at Massingham one evening F/O Ewels observed that after a particularly hazardous operation 'the Wing Commander and other 107 Squadron pilots in the mess sat for a long time in silence and then quietly got out notepaper and wrote out their wills. Not long afterwards all were gone.'

F/L Anthony Richardson put it into words very succinctly when he penned 'Address to the Mother of a Dead Observer':

'Madam, this war is scarcely of my making –
Why pick on me? I'm sorry about Jack.
There was a gunner and a pilot, too,
Who won't come back . . .'

On 31 May the England and Middlesex cricketer, Bill Edrich, a P/O, his observer, Vic Phipps, and his WOP/AG, Ernie Hope, joined 107 Squadron. On 7 June they were one of nine crews briefed to take part in a raid on a heavily defended convoy en route from Hamburg to Rotterdam. S/L Peter Simmons DFC, who was flying the last operation of his second tour, led the formation off and they formed up in the usual three vics of three aircraft, flying low over the sea. Shortly after leaving the Norfolk coast they flew into dense fog, which was right down to sea level, making it almost impossible to judge the height of the aircraft above the sea or to see the next aircraft in formation.

Simmons flew on with Edrich sticking as close to him as possible until, after what must have seemed an eternity, the fog thinned, then dispersed. Unfortunately there was no sign of the other aircraft in their vic of three; Sgt Harry F.

107 Squadron pilots and their crews, May–June 1941, posed before the camera in the garden of the Dixon-Spains' house, which at that time served as the 107 Squadron Officers' Mess. The pilots are in the back row, their observers in the middle, and air gunners in front. Back row: Unknown F/Sgt pilot; F/O Dudenay; F/L F. Wellburn; S/L Peter Simmons; W/C L. V. E. Petley, CO; S/L Zeke Murray RNZAF; P/O Bill Edrich; F/O M. V. Redfern-Smith; and an unknown F/Sgt pilot. Other ranks identified are: in front of Wellburn (PoW 4.7.41) his observer, Sgt D. A. Dupree, and his air gunner, Sgt A. E. Routley (both KIA 4.7.41, Bremen); in front of Petley, F/L R. A. Bailey DFC and Sgt W. M. Harris, air gunner (all three KIA 4.7.41, Bremen); in front of Edrich, Sgt Vic Phipps, observer, and Sgt Ernest Hope, air gunner; and in front of Redfern-Smith, Sgt J. A. Rudkin, observer, and Sgt K. T. Noakes (all KIA 22/23.6.41, Dunkirk). (Mrs Vera Sherring)

Fordham, Simmons's No 2, had hit the sea and was lost without trace, highlighting the dangers of low-level flying over the sea in such conditions. The other six Blenheims had abandoned the operation and returned to base.

The convoy eventually came into view, about a dozen ships, some 2 miles away. Simmons climbed to 250 feet, followed by Edrich, putting on full boost before diving towards their quarry, Simmons aiming for a large merchantman in the centre, while Edrich aimed for another. They were met with a terrific barrage of flak, the two pilots skidding and jinking their aircraft to present a difficult target to the gunners. In the turret Ernie Hope fired at the nearest flak ship, Edrich joining in with his front gun as they drew closer. As they closed on to their targets, just clearing the masts, the two observers released their four 250 lb armour-piercing bombs. As they flew off, keeping as low as possible, they were delighted to see one merchantman wreathed in flames and the other listing. During the attack a great deal of the rudder on Edrich's aircraft had

been shot away, yet they both returned to base safely. Simmons was awarded a well-deserved bar to his DFC.

The same afternoon Edrich played cricket for the squadron against a local village team – quite a contrast, although typical of the strange existence of all operational aircrew, one minute in the thick of battle then back to the comforts of their base with a trip to the local or whatever took the individual's fancy.

June had begun badly with four frustrating missions, none of which were completed due to the weather, and the 'Met' Officer bore the brunt of the crews' frustrations. Then, on 15 June, W/C Hughie Edwards, CO of 105 Squadron, led six crews on a shipping sweep, when they found a convoy of eight merchant ships off Den Haag. Edwards carried out a successful attack on a 4,000-ton merchantman, Sgt Jackson bombing another large ship. (A squadron of ten E-boats was seen and avoided by most of the formation, but F/O Peter H. Watts, on his first operation with the Squadron, mistook the heavily armed

A Blenheim of 21 Squadron, returned from an operation. F/L H. Waples DFC (KIA 23.6.41) in flying kit; acting Squadron CO, S/L Doug Cooper, with a plaster on his face; G/C Sinclair, Station Commander, RAF Watton, with hands in pockets, back to camera; and F/O Tonks, Intelligence Officer, without a cap beside the aircraft, next to F/O Duncan, 21 Squadron MO, and S/L Buckler, facing camera. (Wartime Watton Museum)

and manoeuvrable craft for merchant shipping. He went in low, and although he hit one, he was shot down in flames. On 1 July Edwards was awarded the DFC for this daring low-level operation.) F/Sgt Arthur Guseford in 110 Squadron, who was shot down by Uffz. Barein of I./JG1 in a Bf109F, and another Blenheim, were lost on shipping beats.

Next day, Beats 7 and 10 resulted in the loss of two more Blenheims. During an attack on a 'squealer' off the Frisians, F/Sgt E. A. Rex Leavers DFM of 21 Squadron, went in so low that his Blenheim hit the ship's mast and he cartwheeled into the sea. P/O Ian Watson and P/O Ernest K. Aires, who had cheated death on 25 May, were lost when they were shot down by flak from a German convoy off the Hook of Holland. WOP/AG Sgt Tom Dean, was the third member of the 18 Squadron crew.

'Dinty' Moore describes another June raid:

'On 17 June we flew over to Horsham St Faith for a briefing for a raid that we would never forget. We found that we were to take part in a *Circus* attack on the Kuhlmann Chemical Works at Chocques near Bethune in northern France, accompanied by a large fighter escort. We were to fly in one large formation of

Sgt E. A. R. Leavers DFM (right), pictured during an earlier detachment to Malta, with Sgt Mike Cleary. (Wartime Watton Museum)

24 aircraft in eight vics of three stacked up one slightly below and behind the other. We also discovered that we had drawn the "short straw" in our position, as we would be the last aircraft in this large and unwieldy formation. [105 Squadron, meanwhile, would fly their first *Circus* operation with a formation of six in a high-level attack on shipping at Le Havre]. Later in the war, no matter how many bombers took part in a raid, we never flew in boxes of more than six aircraft, which could manoeuvre sufficiently to carry out evasive action in response to attack by flak or fighters.

At 1745 hours we taxied out, with my excitement having some difficulty overcoming my fear, and took off, the last in the queue, gaining height and getting into formation. Flying down to our rendezvous with our escort, looking forward I could see this enormous formation of Blenheims, while looking back over the tail there was an empty sky. Whenever I see a flock of birds I am always reminded of that moment. Our escort of Hurricanes, who were our close escort, closed in around us while the Spitfires flew high above forming a protect live umbrella. They certainly were a most comforting sight.

We droned on towards the French coast, having climbed to our operational height of about 10,000 feet before being met by a heavy barrage of flak. We carried on towards the target, by which time our vic was lagging behind the main formation and we attracted the unwelcome attention of a number of German fighters who had managed to avoid our escort, which itself was also under attack. The sky was full of fighters whirling around in combat while we were under constant attack. One determined character actually flew up between us and the No 2 in our formation, but although I was surprised, I was astounded to find that I immediately reacted and managed to fire a burst as he went past. My instant reaction must have been due to the training I had received.

The fighters were armed with cannon, so on occasions they could stay off out of range of our machine guns and take pot shots at us. Doing this they hit us in both wings and put our port engine out of commission. If that was the bad news, the good news was that the power for the landing gear and the turret was supplied by the starboard engine, which, thankfully, was undamaged. Losing power on the port engine initially made our kite swing to the left, although George somehow managed to manoeuvre underneath our colleagues for mutual protection. Sadly, they gradually pulled away from us, leaving us an unfriendly and persistent Messerschmitt for

Bristol Blenheim IVs of 139 Squadron from Horsham St Faith off on a Circus *operation in 1941.* (Eric Atkins)

company and a heavy flak barrage to speed us, if that is appropriate in this instance, on our way as we crossed the coast at Cap Gris Nez. Fortunately one of our escorting Hurricanes came to our aid and we heard later that he had shot down our "German friend" near the English coast.

The Blenheim was not noted for its ability to fly on one engine, and George had to fight with the controls to keep us in the air and on course. Apart from sending a message back to base notifying them of our problems, there was little I could do but cross my fingers. We could have landed at any aerodrome, once we crossed the coast, but George was determined to get us back to Horsham St Faith, which he not only did but also brought us in for a perfect landing. It was, by any standard, an example of marvellous flying, so there was no wonder that Ron and I were happy with our pilot. The flight actually lasted for 3 hours 10 minutes, although it seemed a great deal longer.'

Much of June was a little of an anti-climax, for several operations were abandoned through the lack of the cloud cover so necessary for the survival of the poorly armed Blenheims. On Thursday 27 June ten crews from 107 Squadron were ordered to fly to Swanton Morley for a special briefing where they, and ten crews from 105, were told that they would carry out a low-level attack in daylight on the docks at Bremen the following day. This meant flying over the German mainland for some 105 miles, far beyond the range of fighter protection. The formation was to be led by W/C Laurence Petley, but when it was time for take off, at 0430,

'Petters' was unable to start his starboard engine. The remaining 19 aircraft took off on time, so it fell to the lot of P/O Bill Edrich, flying his 11th operation, to take over the lead.

They had been flying for some time when Petley, having persuaded his faulty engine to start, caught up with them and took over the lead, much to the relief of Edrich. When they reached a point opposite Cuxhaven they saw a large enemy convoy, which opened up on them, so the essential element of surprise had been lost. Reluctantly, therefore, Petley turned round and brought the formation back home. Hughie Edwards, at the head of the 105 formation, said afterwards that having got so far he thought they might have gone on. Command thought so too, as Bill Edrich explains:

'After landing back at Massingham we went straight over to the cottage that housed our tiny ops room and headquarters, and there the adjutant, Tony Richardson, was standing with the telephone in his hand. He called out to "Petters", "Sir, the AOC's on the line."

We were all feeling pretty glum, and the chatter that normally succeeds an operation was absent. All eyes were watching "Petters" as he took the receiver. We saw his face blanch and tauten with anger and humiliation as he listened to the voice that we ourselves couldn't hear. In the silent ops room we were watching our leader being accused of cowardice, and we knew that in Stevenson's mind we were all tainted with it. Watching "Petters" and remembering how nearly the leadership had fallen to me, I wondered again what I would have done, and I saw myself, like "Petters", arraigned before the entire squadron by a contemptuous AOC.

"If that's what you think," we heard "Petters" say, "we'll do the whole bloody show again this afternoon."

We didn't doubt that he meant it. And we didn't doubt that Stevenson was capable of sending us. The political pressures he was being subjected to, six days after Hitler's attack on Russia, must have been enormous. We hung around to hear our fate, but when it came through it was an anti-climax. We were to fly up to Driffield, a bomber station in Yorkshire, that afternoon and await orders.'

Petley led nine crews to Driffield but was ordered not to fly on the subsequent operation. 107 Squadron was informed that six Halifax bombers, the first ever to operate, were to bomb Kiel the following morning as a diversion, while the Blenheims were to mount a low-level raid on the Luftwaffe base at Westerland on the island of Sylt. The news was received in silence, for Sylt was renowned for its formidable defences. The Station Commander at Driffield did his best to boost morale, claiming that it was no accident that the raid was timed for midday Sunday, 'when the German fighter pilots, creatures of habit, will be enjoying a pre-lunch lager'. This inspired planning was invalidated when the operation was delayed for 24 hours, until 1000 hours on Monday 30 June.

Seven Blenheims, led by a New Zealander, S/L Zeke Murray, took off and headed out over the North Sea. Eventually the island came into view and the crews soon experienced the intensity of flak for which the island was famed. In describing it, Edrich says:

'I have seen paintings of naval battles, with gun flashes illuminating the scene and the water being thrown up on all sides by shell bursts, but never have I seen such an inferno of fire power as was directed at us in the next few minutes.'

Despite the intense opposition the formation flew on towards their target, though one of the Blenheims had been shot down, and three others were missing by the time the survivors arrived over the airfield where they dropped their bombs, with understandable haste, before turning for home.

The survivors held close together when, about 100 miles from Sylt and feeling reasonably safe, they were attacked by four Bf 109s. The WOP/AG in Murray's aircraft took over fire control over the radio, giving directions for evasive action and directing the fire of his colleagues. The battle continued with fire being exchanged, the Blenheims soaking up a lot of damage, one cannon shell hitting Murray's port engine, holing his petrol tank, though he was still able to stay in the air. Soon the guns on the Blenheims stopped, either because their guns had jammed or they had run out of ammunition, though fortunately the same fate had befallen the Germans, who broke off the engagement.

Finally they reached Driffield, where Murray and one other pilot crash-landed, the remaining aircraft being so badly damaged that they were found to be unfit to fly. Shortly after they had landed another Blenheim, obviously in trouble, came into the circuit and landed. It was piloted by Sgt Levers who, flying through the concentration of flak over Sylt, had collided with one of the missing Blenheims, his flaps and ailerons on one side being chewed up. Somehow he had managed to regain control and quite remarkably had managed to guide the aircraft, using limited cloud cover, back across the North Sea to Driffield, keeping it level by holding the aileron control in the vertical instead of the horizontal position. When it had become too much of a strain he had borrowed a leather belt from his navigator and strapped up the controls. He received the immediate award of the DFM.

When, on the evening of 3 July, crews in East Anglia went to bed, Bremen had already been scheduled as the target for the morrow. Operation *Wreckage*, as it was code-named, would be led by W/C Hughie Edwards, who had followed behind Petley to the same target ten days earlier. As usual sleep was difficult, probably more so given the nature of the difficult and dangerous operation. F/L Tony Richardson RAFVR, 107 Squadron adjutant at Massingham, had already witnessed too many such days, and nights, at close hand. His was the painful duty to write to the bereaved relatives of his brother officers and men who never returned. He later dedicated a poem, 'Night Before Bremen', to his CO and the crews of 107 Squadron, who would fly the *Wreckage* operation.

At least one man relished the thought. Irishman W/O Samuel Joseph Magee, the legendary 107 Squadron Armament Officer, had persuaded Petley to let him go along as an extra gunner aboard one of the Blenheims. During low-level raids by German intruders at Wattisham, while everyone else took cover, Magee had calmly set up his .303 Vickers Gas Operated with its wooden butt and special trigger and had blasted away at incoming Dorniers and Junkers 88. Off duty Magee ran an 180 hp Wolseley around the narrow country lanes at alarming speeds, on seemingly inexhaustible supplies of petrol.

On the morning of 4 July Magee joined F/L Wellburn and his observer, Sgt D. A. Dupree, and Sgt A. E. Routley, air gunner, and together they boarded V6193, one of six 107 Squadron Blenheims taking part. Magee entered the almost dark compartment aft of the bomb well armed with his beloved VGO, and several magazines containing 100% tracer. He settled on to the uncomfortably small ledge behind the bomb well camera hatch so he could see through the small perspex panel in the centre of the door, which he would remove just before the target and hurl a 40 lb GP bomb through it before blasting away with his VGO!

Edwards took off at 0521 hours from Swanton Morley and led nine Blenheims into the clear blue Norfolk sky. It was his 36th operation of the war. His observer, P/O A. S. Ramsay, and his gunner, Sgt G. D. P. Quinn, settled down to their tasks and the crew kept their eyes peeled for the six crews of 107 Squadron led by Petley, who would be joining them after take-off from Massingham.

However, mist and fog, which was to dog the first 100 miles of the operation, shielded them from view as the formation droned low over the sea, maintaining radio silence. Edwards could see his two wingmen but little else. Meanwhile, diversions were in progress: W/C Hurst was leading five crews of 226 Squadron to bomb gun emplacements on Nordeney, and six Blenheims of 21 Squadron were flying a *Circus*, with the customary fighter escort, to the Chocques Chemical Works. Hurst's Blenheim, hit by flak, literally blew up.

When the *Wreckage* Blenheims finally made landfall at the German coast, one sub-flight of three aircraft of 107 Squadron was no longer with them; S/L Murray and F/O Charney had returned to Massingham with mechanical problems, while a third had aborted when F/L Jones, the pilot, became ill. The remaining 12 tightened up formation and pressed on.

Just before 0730 hours the formation was sighted by a coastal convoy near Nordeney, but Edwards pressed on. As the formation crossed into Germany a few miles south of Cuxhaven, people working in the fields, mistaking the low-level bombers for German aircraft, stopped and looked up to wave. Still at a height of between 50 and 100 feet, Edwards turned the formation south towards Bremen. The attack, timed for 0800 hours, was to be made in a 1¼-mile-wide line-abreast formation, the aircraft spaced 100–200 yards apart and flying at tree-top height. Edwards and his crews weaved between the barrage balloons hoisted to 50 feet above the port and braved the tremendous ack-ack fire that greeted their arrival. As Edwards was to recall later:

'As we rightly assumed, the flak and balloons split up the formation and it became every man for himself. The flak was terrific and frightening. It was bursting all around me for 10 minutes. There was a distinct smell of cordite in the air. I was flying so low that I flew through telephone and telegraph wires.'

About 20 shells found their mark on Edwards's Blenheim and Quinn was hit in the knee by shrapnel. Behind them two 105 Squadron machines were shot out of the sky; Sgt W. A. Mackillop's Blenheim was hit by flak and crashed on to a factory, Sgts E. G. Nethercott and F. G. Entwhistle dying with him, while F/O M. M. Lambert's aircraft was last seen by other crews heading away from Bremen, burning fiercely, later to crash, killing Lambert, Sgt R. Copeland and Sgt F. W. R. Charles.

107 Squadron also lost two Blenheims. Petley was shot down by flak in the target area, killing him, his observer, F/L R. A. Bailey DFC, and Sgt W. M. Harris, air gunner. F/L F. Wellburn was also shot down by flak, and he crashed in the target area. Sgt D. A. Dupree, Sgt A. E. Routley and W/O Magee, the latter no doubt firing to the end, died in the crash, but Wellburn survived to be made a PoW. Dupree, Routley and Magee

were buried on 7 July in the Hollefriedhot cemetery, but in 1945 were exhumed for reburial at Becklingen War Cemetery, Soltau, where all the other crews were buried after the raid.

All the aircraft were damaged. After the target Edwards proceeded to circle Bremen and strafed a stationary train that had opened up on them, before leading the formation out of Germany at low level. He recalled, 'I had great pleasure in using up the ammunition from my one front gun, which silenced the opposition.'

Edwards, his aircraft minus part of the port wing, the port aileron badly damaged, a cannon shell in the radio rack and a length of telegraph wire wrapped round the tail wheel and trailing behind, headed for Bremerhaven and Wilhelmshaven. More flak rose to greet them at Bremerhaven until finally the coastline at Heligoland came into view and the Blenheims dived down to sea level again. The battered formation flew north of the Frisians for a short time, then headed westwards for East Anglia. At

Swanton Morley Sgt W. H. A. Jackson had to belly-land with the observer and gunner wounded. Edwards brought his ailing bomber home and put down safely at Swanton Morley, where Quinn had to be lifted out of the aircraft with a Coles crane.

Although four crews were lost, successful attacks had been made on the docks, factories, a timber yard and railways, and great damage was caused to the tankers and transports that were loaded with vital supplies. Operation *Wreckage* received considerable publicity, and congratulations were sent from the C-in-C Bomber Command and the Chief of Air Staff, Sir Charles Portal, downwards. ACM Stevenson sent a telegram that read, 'This low-flying raid, so gallantly carried out, deep into Germany, without the support of fighters, will always rank high in the history of the Royal Air Force.' One Sergeant even had to broadcast his impression of the raid on the BBC Home Service.

An immediate signal from the C-in-C Bomber

V6028 'D' of 105 Squadron, flown by W/C Hughie Edwards, CO 105 Squadron, on the Bremen raid on 4 July 1941, pictured after the return to Swanton Morley. (RAF)

107 Squadron pilots and observers, May–June 1941. Back row, F/O Youalls; F/O Leach; F/O Bryce; F/O M. V. Redfern-Smith; F/O Dudenay; P/O Sammels; P/O Bill Edrich. Front row: F/L R. A. Bailey DFC (KIA 4.7.41, Bremen); S/L Clayton; S/L Peter Simmons; W/C L. V. E. Petley CO (KIA 4.7.41, Bremen); F/L Zeke Murray RNZAF; F/L Anthony Richardson, adjutant; F/L F. Wellburn (PoW 4.7.41). (Mrs Vera Sherring collection)

Command, Sir Richard Peirse, read: 'YOUR ATTACK THIS MORNING HAS BEEN A GREAT CONTRIBUTION TO THE DAY OFFENSIVE NOW BEING FOUGHT. IT WILL REMAIN AN OUTSTANDING EXAMPLE OF DASH AND INITIATIVE. I SEND YOU AND YOUR CAPTAINS AND CREWS MY WARMEST CONGRATULATIONS AND THE ADMIRATION OF THE COMMAND'.

Amid all the bravura, at Massingham Adjutant F/L Anthony Richardson quietly sat down and penned letters of condolence to the relatives of the crews lost on the raid. He also penned 'Lines to A Widow', which began:

'Lady in your faithlessness,
Do you seek to make redress
To the little one who's down,
In his grave in Bremen town?
. . . I served him once and served him well!
I saw him pick his path to hell!
I knew the very hour he died
Over Bremen crucified!'

After the war the gifted Richardson would write 'Wingless Victory', the story of Basil Embry, his CO when at Wattisham earlier in the war.

Bill Edrich, who returned from leave, had read the reports of the raid in the newspapers.

'When I got back to Little Massingham, the mess that had always been so full of life and personality was silent and empty.

"I'm afraid there's no one from the squadron here," said the Mess Sergeant. "We lost nearly all the officers on the Bremen raid. Those who are left have moved over to West Raynham."

He promised to lay on some transport and I went to my room to collect my things.'

On 7 July 101 Squadron converted to Wellingtons and transferred to 3 Group. Two days later 88 Squadron joined 2 Group at Swanton Morley. At this time the other Blenheim squadrons operating from the UK were: 110 Squadron at Wattisham (226 Squadron had joined 2 Group at Wattisham in May); 18 at

Oulton (which sent a detachment to Malta in October and saw out the rest of the war in the Mediterranean theatre); 105 (detached to Lossiemouth as well as Malta); 21 at Watton; 82 at Bodney (which also sent a detachment to Malta); 139 at Horsham St Faith; 107 at Massingham; and 114 at Leuchars (attached to 18 Group Coastal Command).

'Dinty' Moore flew one op with 114 Squadron, having flown his last op with 18 Squadron on 5 July, another shipping patrol. 'My abiding memory of these operations was the seemingly endless sea, which looked both cold and cruel, rather than the three attacks we had made on enemy shipping.' (Having taken part in 20 ops, his crew's tour was complete and he was posted as an instructor to OTU, Bicester, while the rest of his crew were posted to an OTU in the Middle East. He could not go with them because of his recent bout of pneumonia.) He had completed 49 operational sorties without a scratch, whereas between 12 March and 14 July that year 2 Group had lost 68 Blenheims and their crews (15 from 18 Squadron). There were only 12 crews on a squadron and eight squadrons in the Group, so it represented a very heavy loss rate. Losses to the Blenheim detachments in Malta during 1941–42 were almost 100%. On 18 July 20-year-old Freddie Thripp of 82 Squadron (attached to 110 Squadron) was shot down and killed by an Italian fighter after attacking a power station at Tripoli.

On 21 July Edwards was awarded the VC for courage and leadership displayed on the Bremen operation. He thus became only the second Australian to receive this award (the first having been awarded to Lt F. H. McNamara of the RFC during the First World War). On 28 July P/O Ramsey was awarded the DFC, Sgt Quinn was awarded a bar to his DFM and Sgts Jackson, J. A. Purves and W. N. Williams were each awarded the DFM for their part in the raid.

By this time 105 Squadron was in Malta for operations in the Mediterranean. At the end of August Edwards was posted to AHQ Malta and was replaced by W/C D. W. Scivier RAAF of 107 Squadron. Scivier was in action on his first day, but on 22 September his aircraft collided with another Blenheim and crashed into the sea after his tail fell off. Five days later the last sortie was flown. On 28 September the surviving

squadron members sailed home in a cruiser.

After *Wreckage* 107 Squadron needed to be reformed before it could participate in further raids. Bill Edrich, now with the rank of Flight Lieutenant (a double promotion only six weeks after first becoming operational), still had a serviceable plane and a full crew, so they were loaned to 21 Squadron, where in fact they stayed. Edrich was promoted to Squadron Leader (he had gone from P/O to S/L in 19 days) and flew the rest of his ops with 21 Squadron.

Meanwhile, at West Raynham, 107 Squadron took shape again after its mauling. On 6 July W/C A. F. C. Booth took command; previously he had been a Squadron Leader with 105 Squadron under Hughie Edwards. However, senior rank was certainly no protection. Within a week of his new posting, on 12 July, he was killed during an anti-shipping strike. The new CO was W/C F. A. 'Bunny' Harte DFC SAAF, who was killed in action on 9 October 1941 leading the squadron in Malta. In fact, 2 Group lost six wing commanders in one week. One of them was W/C Thomas N. 'Tim' Partridge DFC, CO of 18 Squadron, who piloted one of four Blenheims that were shot down by flak, on 16 July, when 36 Blenheims from 18, 21 and 139 Squadrons carried out a low-level daylight raid on the docks at Rotterdam. W/C P. F. 'Tom' Webster, 21 Squadron, who led the first wave, was rested and replaced by W/C John C. Kercher.

On 23 July Blenheims from 18 and 139 Squadrons carried out a sweep off the Dutch coast without success. As they were turning for home, led by 23-year-old S/L D. J. A. Roe, the youngest officer of the rank in the RAF, whose father was an MT Sergeant on his squadron, Bf110s of 5./ZG76 appeared, damaging every Blenheim and shooting down two. Sgt Peter D. Baker, and Sgt William M. G. Dunham RCAF, both fell victim to a combination of attacks by Oblt. Hotari Schmude, Ofw. Leschnik and FW. Schmidt. A third Blenheim, piloted by Sgt Wood, severely damaged in the attacks, limped back to Horsham St. Faith, where it was crash-landed by Wood. He and his observer Sgt Johnson, were severely injured. Worse, six crews of 21 Squadron based at Manston attacked a 4,000-ton tanker escorted by four flak ships, and three Blenheims were shot down.

On 24 July 36 Blenheims of 139, 18, 107, 226

W/C F. A. 'Bunny' Harte DFC SAAF (centre), who took over command of 107 Squadron on 12 July 1941 from W/C A. F. C. Booth, who lasted just six days before being killed in action. (Harte himself was killed in action on 9 October 1941 at Malta.) To his left is P/O Bloodworth, and to his right is his gunner at Massingham, P/O Wewage-Smith, who had served in the French Foreign Legion, was a fighter pilot in the Bolivian War and who had returned to Europe to fight in the Spanish Civil War as an air observer. When greeted by one of the squadron Intelligence Officers with, 'Well mercenary, what can I do for you . . ?', his reply was, 'Mercenary I may be, but I'll have you know that I'm doing this at strictly cut prices for patriotic reasons.' (Quotation from Air Gunner *by Mike Henry, Foulis & Co, 1964).* (Mrs Vera Sherring)

and 114 Squadrons flew *Circus* operations to cause a diversion for the bombers attempting to stop the 'Channel Dash' by the *Scharnhorst* and *Gneisenau*. On 30 July 12 crews from 18 and 82 Squadrons, led by S/L Roe, were briefed to attack shipping in the Kiel Canal, making use of cloud cover, which, as so often happened, petered out before they reached the target. However, the operation was anything but uneventful, crews from 18 Squadron attacking a ship in convoy off Heligoland with the loss of Sgt H. D. Cue and crew who were taken prisoner. The 82 Squadron Blenheims seriously damaged three ships in another convoy with the loss of two aircraft. 139 Squadron fared even worse, losing four Blenheims to Bf110s of ZG76. So ended July, during which 39 crews failed to return.

During August squadrons in 2 Group were directed to carry out a period of intensive training in low-level flying, which caused much speculation among the aircrew, who wondered what was to be their target. It was not until the 12th that they found out and the speculation was over. They were to fly to Cologne, where they would split into two forces to make simultaneous

attacks on the Quadrath and Knapsack power stations there.

The 56 Blenheim crews who would have the central role in this historic low-level daylight operation entered their respective operations

26-year-old W/C Thomas N. 'Tim' Partridge DFC, CO 18 Squadron, at Blickling Hall shortly before he was killed in action on 16 July 1941 piloting one of four Blenheims that were shot down by flak during a low-level daylight raid on the docks at Rotterdam. (Mrs Vera Sherring)

Blenheims of 21 Squadron run in for the attack on Rotterdam on 16 July 1941. The nearest aircraft is YH-P V5595, which was one of three shot down by ships' flak off Gravelines while on 'Channel Stop' duties from Manston two days later. The pilot, Sgt J. R. M. Kemp, and his crew survived and were taken prisoner. (Wartime Watton Museum)

rooms and their eyes were drawn to the large map of western Europe on the wall, with the proposed routes and targets displayed. Being human beings, with a desire to survive, their reactions must have varied considerably, though if they felt fear they would have made sure it was not evident to their colleagues. At Watton the briefing was attended by the 18 crews of Force 1 (12 from 21 Squadron and six from 82 Squadron), none of whom had probably heard of Quadrath, but they would certainly recognise on the map the city of Cologne nearby. (The huge Knapsack power station was the largest steam generator in Europe, producing 600,000W; the Quadrath station produced 200,000W, and their destruction would significantly affect war production.)

The aircrew listened intently to their station commander, G/C Laurie F. Sinclair, who three months before had been awarded the George Cross for pulling a WOP/AG from a blazing Blenheim after two of its bombs had exploded. The aircraft were detailed to fly in three boxes of six aircraft (each split into two vics of three), led by W/C John O. C. Kercher (lead box), with Bill Edrich (port box) and S/L H. J. Meakin of 82 Squadron (starboard box).

At the same time 38 crews of Force 2 (comprising 18, 107, 114 and 139 Squadrons), led by W/C James L. Nicol, CO of 114 Squadron (KIA 19 August 1941), were briefed for their attack on Knapsack. One 21-year-old gunner later recorded:

'We were keyed up when we went into the briefing room at 0645, and the Station Commander's opening remarks did nothing to lessen the tension. He started off by saying, "You are going on the biggest and most ambitious operation ever undertaken by the RAF." Then he told us what it was. Cologne, in daylight. 150-odd miles across Germany at tree-top height and then – the power house. Our orders were to destroy our objectives at all costs. We were given the course to follow, the rendezvous with other squadrons of bombers, and the rendezvous with fighters. We were given the parting point for the fighters and the moment at which certain flights would peel off the formation for the attack on the second power house, and then – in formation across Germany.'

Each Force would be escorted as far as Doel, just inside the Belgian border, by six Whirlwind fighters of 263 Squadron, and three squadrons of Spitfires would provide withdrawal support from Walsoorden onwards. The operation would also involve four Fortress Is of 90 Squadron, two of whom would make a high-level attack on Cologne, another De Kooy airfield, and the other Emden, while a 5 Group *Circus* involving six Hampdens of 106 Squadron and six of 44 Squadron, and several squadrons of Spitfires and Hurricanes, would make attacks on Gosnay power station and St Omer-Longuenesse aerodrome respectively.

The gunner takes up the story:

'While pilots and observers were getting all they could from the weather man, we rear gunners gathered round the Signals Officer for identification signs, then hurried out to get ready. Someone said "What a trip!", and got the answer, "Yes, but what a target!"

Knapsack, we were told, was the biggest steam power plant in Europe, producing hundreds of thousands of kilowatts to supply a vital industrial area. If we got it, it would be as good as getting hold of a dozen large factories. One of the pilots on the raid was in civil life a mains engineer for the County of London Electricity Supply. He came away rubbing his hands and explained to us that, with turbines setting up about 3,000 revolutions a minute, blades were likely to fly off in all directions at astronomical speeds, smashing everything and everyone as they went.'

Bill Edrich recalls that it had been hoped, by synchronising the two attacks, to confuse the enemy. As one of the leaders of Force 1, he flew low over a fairly choppy sea to the mouth of the Scheldt, following a series of dog-legs on the way to the target, hoping that the enemy would not guess their intentions. As they flew across Holland, pulling over trees and church spires, people everywhere waved them on. Crews looked down at fields planted out in the pattern of the Dutch flag.

On the way in three Blenheims were lost. T2437 of 82 Squadron, piloted by 18-year-old P/O Graham C. Rolland, was hit by flak and crashed at Strijensas, near the Moerdijk bridge at 1210. He and his two crew, P/Os Hugh M. Clark and Sgt Ernest Bainbridge, were killed. V6423 of 18 Squadron, which was being flown by P/O G. H. Hill, crashed at Diest, Belgium. All three crew survived and were taken prisoner. V7451 of 21 Squadron, piloted by P/O Jim Langston, was hit by a burst of flak, which knocked rear gunner Sgt Ken Attew, WOP/AG, out of his turret before the aircraft crashed at Potz, near the target.

Langstone and Sgt Dave Roberts, observer, survived and were taken prisoner.

As the formation neared the German frontier crews noticed that people were no longer waving, they just watched. In Germany itself people scuttled off to their shelters.

Bill Edrich remembers the operation:

'We had practised our attack many times over a power station at St Neots, and now we prepared to put it into effect. With four 250 lb, 11-second-delay bombs each, we had to clear the target in fairly quick time. My box of six was going in last. At St Neots we had got everyone across the target in less than 3 seconds. Could we manage it now?

The tall chimneys of the power station stood out ominously, forcing us up to 400 feet and more. The three sections were stepped up slightly from front to rear. There was some light flak coming up from the target area, but otherwise we were unopposed – we had achieved complete surprise. Kercher and Meakin flew their formations in like regiments, directly in front of us and slightly below. All we had to do was to keep our position.

We were well past the target when the first bombs went off. Rear-facing cameras in each Blenheim were recording our results. But we could see that the attack had been successful. The core of the power station was in flames when the first bombs went off.'

In his rear turret the 21-year-old Blenheim gunner did not know that they were over the target until he saw the power-house chimneys above: four on one side, eight on the other.

'Then the observer called out "Bomb gone!", and as I felt the doors swinging to, the pilot yelled "Machine gun!" I burst in all I could as we turned away to starboard. Three miles off I had a good view of the place. We had used delayed-action bombs, and banks of black smoke and scalding steam were gushing out. Debris was rocketing into the air, and I thought of those turbine blades ricochetting around the building.'

All 17 aircraft of Force 1 dropped their bombs within the target area. They all came off the target unscathed, then drove off some Bf 109 fighters that approached them before, purely by chance, the Blenheims crossed a Luftwaffe airfield near Antwerp. They machine gunned some Bf 109s on the ground and shot one down

On 12 August 1941 56 Blenheims, split into two forces, attacked the Quadrath and Knapsack power stations at Cologne. Four Blenheims of 139 Squadron, three of 18, and one each from 21, 82 and 114, plus two Blenheims of 226 Squadron, which were used as fighter navigators for the Spitfire withdrawal support, and four Spitfires, failed to return. (Wartime Watton Museum)

that was taking off. Still unopposed, they flew into a heavy thunderstorm near the Scheldt estuary, which broke up the formation and caused the loss of a Blenheim.

On clearing the storm Edrich was joined by several other Blenheims and together they sped across the shallows and mudflats of the estuary towards their rendezvous with the Spitfires. It was then that they experienced their most serious opposition, partly from intensive fire from coastal batteries and even more seriously from a huge flock of seagulls that they had disturbed.

W/C James L. Nicol, leading Force 2, recalled flying below the level of the trees and, when they were only 7 minutes away from their target, seeing the Blenheims of Force 1 crossing their path. It seemed to him that the air was alive with Blenheims. They had nearly reached the target when his WOP/AG called out over the intercom 'Tallyho – fighter to port', and he felt cannon shells hitting his port wing. He led his formation into evasive action when they ran into intensive flak. He could see the flak bursting among the Blenheims in front of him, so looked to see where it was coming from. Seeing flashes from a gun emplacement, he went straight for it, firing with his fixed front gun. Nichol went on:

'You couldn't miss the target. There were 12 chimneys – a row of four and a parallel of eight –

standing stark against the sky. There was smoke and flames coming from the plant, so we climbed to attack. The flames were 50 feet high and the smoke was too thick to let us bomb accurately from any lower. Inside the buildings we could see the sullen glow of explosions under the smoke. I flew straight between the chimneys when I heard my observer call "Bombs gone!".

I did a steep turn over a belt of trees down into a sandstone quarry to get away from the flak. I should think we were about 30 feet below ground level. As we came up I heard my WOP/AG call "Fighter again", and at the same moment a piece of my port wing fell away. I heard no more from my WOP/AG and it must have been then that he was wounded. I tried once more evasive action. A bullet came in behind my head and another smacked the armour plating at my back. My observer said that he could see a stream of bullets coming between his legs. I turned to the right to give the fighter a more difficult angle of fire and this seemed to work; he sprayed the air below us. While we twisted about I hit the top of a telegraph pole and clipped the airscrew, yet remarkably this didn't seem to affect our flying. There was, however, a film of oil over my perspex, which impeded my vision, and we would have hit a church spire had my observer not warned me just in time. I banked sharply to avoid this obstruction, catching the tip of my wing on a tree. Once more we were lucky and managed to catch up to the others.

The worst of the attack was over, but I have never known anything so welcome as the squadrons of Spitfires waiting for us, who warded off the attacks of even more Messerschmitts, then I had to think of my WOP/AG. I tried to call him up, then was passed a note that read, "Please get here quickly. Bleeding badly". I gave my observer a bandage and he crept through the bomb bay to give the gunner first aid. I flew on back in an interval between two storms and made straight for base. Our undercarriage had been damaged and would not go down. My observer held our WOP/AG as I made a belly-landing.'

Seven days later W/C Nicol, who was awarded the DSO for the Knapsack raid, F/Sgt Edward T. W. Jones, observer, and F/O Herbert J. Madden DFC were all killed when their Blenheim was shot down by a Bf 110 of 5./ZG76 near Vlieland. W/C Kercher also received the DSO for the Quadrath raid.

Force 1 had lost two Blenheims, and Force 2 eight Blenheims. V5725 of 139 Squadron, flown by Sgt Harry Ingleby RCAF, was shot down by flak over the target and crashed at Berrenrath; all three crew were killed. A few moments later Z7448, also of 139 Squadron and flown by Sgt G. Coast, crashed at Hücheln; he had probably been hit by flak over the target. Coast and his observer, P/O K. J. Mackintosh, survived and were taken prisoner, while Sgt Dennis A. Wilson, WOP/AG, was killed. Nearing the Dutch coast P/O Malcolm T. K. Walkden's Blenheim from 18 Squadron hit high-tension cables, which sheared off the tail; the aircraft crashed in the mouth of the Scheldt with no survivors. P/O Jim Corfield of 21 Squadron also hit high-tension cables in the Dutch coast area on the way back and crashed into the sea off Texel; he died together with P/O Arthur L. A. Williams and P/O Maurice Williams, WOP/AG.

The Blenheim flown by New Zealander F/L George A. Herbert of 139 Squadron was damaged by light flak over the target, and at 1318 was finished off by Oblt Adolf Galland of Stab./JG26, his 77th victory. It crashed into the mouth of the Scheldt, killing all three crew. Two minutes later Z7281 of 114 Squadron, flown by Sgt Douglas J. Wheatley, was set upon by Oblt Kurt Ruppert in a Bf 109 of III./JG26, who shot it down in flames. The Blenheim hit the sea off Flushing and there were no survivors. At 1328

Oblt Baron Freiherr Hubertus von Holtey of Stab./JG26, in a Bf 109E, shot down the Blenheim flown by S/L A. F. H. Mills RCAF, who ditched in the sea south of Flushing. All three crew were taken prisoner.

Among the withdrawal forces, Spitfire P8446 of 152 Squadron was shot down at 1312 by the Luftwaffe Flakabteilung 43/XI near Biervliet, and pilot George White was killed. Two minutes later the same battery shot down P6793 of 19 Squadron; the pilot belly-landed near Breskens and was taken to hospital. Two Blenheims from 226 Squadron, navigating as fighter leaders, were lost. At 1253 V5859, piloted by F/L Gwilym I. Lewis, was hit by flak and crashed near Philippine in Zeeuws-Vlaanderen, Belgium. Lewis, F/Sgt Neville Cardell, observer, and F/Sgt Jack Woods, WOP/AG, were killed. At Katwijk at 1245 the Flakalarm was sounded, pilots of I./JG1 climbed into their Bf 109s and took off in the direction of Zeeuws-Vlaanderen, while at the same time Bf 109Es of JG26 took off from Wevelgem and Woensdrecht. As the returning aircraft approached, the flak guns opened up, only breaking off their barrage when Uffz Zick of I./JG1 dived his Bf 109E on to the tail of Z7352 piloted by F/L Hugh S. Young, and dispatched it with a burst of gunfire. The Blenheim crashed at 1300 hours in the mouth of the Scheldt with no survivors.

The 12 Blenheims that were lost represented 15.4% of the force. This would have been acceptable had the damage to the power stations reported by the aircrews been confirmed by later reconnaissance, but they were both soon back in commission again.

Six days later, on 18 August, 88 Squadron, which on 1 August had moved from Swanton Morley to Attlebridge, received 19 Blenheim Mk IVs from 105 Squadron for anti-shipping operations off the Dutch coast. Results were poor, however, and were little better on 21 August when cloud obscured the chemical works at Chocques; crews dropped their bombs on factories and railway junctions near St Omer instead.

Shipping was again the target on 26 August when 21, 82, and 88 Squadrons all suffered loss. Worst hit was 82 Squadron, which lost four Blenheims to Bf 109s of 2. and 3./JG52. Nine crews from 88 Squadron took part. S/L Alan

Lynn, the CO, and F/L Alexander caught a 4,000-ton motor vessel travelling in convoy, which they attacked, scoring direct hits. The vessel was aflame and dead in the water as the Blenheims sped away. P/O G. B. Dunn's Blenheim was hit by flak and exploded as it hit the water; Dunn, his observer, P/O Jones, and F/Sgt Davies were listed as missing. When P/O T. G. Edwards's Blenheim was attacked by two Bf 110s, F/Sgt F. Tweedale kept the Luftwaffe at bay while his pilot jettisoned the bomb load and the crew made it back safely.

Also on 26 August Bill Edrich recalled a briefing when they were detailed to intercept a southbound convoy off the Dutch coast near Ijmuiden. He led the six Blenheims of 21 Squadron, flying low in two vics of three; S/L R. A. 'Dick' Shuttleworth led the second, in what was for him his first shipping strike. The convoy came into sight and Edrich decided to make their approach from the direction of the Dutch coast and to attack the flak ships, opening the way for the second vic to attack the merchantmen. He gained height on his approach before diving over his target, just clearing the masts as he released his bombs and returned to nought feet. There had been no flak on the run in, but as they pulled away the tracer overtook them, racing past like a blizzard. His No 2 survived the attack but he saw his No 3 plunging towards the sea with his port wing a blazing torch. Shuttleworth and the other two members of his vic attacked the merchantman, scoring several hits without further loss.

The following day Edrich, who was then in charge of 21 Squadron, was informed that he was to supply six aircraft for a low-level strike on the docks at Rotterdam on 28 August. The order further specified that the aircraft were to be led by the inexperienced Shuttleworth. Edrich had a justifiable premonition that the Germans would be more than ready for such a raid following the successful operation that had taken place only six weeks earlier. He was so concerned that he requested to be allowed to lead the mission instead of Shuttleworth, a request that was turned down. Reconnaissance had shown that the Germans were once again assembling many ships in Rotterdam to carry war materials and food along the coasts of the occupied countries. It was therefore decided that the second raid,

which went ahead on the 28th, was imperative. Crews must have been pleased to learn that they were to have Spitfire IIas of 19 Squadron from Coltishall and 152 from Swanton Morley for fighter escort.

The first attempt, just after 1440, was re-called at 1530. At around 1720 18 crews – six from 21 Squadron at Watton, six from 88 Squadron at Attlebridge, three from 110 Squadron at Wattisham and three from 226 Squadron at Swanton Morley – were successful, though 'F-Freddy' crashed on take-off at Attlebridge. The Spitfires were picked up and the formation flew to a point 4 miles south of Oostvoorn, where they would turn to their second point 5 miles south of Waalhaven where the three boxes of aircraft would come into line abreast and speed in at roof-top height.

The formation made landfall at the Dutch coast, but as soon as they reached the mouth of the Nieuwe Waterweg, the canal that links Rotterdam to the sea, destroyers and anti-aircraft batteries threw up a terrific barrage of flak. As soon as they were clear of the flak they came under attack from enemy fighters, but the 17 Blenheims scraped through and flew on, hugging the ground all the way to the docks. Their arrival was greeted with a hail of light machine gun and flak fire as they swept across Rotterdam at roof-top height in line abreast. The Spitfires, meanwhile, had climbed to 1,500 feet to provide top cover while the Blenheims hurled their bombs into shipping and construction yards.

21 Squadron hit two large ships and dock buildings. Sgt Kenneth Hayes, and P/O W. L. MacDonald, were shot down by Lt. Hans Müller of 6./JG53 in a Bf109f. None of Hayes' crew survived but MacDonald and his WOP/AG survived and were taken prisoner. One of two flak victims was the Blenheim flown by Dick Shuttleworth, which crashed in Scheurpolder. He died later in the Wilhelmina Hospital in Amsterdam. Edrich's premonition had been fulfilled, and he would have to break the news to his friend's wife. Two Blenheims of 226 Squadron joined three from 110 Squadron and made a run on shipping at just 20 feet. P/O F. M. V. Johnstone of 226 Squadron flew so low that he crashed headlong into a warehouse on the north-west corner of Masshaven and exploded into a ball of fire. Incredibly, Johnstone and his

two crew survived and were made PoW. An 88 Squadron Blenheim crewed by P/O Tudor G. Edwards, P/O Fred A. Letchford, and F/Sgt Frank Tweedale, who had returned after the brush with Bf110s two days earlier, were shot down and killed, as were F/L James O. Alexander and crew.

Nineteen-year-old F/L Mayer H. R. 'Dickie' Namias of 88 Squadron spectacularly sank a 10,000-tonner when one of his bombs bounced from the dockside and hit under the stern of the ship, which exploded and sank. S/L Alan Lynn caught a 5,000-ton vessel, while F/L Stewart bombed a 4,000-ton ship, which he missed. Stewart then turned to the shipyards, but was attacked by a trio of Bf 109s of 6./JG53. His gunner, F/Sgt Mills, was wounded and the aircraft was badly damaged. After the attack the Blenheims joined up with their escorts, now reinforced with a dozen Spitfires of 266 Squadron.

In a minute to the Chief of Air Staff on the 29th, Churchill, obviously perturbed by the losses sustained in the operation, wrote: 'The loss of seven Blenheims out of 17 in the daylight attack on merchant shipping and docks at Rotterdam is most severe . . . While I greatly admire the bravery of the pilots, I do not want them pressed too hard. Easier targets giving a high damage return compared to casualties may be more often selected.'

The following day he drafted a message to the crews: 'The devotion and gallantry of the attacks on Rotterdam and other objectives are beyond all praise. The Charge of the Light Brigade is eclipsed in brightness by these almost daily deeds of fame.'

The comparison with the unfortunate Charge of the Light Brigade may well have been appropriate, but was hardly encouraging to those taking part. During August the loss rate was as high as 30%. Of 77 Blenheims that attacked shipping, 23 were lost, while of 480 sorties flown, 36 failed to return. Coupled with their losses in Malta, it was a very demanding and fateful period for 2 Group.

The anti-shipping role and shipping 'beat' patrols of 2 Group Blenheims were coming to an end by September, but not before they inflicted a terrible penalty on the crews taking part. On 6 September 88 Squadron moved on detachment to Manston in Kent to take part in 'Channel Stop' operations. (Further detachments, to Long Kesh in January/ February 1942, Abbotsinch in May, and Ford in July 1942, were made before the whole Squadron moved from Attlebridge to Oulton, Norfolk, in September 1942.)

On 17 September ten Blenheims from 139 Squadron flew a *Circus*, their target being the Grand Quevilly power station near Rouen, on which they claimed three direct hits. They too came under attack from enemy fighters, one of the Blenheims being damaged while the Spitfire escort claimed to have shot down four of the 109s for the loss of four of their own. In 82 Squadron meanwhile, P/O C. J. Harper and crew failed to return from an attack on Mazingarbe power station and chemical complex.

Three days later, on 20 September, in an attempt to confuse the enemy defences, *Circuses* were directed at three different targets. Three Blenheims of 18 Squadron went to the marshalling yards at Hazebrouck, nine from 82 and 114 Squadrons to the shipyards at Rouen, while Hampdens bombed Mazingarbe. On the same day, at a much lower level, shipping 'beats' were flown off the Dutch coast by 22 Blenheims

Blenheim IV GB-X of 105 Squadron. Anti-shipping 'beats' during March–May 1941 continued to show scant reward for the high losses suffered. (RAF)

A Blenheim IV of 88 Squadron coming in to land while a Boston sits it out on a hardstand. In October 1941 88 Squadron began re-equipping with the American medium bomber. (IWM)

of 18, 139 and 226 Squadrons, Spitfires of 66 and 152 Squadrons flying escort. Twelve Blenheims flew straight into an enemy convoy of 14 ships and attacked it. The crews from 18 Squadron found a motor ship and a tanker, which they seriously damaged for the loss of Sgt John M. Nickleson RCAF and his crew, who were shot down in flames.

Meanwhile, off the Hook of Holland the crews from 226 Squadron found a convoy of 14 ships flying protective balloons, which they attacked, setting fire to four of them and breaking the back of another. Sgt J. C. V. Colmer's Blenheim was destroyed in one of the bomb bursts and, following his attack, the aircraft flown by F/L Dickie Namias was hit in the starboard engine; yet despite this he dropped his bombs before ditching in the sea. All the crew died Another Blenheim, piloted by F/L Digger Wheeler, an incredibly tough New Zealander who had been a sheep rancher in the Argentine, was also hit in one engine, and although he twice bounced off the sea, he somehow managed to bring his aircraft and his crew home safely. The search for a target by the crews of 139 Squadron had been fruitless.

On the 21st *Circuses* were flown by six Blenheims from 18 Squadron, whose target was the power station at Bethune, and six from 139 Squadron, who unloaded their bombs on the power station at Gosnay. On the 27th the last

Circuses of the month were flown by 110, 226 and 114 Squadrons when the new Fw 190 was encountered for the first time. In October the last shipping 'beats' were flown by Blenheims in the UK, the Air Staff at last having concluded that the aircraft was just not suitable for this role. (Anti-shipping operations were taken over by Hurricane fighter bombers of 402, 605 and 607 Squadrons.)

During October the most successful *Circus* flown took place on the 12th. It was directed at the docks at Boulogne and involved 24 aircraft from 21, 110 and 226 Squadrons. Elsewhere on the same day three or four ships in a convoy off Den Haag were hit, and 82 Squadron found a convoy of seven merchantmen protected by three flak ships 8 miles off the Dutch coast between Ijmuiden and Scheveningen. Led by S/L H. J. Meakin, the aircraft swept into the attack, scoring a direct hit on a 5,000-ton tanker and leaving a freighter on fire. The flak was, as always, fierce; one severely damaged Blenheim ditched in the sea close to the convoy, another plunged into the sea with the loss of all on board, while a third, more fortunate, having lost an airscrew, somehow managed to stagger back to base.

Next day, 13 October, the Blenheims were out on another *Circus*, this time once more to the Mazingarbe ammonia production works. Pilot Sgt Eric 'Tommy' Atkins, of 139 Squadron (whose second op this was, his first having been a shipping attack on the Heligoland Bight on 11 October, when the squadron lost three of six Blenheims), viewed it philosophically:

'The fact that the target had been pranged before on *Circuses* made it a less difficult "second guessing" game for the Germans when they saw the formation approaching. They were well versed in retaliation methods. German radar in the Pas de Calais area had been vastly improved, and this enabled their fighters to be high and waiting. They also knew that the Blenheim could do limited damage at 17,000 feet with only four 250 lb bombs and without the latest bomb sights. Our own firepower against fighters was two Browning guns in the turret, one in the port wing and another in the nose.

It was not a long trip as operations went: 3 hours, there and back. We took off from Horsham St Faith for West Raynham and quickly formated with one another in the box of six – two vics of three with the second vic slightly lower than the first to co-ordinate firepower. At the same time we climbed steadily and headed towards our first rendezvous point with our fighters. There was some ribald comment in the cockpit.

"Steer due south, Tommy, if No 1 gets lost," said Jock Sullivan, my navigator.

"That'll take us to the Costa del Sol," I replied.

"Can't see any of our fighters," said Bill Harrison, the WOP/AG. "Probably still having their breakfast."

"Just don't shoot any of ours down, Bill," I replied.

By this time, dressed in my altitude clothing, I was sweating from my exertions in keeping in the formation and still climbing. Still no sign of our fighters. We knew that they had limited fuel and range, and we hoped that they were already in their positions, shadowing us in the clouds. Our leader had given up circling and set course for the target. As we climbed to 16,000 feet the earth looked strangely remote and unreal below, patchwork quilt in design. It was our first *Circus*, and now that we were approaching the amphitheatre where the action would take place we felt vulnerable.

It wasn't easy to keep in formation in the thin atmosphere, and the Blenheim wallowed on the controls. We were No 2 in the front vic and Bill shouted out to me that the second vic had strayed and were line astern of us instead of stacked just below. "Do they want their bloody heads shot off?" he said.

But there was constant movement of aircraft and

Sgt pilot Eric 'Tommy' Atkins of 139 Squadron at Oulton in September 1941. His first op, a shipping attack in the Heligoland Bight on 11 October, cost the squadron three of the six attacking Blenheims. (Eric Atkins)

vics, and I wondered what would happen when we were attacked.

Suddenly heavy flak bursts surrounded us – subdued thuds and thick smoke, masking the deadly shrapnel flying about. I knew then why there were no fighters – both ours and the enemy's were keeping their distance and waiting for the flak to wilt before the air attack began. The flak was so heavy that it threatened to turn the Blenheims on their side. We were issued with a steel helmet to wear over our flying helmet when flying, as extra protection against flak, but we preferred to sit on it – most of the flak comes upwards and not downwards! The bangs under the aircraft suggested that we had been hit, but there was no visible large damage and the flying controls were not affected. The formation was being jostled about alarmingly in the air and we kept asking each other "Are you OK?".

I said to Bill, "Keep a good look out – after the flak will come the fighters."

It was almost a clear sky with a winter sun and the scene was set for the next action. Our leader was losing height and we followed him to 14,000 feet, the bombing height, in between the light and heavy flak perimeters. Jock shouted, "Target below and to port, Tommy!" I couldn't see it and I was too busy formating. The leader's bomb bay doors were open. Jock opened ours too. On the signal we let go our four 250 lb bombs. Jock and Bill sighted them down and reported bursts in the target area. We were too high to see what we had achieved. We were not allowed more than one run-up to the target, so we prepared to get the "hell out of it"!

The leader headed home. The flak had ceased. Then Bill shouted, "Enemy aircraft at 8 o'clock!" It was on the port side of us, but it turned out to be one of our close escort Hurricanes. There were others about, but they were busy elsewhere. Jock saw a yellow-nosed fighter diving towards us, but it veered away from the formation as it was engaged by a Spitfire. This was probably one of the new Fw 190s [one of which was caught on camera-gun film for the first time on this day by a 129 Squadron Spitfire], superior to our Spitfires in performance, but not in pilot skill. We never saw it again.

The journey back was mostly uneventful, apart from a burst or two of light flak as we approached the coast. Our formation up to this point had been rather straggled, but over the sea we closed up to prove that we could formate more effectively. At this point Spitfires appeared to cover our withdrawal.

On the ground back at Horsham St Faith we examined the aircraft. Five out of six aircraft, including our own, had flak damage. My steel helmet had a "scar" on it adjacent to some flak damage to the airframe. It looked as though it had "saved my bacon" or, more accurately, my "privates"! Another piece of flak had pierced the perspex of the observer's compartment and must have just missed Jock's head. Bill was unscathed, but frustrated because he had not had a real opportunity to fire at an enemy aircraft;

however, he was mollified when he saw the flak holes peppering the outside of his turret! All the Blenheims got back safely.

We didn't like *Circuses*. They were for freaks and animals, not airmen! It didn't seem right that the Blenheim should be used as bait. Such tactics were far from being successful – the enemy often lacked presence. Better co-ordination was needed between our escort and ourselves. It wasn't easy for bombers under fire to give our fighters tactical co-operation.'

Eric Atkins later flew Mosquitos, Jock Sullivan was killed in action, while Bill Harrison survived the war but died of pneumonia soon after.

On 15 October W/C V. S. Butler DFC led a formation of 226 Squadron Blenheims to Le Havre harbour. In a clear blue sky the CO began his bombing run 8 miles from the docks, making the aircraft an ideal target for the anti-aircraft gunners, who not unnaturally responded not only with enthusiasm but also accuracy, literally shooting two of the bombers out of the sky. The escorting fighters, meanwhile, found themselves doing battle with Bf 109s. Butler led the remains of his formation down to low level and they made good their escape, though the aircrew undoubtedly could not forgive their leader for taking them on a ridiculously long bombing run.

Altogether 160 Blenheims and 480 airmen in 2 Group were lost between 24 March and 31 October 1941. This figure does not include aircraft that crashed on their return to the UK or the crippling losses by the squadrons detached to operate from Malta. However, new aircraft were coming. Meanwhile, on 17 December, AVM A. Lees replaced AVM Stevenson at Group HQ; Stevenson was posted overseas and later commanded the RAF in Burma. On his departure, he said:

'Since February 17th I have watched with admiration the courage, determination and war efficiency displayed by squadron commanders, flight commanders, leaders and crews. These fulfilled the highest traditions of the service, and were maintained throughout the vigorous day offensive against the enemy. Many hundreds of thousands of tons of Axis shipping, both here and in the Mediterranean, have been sunk and damaged, while such daylight raids as Bremen, Cologne and Rotterdam already have their place in the history of the air war . . .'

Chapter Five

Boston Boys

*'We're flying binding Bostons
At 250 binding feet,
Doing night intruders
Just to see who we might meet.
And when the daylight dawns again
And when we can take a peek,
We find we've made our landfall
Up the Clacton binding Creek.'*

At the beginning of 1942 2 Group possessed just five bomber squadrons in East Anglia. On 5 January W/C L. Alan Lynn DFC, a South African, took over command of 107 Squadron at Great Massingham, while in Malta, W/C Dunlevie RCAF and what was left of the squadron's Blenheims were waging war in the Mediterranean, where they would remain until the 12th. Training on the Blenheim continued until the first Boston III arrived at Massingham on 5 January. The new role for 107 Squadron (and 88 and 226, which also re-equipped with the Boston) was to be high-level, pin-point bombing with a dozen or more aircraft. For two months 107 and 226 Squadrons converted together, using the range at Brancaster on the Wash for firing practice.

Meanwhile, at Swanton Morley, crews in 105 Squadron, now commanded by W/C Peter H. A. Simmons DFC (later killed flying a Turkish Air Force Mosquito) were to take delivery of the first Mosquito B Mk I bombers in the RAF. However, models were slow to arrive, and Swanton Morley's grass airfield proved unsuitable, so in early December they moved to Horsham St Faith, near Norwich. 105 was replaced by 226 Squadron, commanded by W/C V. S. Butler DFC; they arrived from Wattisham where they had been flying Blenheims. S/L John Castle, a pilot in 226 Squadron, recalls:

W/C Alan Lynn DFC, a South African, had joined the RAF just before the war on a Short Service Commission, and in 1940 had flown Fairey Battles in France, but had taken a dislike to the single-engine machine and was sent home and put into Training Command. However, he somehow eventually persuaded his seniors to release him for operational duties on twin-engines. On 5 January 1942 Lynn took command of 107 Squadron and remained with it until 13 September 1942. By late 1944 he had completed at least 150 ops and had been awarded the DSO and bar and DFC and bar, together with a Dutch Gallantry medal. (via John Bateman)

The first Boston IIIs arrived at Great Massingham on 5 January 1942, as the new role for 107 Squadron (and 88 and 226, which also re-equipped with the Boston) was to be high-level, pin-point bombing. These Boston IIIs were photographed at a press day on 8 April 1942, the nearest aircraft being AL280, and the next W8373. Note the huge 12-inch exhausts to which flame dampers were fitted later, and the 'hooked' pitot head on top of the fins, which proved difficult to cover to stop insects crawling in. (Tony Carlisle, via Nigel Buswell)

'It's difficult to imagine now what a rowdy, rumbustious squadron 226 was when it arrived at Swanton Morley on a grey 9 December 1941. We had

come from all over the world: New Zealand, Canada, Australia, the USA, the Argentine, a Catholic from Northern Ireland, and a Protestant from the South. The only officer left from the squadron that had been in France in 1940 was our CO, Bobbie Butler; the two flight commanders, MacLancy and I, were two of the five pilots surviving a tour of Malta with 110 on Blenheims; 105 came out from Swanton to take over from us. 226 had led the first low-level daylight raid on Cologne and had taken a fair pasting on shipping strikes.'

Training in their new role took time and the Boston crews of 107 Squadron were not considered ready when Operation *Fuller* was mounted on 12 February in a vain attempt to prevent the 'Channel Dash' by the battle cruisers *Scharnhorst*, *Gneisenau* and *Prinz Eugen*, which were slipping through the English Channel from their French berths to Germany. However, six of

F/O J. P. Crump climbs aboard his Boston III at Massingham on 8 April. Note the tube for the trailing aerial, the twin belt-fed Browning .303-inch machine guns and, through the oval window, the armoured shield on a VGO 'K' drum-fed machine gun for use out of the bottom hatch. The pilot's seat-type 'chute lies on the ground, while W/O Dotteridge, navigator, carries his chest-type 'chute and a steel helmet. The gunner is WOP/AG Sgt Gus Vevier. (Tony Carlisle, via Nigel Buswell)

226 Squadron's Bostons and four from 88 were involved (as were nine Blenheims of 118 Squadron, 12 of 82 and 16 of 110), but only Digger Wheeler and his crew in 226 Squadron found the German ships, and they were beaten off by six of the escorting fighters. Wheeler landed at Swanton Morley with two holes in the fuselage and an unexploded 20 mm cannon shell in the starboard wing.

The first Boston operation took place on Sunday 8 March with three raids on targets in France. In the early afternoon six Bostons of 226 Squadron at Swanton Morley, led by W/C Butler, and six from 88 Squadron at Attlebridge, took off to make the first daylight bombing raid of the war on Paris. The target, the Ford Motor Works at Matford, near Poissy, on the banks of the Seine, was turning out tanks and military vehicles for the Germans. Meanwhile, 107 Squadron provided six crews for a *Circus* operation to the Abbeville marshalling yards, escorted by the Kenley and Biggin Hill Wings in 11 Group, while fighters of 10 Group flew a diversionary operation, and six more Bostons, three each from 88 and 107 Squadrons, would attack the Comines power station.

The Matford works were at the extreme limit of the Bostons' range, so 88 and 226 Squadrons used Thorney Island on the South Coast as a forward re-fuelling base. They had to fly at very low level to and from the target without fighter escort, which did not have the range to accompany them. Meanwhile, a second *Circus*, using six Bostons from 88 and 226 Squadrons,

The smiles on the faces of 114 Squadron aircrew at West Raynham on 12 February 1942 conceal the unsuccessful attempts to bomb the German warships in the 'Channel Dash'. Left to right are Kendrick; John Newberry; 24-year-old W/C John F. G. Jenkins DFC DSO, 114 Squadron CO, who led six Blenheims on that day; King; 31-year-old F/O Henry Paul Brancker DFC; and F/Sgt C. H. Gray DFM. Jenkins, who received the DSO for leading 13 Blenheims in a strafing raid on Herdls airfield, Norway, on 27 December 1941, when British commandos stormed Vaagso Island, was killed on 27 March, when his Blenheim, Z7276 'N-Nut', failed to return from a night intruder attack on Soesterberg airfield. Paul Brancker, observer (cousin of AVM Sir William Brancker, who lost his life in the R101 airship disaster in December 1930), and Gray, died with him. (Mrs Vera Sherring)*

A Blenheim IV V550 intruder of 18 Squadron at Horsham St Faith, Norwich, in the winter of 1942. In March of the year 82, 139 and 110 Squadrons were dispatched to the Far East. The remaining Blenheims, of 18, 21 and 114 Squadrons, were employed in night intruder operations against enemy airfields, which was to last until the final Blenheim of 18 Squadron came in to land at Wattisham at 0145 on 18 August. (Alan Ellender, via Dr Theo Boiten)

covered by fighters, attacked Comines power station.

P/O Peter Saunders, navigator-observer in P/O W. J. 'Bill' O'Connell's Boston in 226 Squadron, looked out at the other Bostons on his port side and was thrilled at the sight.

'They were flying along wing-tip to wing-tip and they looked like the arm of a gigantic flail sweeping across fields and skimming the hedgetops. The Bostons were lovely machines, powerful-looking with their big, blunt engines, yet smooth-flying, sleek, graceful – and they were beautiful to watch, racing along side by side, fast and low, rising and falling to the contour of the ground like darting swallows. We were accustomed to low level, but this was the very lowest that we had ever flown.

As we stuck close to the Wingco's plane in formation, my heart jumped involuntarily from time to time as we swept over hedges and fields, as houses and trees slithered close past our wings and as we pulled ourselves precariously over the lip of gullies and embankments. It seemed at times recklessly and unnecessarily low, but the whole success of our mission – and our survival too – hung upon the surprise that we must achieve, and flying low was the best method of ensuring that a gunner would have little time to draw a bead on us or an enemy fighter spot us.'

Peter Saunders could hardly believe their luck. It continued right to the target, for no fighters showed at all as Butler led the formation 'daisy-cutting' all the way, past Evreux, Mantes-Gassincourt and finally to Poissy on the outskirts of Paris. At bombing height – 400 feet – the Bostons' bombs went winging down.

Peter could see the Matford Works perfectly clearly:

'A huge, long rectangular building lying close to the river bank and a tower nearby with the name "MATFORD" on it. How obliging to mount it there, to help make doubly sure that this was our target! I saw the Wingco's bombs land smack in the middle of a concentration of lorries alongside the factory, the rest on the factory itself. We swept in behind him. Just as our bombs went down, his exploded. The terrific blast shook us and lifted us bodily upwards. Debris rose high in the air and dust swirled around. Some flak was streaming up towards us from the ground. There was a sharp crunching against our starboard wing and the aircraft shuddered violently. Then we were past. The other boys were coming in behind us. "Chappie" Chapman, the WOP/AG, was looking out to watch our bombs burst. He yelled jubilantly, "Plumb in the middle! Good work!" We knew our bombs had hit.

We had a long way to go to get there, but happy thoughts filled our minds. What a perfect day. What an experience. The target decidedly "pranged"! What an achievement for Wingco, and for George, to have led this show; to have carried it off like this! What a thrill for them. What a feather in their caps. What ragging. What back-slapping for them when we get back! They deserve it, they can be proud . . .

It was then that we saw that the Wingco was having trouble with his bomb doors – they were still hanging open. He was trying to close them, for we saw them come up, stick, then fall open again. He made two more attempts with no success. Had they been damaged by the flak, or could it be that the Wingco was hurt? A stretch of thickly-wooded ground loomed ahead of us. We swept up and over it. The Wingco's props seemed to trail on the branches below. The Boston tottered, slipped heavily sideways and crashed into the trees. Still on its side, it went hurtling on.

The first Boston Circus operations (C-112A & B) took place on 8 March when six aircraft of 107 Squadron attacked the Abbeville marshalling yards, and three of 88 and three of 107 attacked the Comines power station. In the afternoon six from 226 and six from 88 Squadron carried out the first daylight bombing raid of the war on Paris with an attack from 400 feet on the Ford Motor Works at Matford, which is seen here burning after the raid. W/C V. S. Butler DFC, CO 226 Squadron, who led the operation, was killed. (RAF)

Trunks splintered and broke in its path. There was a blinding flash of white-blue flame and then the horror of the scene was cloaked in fierce red fire. We could not stop. Our thoughts crowded in on each other. "Chappie" was the only one, from his gunner's turret, who could see. He said nothing. Neither could we. We sped homewards.'

All six 226 Squadron Bostons placed their bombs on the factory, though only two crews in 88 Squadron bombed the target, but damage to the Matford Works was later estimated at 35–40 million French francs, and it was out of commission for three months.

Circus operations remained the order of the day, and casualties were heavy. In April 107 Squadron alone lost seven aircraft from 78 sorties dispatched, and 11 aircrew were killed. On 17 April 88 and 107 Squadrons flew diversionary raids in support of Lancasters

On 14 April 1942, in Circus *123, 12 Bostons of 88 Squadron led by S/L Shaw Kennedy attacked the power station at Caen/Mondeville from 8,000 feet and practically all bombs fell on some part of the power station or the adjoining Thomas & Martin steelworks. (RAF)*

On 16 April, in Ramrod 20, 12 Bostons of 226 Squadron led by S/L John Castle (who received the DFC for this raid) attacked the power station at Le Havre. The second box of six bombed from 14,500 feet, 500 feet above the leading box. Direct hits were scored on the power station, interrupting the electricity supply for 48 hours and gutting 75 feet of the northern end of the main building. A direct hit was also obtained on the bridge between the Bassin de la Barre and the Bassin Vaubin. All the Bostons returned safely, although 11 of the 12 received Flak damage. (RAF)

Following reports of plans to load Ju 52s with torpedoes, on 30 April 1942 six Bostons of 226 Squadron in Circus 148 flew to Exeter, thence to Morlaix, France, where they bombed the airfield from 12,000 feet. No Ju 52s were present, but a mixed load of 500 lb and 40 lb bombs were dropped on the main SE dispersals. Aircraft visible are two Ju 88s, two small machines to the south of the airfield and three fighters, probably Bf 109s, to the west of the runway. (RAF)

On 6 May 1942 six Bostons of 88 Squadron led by S/L Dickie England attacked an armed merchant vessel alongside the outer mole at the docks at Boulogne from 12,700 feet. (RAF)

attacking Augsburg. Six Bostons from 88 Squadron bombed the Grand Quevilly power station near Rouen, while another six hit the shipyards nearby. Meanwhile, 107 Squadron attempted to bomb an artificial silk factory at Calais, but their bombs were dropped on railway lines nearby, and one of the Bostons was shot down into the sea by Bf 109s.

On 25 April all three Boston squadrons operated in concert with one another with two operations against French ports. 88 Squadron attacked Le Havre, while 107 bombed Cherbourg and six Bostons from 226 bombed the dry docks at Dunkirk from 14,000 feet; buildings on the northern end of the Citadel Quay were hit. On the second raid of the day 107 Squadron's Bostons were attacked by Fw 190s, and they also came under a heavy flak barrage. One of the Bostons, badly damaged, nevertheless managed to make it home minus part of its tail.

May followed much the same pattern, except that on the 31st the first Mosquito bombers, from 105 Squadron, now entered the fray, five aircraft being dispatched to Cologne to photograph damage caused by the first '1,000' raid. In June the second Mosquito squadron, 139, at Horsham St Faith, became operational. On their first operation on 1/2 July, W/C A. R. Oakeshott, the CO, and one other Mosquito crew were lost. (The story of the two squadrons' sojourn in 2 Group is covered in the author's *The Men Who Flew the Mosquito* (PSL, 1995).) On 7 May,

On 7 May six Bostons of 226 Squadron led by P/O W. J. O'Connell attacked the power station at Ostend from 11,000 feet in Circus 164. 226 Squadron were bracketed by intense flak and the base of a shell lodged just behind the head of Sgt Parsons, pilot of one of the Bostons; three gunners were also wounded, and immediately after the bombing Sgt Goodman broke formation, out of control, and his WOP/AG, Sgt Burt, bailed out (he became a PoW). The photo shows the Boston (AL750 MG-Z) immediately after Burt had bailed out. Goodman regained control and flew back to make a safe landing at Swanton Morley. A report received later stated that 22 coffins were delivered to the Germans by the local undertaker, a bomb having hit a listening post. (RAF)

On 9 May 1942 in Circus *170, six Bostons of 88 Squadron led by S/L Dickie England dropped bombs on two oil tanks with a capacity of 700,000 gallons at Bruges from 13,500 feet (which undershot), while six of 226 Squadron attacked the marshalling yards at Hazebrouck in C-168, and 12 from 226 attacked the docks at Boulogne in* Ramrod 33. *(RAF)*

meanwhile, six Bostons in 226 Squadron attacked a power station in Ostend. The German defenders put up a large flak barrage and Sgt Goodman's Boston was hit and fell out of

On 2 June in Circus *182 six Bostons of 88 Squadron led by S/L Griffiths bombed the docks at Dieppe from 8,000 feet; hits were obtained on the New Dry Dock, railway lines and cranes on the Quai de Norvege, two on buildings and the storeyard of the Ste Franc-Graigola-Merthyr. (RAF)*

control. Sgt Burt, the rear gunner, thought the aircraft was doomed and promptly bailed out, but Goodman wrested back control and crossed the North Sea safely. Burt was later reported to be a PoW. On 17 May 12 Bostons led by W/C W. E. Surplice DFC raided the docks at Boulogne. Six of the aircraft were hit by flak and one pilot was wounded. A week later 14 Bostons of 226 Squadron took a much-needed break from operations when they left for Thruxton for a week-long Army Co-Operation Exercise.

In June 226 Squadron at Swanton Morley hosted the A-20 crews of the 15th Light Bombardment Squadron USAAF, who, being the only American unit in the UK at the time, and with Independence Day looming, were needed for a flag-waving curtain-raiser to an American offensive in Europe. Both squadrons found that the other flew the Boston differently, even during take-off. While the RAF leader approached the end of the field still on the ground, the US pilot wingmen would be airborne and flying alongside with their wheels drawing up into the wheel-wells. The RAF mechanics were particularly grateful; damaged nose-gear wheels and struts had become a major headache for them.

On 4 June the Americans sat in at a 107 Squadron briefing at West Raynham. The target was a 480-foot tower in the docks at Dunkirk. Bill Odell, one of the American pilots, remembers the operation:

'The route was almost direct using the tactics of sea-level flight to foil the radio aircraft detection system until about 13 minutes from the coast. At that point a 1,000-foot climb was to begin, dropping four 500 lb bombs at 10,000 feet. All kinds of fighter protection was going over. Immediately after bombing we were to take pictures, make a steep diving turn to the right and continue down to sea level and come straight home. Twelve fighters would escort the return flight.

I watched the RAF take off procedure, which was much different from ours. Their engines were run from 10 to 20 minutes on the ground before flight. The crews were all Blenheim trained, which may have accounted for such a procedure. The Bostons were kept on the ground with all three wheels until a bounce forced the pilot to fly it. One new pilot took off with upper cowl flaps open and reported back to the Squadron CO that he thought for a long while it was the bomb load causing the different flight characteristics. They attempted to take off in formation but didn't seem to hold it very well and did not become organised until after 4–5 minutes of flying. They had a much more open formation than us.

W/C Lynn kept a close check on the flight by checking his watch. As soon as they left the target we left the mess. Back at "Ops" we learned very shortly that only five of the six that went on the run would be back. P/O ["Goolie"] Skinner and crew [who were on their first op] had ditched their ship and were all in the dinghy. [Skinner and Sgt Bernstein, WOP/AG, survived, but Sgt Paddy Foster, observer/navigator, died a month later of his wounds.] Shortly the five showed up over the field; one circled and shot a red flare to show he was in trouble.'

On 5 June 24 Bostons bombed Morlaix airfield and power stations at Le Havre and Ostend again. A direct hit was achieved at Ostend, but bombing from 10,000 feet meant that German flak gunners had fairly easy targets at which to shoot, and every Boston was hit by flak during their bomb runs. Still the losses mounted. On 11 June P/O T. B. Skinner and his crew in 107 Squadron failed to return after they were stalked by an Fw 190 5 minutes from the English coast after a raid on Lannion airfield. Their Boston was raked by machine gun fire from 800 yards; the tail fell off and they fell into the Channel. All the crew perished.

Raids on French and Belgian ports, airfields and power stations continued. Then, on 25/26 June, when the second '1,000 bomber' raid took place, on Bremen, low-level bombing and strafing attacks were at dusk made on 13 airfields in Germany by 16 Blenheims, 27 Bostons from 88, 107 and 226 Squadrons (making their first *Intruder* sorties) and four Mosquitos from 105 and 109 Squadrons, which attacked Stade. Extra bomb bay tanks were provided, carrying 100 gallons. Overall the raids were a success, though one flight in 226 Squadron bombed a dummy aerodrome. Six Bostons went to Leeuwarden and three more flew to Bergen-Alkmaar, but it was darker than anticipated and four aircraft were unable to find their targets. The others attacked at 2230 with 11-second and 30-minute delayed-action 500 lb bombs and incendiaries.

F/L A. F. 'Tony' Carlisle's aircraft was caught in the explosion of one of the bombs, which holed the tail of his Boston. His rear gunner had his guns blown overboard as the aircraft was overturned, but Carlisle regained control and managed to return safely, his flying skill earning him a DFC. Light flak prevented W/C Lynn and P/O Allen from attacking, but F/L R. MacLachlan flew low at 75 feet and P/O Rushden dropped his bombs from 100 feet near a hangar. Both aircraft were damaged by ground fire, but they returned to base safely. W/C Lynn, meanwhile, was forced down over the coast.

On Monday 29 June 12 Bostons of 226 Squadron, led by S/L Shaw Kennedy, attacked the marshalling yards at Hazebrouck, escorted for the first time on a *Circus* raid by Hawker Typhoons. One of the Bostons was flown by a US crew, captained by Capt Charles Kegelman, for the first ever US sortie from England. Bombing from between 12,500 and 13,000 feet, the formation recorded two hits on the railway lines at the eastern end of the yard, and one or two were seen to burst on railway lines and sheds at the western end. The rest of the bombs fell on

Captain Charles Kegelman USAAF, with an American crew, piloted one of the 12 Bostons led by S/L J. S. Kennedy DFC that took part in a Circus *(C-195) against the Hazebrouck marshalling yards on 29 June, the first time since 1918 that Americans had operated from England. Also on this operation Typhoons were used as high cover for the first time. Bombing was from 13,000 feet, no flak was encountered and hits were scored on the north-east edge of the yards, and on the railway embankment north-west of the town.* (RAF)

A photograph taken from the rear-mounted camera of the leading Boston (AL679 'Y'), flown by F/L R. A. 'Yogi' Yates-Earl, of the attack on Bergen-Alkmaar airfield, showing the explosion caused by Boston AL741 'V' flown by Lt 'Stan' Lynn USAAF, which was shot down by flak. (RAF)

buildings to the south and north. No flak was encountered by the formation while over the target, and all the aircraft returned. Not so fortunate were the escorting Spitfires, who encountered German fighters en route to the target, claiming three destroyed for the loss of five of their own.

On 4 July six American crews joined six crews from 226 Squadron for Independence Day attacks on De Kooy, Haamstaede, Bergen-

Uffz Johannes Rathenow of IV. Gruppe JG1 returns victoriously to Bergen-op-Zoom airfield in his Fw 190A-3, 'White 12', Wrk Nr 437, to be congratulated by his ground crew and fellow pilots after taking off during the attack by Bostons and pursuing P/O C. F. Henning's Boston (Z2213 'U') for 20 miles out to sea before shooting it down. All the crew were lost. (via Eric Mombeek)

Alkmaar and Valkenburg airfields in Holland. Gen Dwight D. Eisenhower, newly arrived in England to command the US Forces in the ETO, was at Swanton Morley to see them off, at around 0710. When they returned it was immediately obvious that the raids had been less successful than the occasion had demanded. Three aircraft were missing, two of them crewed by Americans. At De Kooy Lt F. A. 'Jack' Loehrl's Boston had been hit by flak and only Lt Marshall Draper, the bombardier, survived to be made a PoW. After bombing Bergen-Alkmaar Lt W. G. 'Stan' Lynn's Boston was also hit by flak; it broke up in mid-air, killing all on board. Unteroffiziers Erwin Grütz and Johannes Rathenow of IV./JG1 took off as their airfield was being bombed and sped after the Bostons. Grütz was shot down and killed by return fire, and his Bf 109F-4 crashed near the base. Rathenow, in his Fw 190A-3, caught up with P/O C. M. 'Hank' Henning and shot him down into the sea at 0830, 20 kms west of Callantsoog. It was IV Gruppe's first success.

The most amazing piece of flying was carried out by Capt Kegelman, whose Boston took a hit

in the starboard engine; it burst into flames and the propeller flew off. Kegleman's right wing-tip struck the ground and the fuselage actually bounced on the surface of the aerodrome, tearing a hole in the belly of the bomber. Kegelman nursed the Boston all the way back to Swanton, a feat that earned him the DSC. F/L 'Yogi' Yates-Earl and his observer, P/O Ken Houghton, were awarded the DFC, and his gunner, Sgt Leaver, the DFM, for their part in the attack on Bergen-Alkmaar.

Crews had bombed and strafed the airfields, but at Valkenberg S/L John Castle, the leader of the formation, found he was unable to open his bomb doors through an error in selection. On the run-in to a target Boston pilots normally had the bomb doors selected to 'neutral', then placed them to 'open' before dropping their bombs. Castle discovered too late that he was still selected to 'closed'; moving the door control had only placed the doors to 'neutral', and they failed to open. The two American crews behind waited in vain for the leader's bomb doors to open as the signal to drop their own bombs. Instead, the formation used their machine guns on airfield

Uffz Erwin Grütz took off at the same time as Rathenow in his Bf 109F-4, 'White 6', Wrk Nr 7423, and was shot down and killed by return fire from one of the Bostons. He was buried with full military honours. (via Eric Mombeek)

buildings and three dispersed Bf 109s, setting one on fire. All three aircraft were forced to bring their bombs back.

The experienced 226 crews were all of the same opinion that the flak encountered was the worst they had ever experienced. At De Kooy the three Bostons led by S/L Shaw Kennedy were forced to fly through 3 miles of flak, the worst he had encountered in over 60 operations, and it

S/L J. C. Shaw Kennedy DFC leaving Boston Z2234 'H' on his return from De Kooy following the 4 July 1942 raid. (RAF)

prevented them from bombing. Kennedy machine gunned anti-aircraft positions and personnel near the airfield, and on the way home he attacked a 250-foot trawler with bombs and machine guns, but his bombs overshot. He also attacked a second trawler with machine guns. Eisenhower and his fellow generals, gathered to fete the heroes' return, were confronted with the stark reality of *Circus* operations, something the RAF had long since come to accept as part of the game of war.

On Sunday 12 July a *Circus* of six Bostons of 226 Squadron, led by John Castle, and six American-crewed Bostons (in the last of 16 sorties with the RAF), led by Capt Bill Odell and escorted by fighters, headed for Abbeville-Drucat airfield, where 150 fighters were reported dispersed in the woods just north of the runways. The crews bombed from 8,500 feet, but owing to 4/10 cloud over the aiming point the accuracy of the bombing could not be observed. Slight to inaccurate flak was encountered from both heavy and light anti-aircraft guns, with two aircraft

receiving hits, but all returned safely. (In September the 15th Bomb Squadron flew a few missions before transferring to the 12th Air Force earmarked for North Africa.)

On 16 July 2 Group ordered the first of a series of low-level attacks by Bostons on power stations, marshalling yards and other industrial targets using cloud cover. Each squadron was to send ten aircraft a day when visibility and cloud cover permitted, escorted by fighters of 11 Group. Each target was to be bombed by a pair of Bostons, with each squadron being given five targets.

On Sunday 19 July 20 Bostons of 88 and 226 Squadrons mounted raids in pairs on ten power stations in the Lille area using low cloud as

On 19 July 20 Bostons of 88 and 226 Squadrons mounted raids in pairs on ten power stations in the Lille area using low cloud as cover. The Boston flown by F/Sgt Matthew G. Johnson in 226 Squadron, with P/O Leonard S. Stewart, navigator, and Sgt Fred C. Thorogood, gunner (pictured), nose-dived into the ground while making a bomb run on Mazingarbe power station and exploded in a wood east of Boulogne. All three men were given a military burial in the Cimetière de l'est at Boulogne. (Ralf Thorogood)

S/L John Castle DFC, who led the attack on Valkenburg in Boston Z2258 'A' on 4 July. (RAF)

cover. The Boston flown by F/Sgt Matthew G. Johnson in 226 Squadron, with P/O Leonard S. Stewart, navigator, and Sgt Fred C. Thorogood, gunner, nose-dived into the ground while making a bomb run on Mazingarbe power station and exploded in a wood east of Boulogne. All three men were given a military burial in the Cimetière de l'est at Boulogne. A second Boston, flown by P/O Aubrey K. C. Niner, of 88 Squadron, was also lost. Niner's aircraft and another Boston, flown by Sgt G. W. 'Ginger' Attenborough, had made for the power station at Lille-Lomme but missed it, so they attacked the aerodrome at Lille-Nord instead. Niner's aircraft was hit in the starboard engine and he had to belly-land on a football pitch in Lille. Niner, his WOP/AG, Sgt George Lawman, and his navigator, F/Sgt Philip Jacobs, were made PoW.

During July the Bostons again intruded after dusk. On the 26/27th, when 400 RAF heavies attacked Hamburg, 226 and 107 intruded over night-fighter airfields at Jever, near Wilhelmshaven, and Leeuwarden respectively. AL746 'M' of 226 Squadron, piloted by P/O Victor N. Salmon RCAF and which had been flown by Capt Odell of the 15th Bomb Squadron on the 4 July Independence Day raid, was brought down by flak en route and crashed on the edge of Langeoog. All four crew were killed, among them P/O Harold F. Deck, the 29-year-old observer, whose two brothers also lost their lives flying with the RAF (one had died on 1 November 1941 in the first ever Typhoon crash, at Roudham, Norfolk, and the other was killed flying a Tempest over Germany in April 1945). On 28/29 July 18 Bostons of 88 and 107 Squadrons intruded over Dutch airfields at Alkmaar and De Kooy. F/L R. MacLachlan of 107 Squadron first eluded a night-fighter and was then fired on by a flak ship, but he and his crew made it home safely.

Early in August the Boston squadrons commenced training for the forthcoming Operation *Jubilee*, which would involve British and Canadian landings at Dieppe on 16–20 August. On the first day 16 crews in 107 Squadron and those of 88 Squadron were dispatched to Ford while 226 Squadron crews

The 19 July attack by Bostons of 226 Squadron on power stations in progress at Chocques. (RAF)

A second Boston, flown by P/O Aubrey K. C. Niner, of 88 Squadron, was also lost on 19 July, when it was shot down while attacking the aerodrome at Lille-Nord. Niner's aircraft was hit in the starboard engine and he had to belly-land on a football pitch in Lille. Niner (pictured here after capture), his WOP/AG, Sgt George Lawman, and his navigator, F/Sgt Philip Jacobs, were made PoW. (Aubrey Niner)

On 28 July 1942 Uffz Karl Bugaj (seen here on his return being congratulated by other members of his Staffel) scored the first victory for 11th Staffel, JG1 (and the second victory for IV. Gruppe) when he shot down a Mosquito of 105 Squadron from Marham over München-Gladbach; the aircraft crashed at Tilburg and the crew, P/O F. A. Hurley and F/O F. W. Weekes, were both killed. (Eric Mombeek)

were sent to Thruxton, all to carry out Army Co-Operation training to become proficient in smoke-laying from low level. On 19 August 107 Squadron carried out 32 sorties over Dieppe without loss, but several aircraft were hit. At 0416 hours W/C Alan Lynn and F/L MacLachlan joined four Bostons of 418 and 605 Squadrons in trying to nullify coastal batteries as a prelude to the start of the Allied landings at 0500 hours, but the light was poor and results were unobserved. Fire was continuing from the Hitler battery, so 107 Squadron was ordered to send 12 Bostons in to silence it. Lynn led the formation in a bombing run west to east, but ground haze reflecting back light from the sun made the target difficult to spot and all bombs overshot. Flak was heavy but none of the Bostons was hit. The last Boston smoke screen action of the Dieppe operation involved four crews from 226 Squadron, led by S/L Graham 'Digger' Magill, and one from 88 Squadron. They flew over the beach-head at 1414 hours, being escorted by 66 Squadron, to conceal the few remaining ships still within gun range of the German batteries.

The Dieppe operation cost the RAF 108 aircraft, 48 German aircraft were lost and 4,000 army and navy personnel. Two Bostons of 226 Squadron, which flew 28 sorties between 0509 and 1500 hours, failed to return from the day's operations. 88 Squadron flew 32 bombing sorties, losing one Boston. The following message from AOC, HQ No 2 Group, was sent to the Boston stations in Norfolk:

'I CANNOT THANK YOU ENOUGH FOR THE WHOLE HEARTED CO-OPERATION OF YOUR SQUADRONS AND HOPE YOU WILL CONVEY MY CONGRATULATIONS TO THEM ON A VERY FINE PERFORMANCE. LEIGH-MALLORY.

'I WISH TO ADD MY CONGRATULATIONS ON ATTACKS PRESSED HOME IN FACE OF HEAVY OPPOSITION, ESPECIALLY IN THE CASE OF 226 SQUADRON ON SMOKE LAYING. THE TIMES OF TURN ROUND AND TAKE OFF AFTER RECEIPT OF ORDERS WERE ALSO OF A HIGH ORDER AND REFLECT THE GREATEST CREDIT ON ALL RANKS, BOTH AIRCREWS AND MAINTENANCE PERSONNEL.'

F/L G. A. Casey (with his daughter), S/L J. S. Kennedy and F/L H. A. Asker pictured in London on 27 October 1942 after receiving awards for their part in the Dieppe operation on 19 August. Casey and Asker were awarded the DFC, while Kennedy received a bar to his DFC. W/C W. E. Surplice DFC was awarded the DSO and P/Os R. S. Rutherford and L. J. Longhurst also received the DFC, as did P/O H. J. Archer of 88 Squadron. (Canadian Military Archives)

On 19 August the Bostons took part in Operation Jubilee, *the Dieppe operation, 226 Squadron working from Thruxton and being engaged on smoke-laying, with 88 Squadron operating from Ford on bombing sorties. This photograph was taken by 226 Squadron while engaged on dropping smoke bombs to blind coastal batteries. Two Bostons of 226 Squadron did not return, and of 14 aircraft only three escaped damage. 88 Squadron completed 32 bombing sorties, losing one Boston. (RAF)*

Returning to Great Massingham, 107 Squadron was again on bombing operations on 27 August when 12 aircraft attacked the airfield at Abbeville. The flak was heavy and accurate and P/O Allen was forced to ditch on the way home. He and two other crew survived, but F/Sgt G. T. Relph, observer, was killed. The ASR launch that arrived on the scene was also attacked by three Fw 190s while it was picking up the downed crew.

Throughout September and October pairs of Bostons from 88, 107 and 226 Squadrons continued low-level attacks on power stations in northern France. On 22 September two Bostons of 226 Squadron, one flown by F/Sgt M. A. H. Demont, the other by Sgt Maurice A. Collins, were shot down by fighters. One was claimed by Hptm Mietusch, CO of 7./JG26, who shot down his victim at 1315 hours 3 kms east of Ostend; it was his 23rd victory. Demont and his crew were killed, but 'Collie' Collins evaded and eventually returned home nine months later via the French Underground and imprisonment in Spain. P/O Harry J. Milford, his observer, and Sgt George Nicholls, gunner, were captured and sent to PoW camps. (Milford was one of the 50 prisoners murdered following the Great Escape at Stalag Luft III in 1944.)

On 13 October 'Dinty' Moore, now a F/O

On 29 August Sgt Simkins and Sgt Savage of 88 Squadron bombed Comines power station, and 11 Bostons of 226 and 88 Squadrons, led by S/L Dickie England, bombed fishing wharfs at Ostend from 9,500 feet. A bomb that exploded in the 25,000-volt switchgear at Comines caused complete stoppage of the power station. The 10,000-volt switchgear was damaged at the same time, thus cutting off all local supplies in the Comines district. Not until 20 September was a temporary low-tension network in operation, and on 19 October the station capacity was still only 10 per cent of normal. Only on 30 November, 13 weeks after the raid, was the capacity restored. (RAF)

Right *On 6 September Fw Erwin Roden of 12./JG1 shot down Mosquito IV DK322 GB-P of 105 Squadron crewed by Sgt K. C. Pickett (PoW) and Sgt H. E. Evans (KIA), which crashed at 1830 hours near Tourines-La Grosse, Belgium. Thirteen days later, on 19 September, Schwarmführer Ofw Anton-Rudolf 'Toni' Piffer of 2nd Staffel/JG1 shot down Mosquito DK326 of 105 Squadron crewed by S/L N. H. F. Messerly DFC and P/O F. Holland (both KIA) of 105 Squadron. Piffer, seen here shortly after recording his 7th and 8th victories over B-17s, was himself killed in action on 17 June 1944. (via Eric Mombeek)*

Below *On 22 September 1942 18 Bostons from 88, 107 and 226 Squadrons set out to attack power stations and secondary targets in northern France. F/O D. Grundy and his observer, F/O F. T. Coxall, of 88 Squadron, were awarded the DFC for their low-level attack on the Aciéries de France Isergues iron foundry, which they left enveloped in flames. (RAF)*

Bottom *Hits can be seen on the Finalens chemical works at Douvrin in this remarkable low-level photograph taken by Sgt Savage's Boston of 88 Squadron, during his attack on 22 September. (RAF)*

Top *Mosquito IV DK337 GB-N of 105 Squadron pictured at Horsham St Faith on 22 September 1942 when it returned hit by light flak. DK337 took part in the daylight raid on Berlin on 30 January 1943, when it was flown by F/Sgt P. J. McLeehan and F/O R. C. Morris. It failed to return from an operation to Duisburg on 31 August 1943.* (de Havilland)

Middle *Fw Fritz Timm of 12./JG1 receives the Iron Cross, Second Class, from his Gruppenkommandeur, Hptm Fritz Losigkeit, after shooting down Mosquito DK339 of 105 Squadron, crewed by W/C C. R. K. Bools and Sgt G. W. Jackson (both KIA) on 9 October 1942. Ofw Timm was killed in his Bf 109G-6 'Yellow 3' (440939) on 28 May 1944 during combat with P-51 Mustangs of the USAAF, at Elsdorf/Köln.* (via Eric Mombeek)

Bottom *On 11 October 1942 Mosquito IV DK317 of 105 Squadron flown by S/L J. G. L. Knowles and P/O C. D. A. Gartside of 139 Squadron, and DZ341 GB-A of 105 Squadron, flown by F/L J. Lang (PoW) and P/O R. P. Thomas (PoW), both failed to return from a raid on Hannover. They were shot down over the sea by Uffz Günther Kirchner (pictured) and Uffz Kolschek, of 5th and 4th Staffel/JG1 respectively. A third Mosquito IV, DZ340, crashed at Marham on return.* (via Eric Mombeek)

gunner in 88 Squadron, was 'ready and raring to go' on his second tour in 2 Group, but they were recalled after only 20 minutes in the air. 'Dinty' had already spent a frustrating time at Bicester, where he had made repeated requests for a posting. However, they continued to fall on deaf ears, so when he was asked by F/L Johnny Reeve, who was in charge of the Gunnery Wing, to crew up with him and P/O Freddy Deeks for another tour of operations, he jumped at the chance.

'Johnny was a rather complex character who I never really got to know, whereas Freddy, who had worked in Fleet Street, was most interesting and easy to get along with. Like myself, they had both completed one tour of operations on Blenheims, Freddy being one of the few who had survived a tour in Malta during the winter of 1941/42 where the loss of aircraft and crews had been absolutely appalling. The air gunner who normally flew with us was an extremely likeable Newfoundlander called Johnny Legge.

   Losses in 2 Group, meanwhile, had fallen. It also meant living in Blickling Hall again, which for me was like going home, except that this time I lived in the Officers' Mess, with the services of a batman! Sadly, my memories of this tour, which was to last 14 months, were of a squadron that, by comparison, was under employed. In the spring of 1943 our aircraft were needed in North Africa, so we spent some time converting from the Boston Mk III to the Mk IIIa. Second, it was a period of preparation for the invasion of Europe and the development of close links with the Army, to which the Group would provide close support. A third reason may have been the sobering experience of the very heavy losses we had experienced in 1941.'

Only two *Circuses* were possible during October, the first on the 15th, when three Bostons of 88 Squadron, 11 from 107 and nine from 226, led by S/L Magill DFC, visited Le Havre, their intention being to bomb a 'Neumark' Class raider, which was reported to be still in dry dock undergoing repairs following damage sustained in an earlier raid. On arrival, however, the Boston crews discovered that the vessel had sailed, so they unloaded their bombs on a 5,000-ton motor vessel in the Bassin de Marée instead.

Next day, 16 October, 'Dinty' Moore and his crew took off at 1155 hours as part of a formation of six Bostons in a *Circus* attack on Neumark-en-le-Havre.

'We flew down to Ford in the south-east where we rendezvoused with our escort, climbing rapidly to our operational height after leaving the coast of Kent. The usual flak barrage was awaiting our arrival over the French coast, although it cannot have been too accurate as we flew on to bomb the target before returning home. The Luftwaffe stayed away from the party and we landed back, unscathed, at Oulton after a flight lasting 2 hours 50 minutes feeling on top of the world after completing our first mission.

Our first flight in the Boston was a revelation, for here we had a fast, manoeuvrable aircraft, with a terrific rate of climb, capable of carrying a bomb load of 2,000 lb, twice the weight carried by a Blenheim. Unlike the Blenheim, the Boston could, with one propeller feathered, still climb without causing the pilot too many problems. Here we had a beautiful,

On 31 October 17 Bostons of 88 and 107 Squadrons headed for power stations in the area of Rijsel and Bethune, while Pont à Verdin was the target of six Bostons of 107 Squadron. P/O George Turner, pictured in the cockpit of Boston 'EST MELIOR DARE QUAM ACCIPERE' ('It is better to give than to receive') with observer George Liddle in the nose, and S/L Philip Rex Barr DFC, dropped their loads on Pont à Verdin, while F/Sgt Nicols attacked Comines. (via Nigel Buswell)

highly manoeuvrable and powerful aircraft, so we were better equipped to carry the war to the enemy than we had been during the summer of 1941. Another factor that struck me was the manoeuvrability of a formation of six aircraft to evade flak or fighters, compared with the old unwieldy formation of 24 Blenheims.'

In the late afternoon of 31 October, 17 Bostons of 88 and 107 Squadrons headed for power stations in the area of Rijsel and Bethune. Four Bostons flew to Mazingarbe, four to Gosnay, six to Pont à Verdin and three to Comines. Of the four who had Mazingarbe as a target, only one reached its destination and dropped its bombs. The same happened to the Bostons at Gosnay: not one of the seven aircraft could find the target. Most of the Bostons dropped their bombs on secondary targets and strafed them with their guns.

Pont à Verdin was the target of six Bostons of 107 Squadron. Over the sea the aircraft of F/Sgt Grant had to return after experiencing problems with his guns. The other five continued in heavy rain and reduced visibility. P/O George Turner and S/L Philip Rex Barr DFC dropped their loads on Pont à Verdin, while F/Sgt Nicols attacked Comines. In the two remaining Bostons, Sgt Simpson and P/O Henry Collings headed for Pont à Verdin. Simpson could not find his target, so dropped his bombs on an alternative. Collings did the same before, over Jonkershove, his Boston was picked up by two incoming Fw 190s of 8./JG26 from Wevelgem-Kortrijk. The leading fighter was being flown by Lt Paul Galland, one of two younger brothers of Adolph, and his wingman was probably Ofw Johann Edman. They attacked as soon as the Boston came within range. Stanley Nash and Francis Pickering, the two air gunners, returned fire, but shells from Galland's guns set the aircraft on fire. The other crew member was Ronald Tebbutt, the 32-year-old navigator.

Michel Hoornaert, a farm-hand, looked up and witnessed the air battle.

'The Boston flew at about 50 metres over me and I saw the crew up front through the plexiglas nose. They turned their heads to the left and right all the time. The aircraft climbed again to the farm of André Spruytte. There it had reached about 300 metres when I saw for the first time the flames coming from the aircraft. Over

the farm the Boston turned to the right, then turned east and took the direction from which it came. The pilot was clearly looking for a place to land.'

Farmer Odiel Vanbiervliet saw the Boston come straight towards him and his farm.

'Between the aircraft and me was a haystack and I thought that it would hit it, but it went over . . . then I fled to a barn to protect myself. It touched 200 metres before a stream, slid through a fence in the middle of the meadow till the edge, where it flipped over in the willows.'

Hoornaert adds:

'The wings broke off and two willows were carried

Francis 'Rex' Pickering, air gunner (KIA) on P/O Henry Collings' (KIA) Boston, which was shot down on 31 October by Lt Paul Galland of 8./JG26 from Wevelgem-Kortrijk in his Fw 190. (via Nigel Buswell)

A photograph of Comines power station taken by a retreating Boston at 50 feet. (via Nigel Buswell)

along . . . the fuselage screeched for a few hundred metres till the Schrevelstreet, where it came to a stop.'

Vanbiervliet continues:

'Then it carried on for a long way through the field and exploded. One of the crew members was still alive but he died shortly afterwards. I did not see any other bodies. Somebody wanted to take away a parachute. Then the Germans came and we all had to leave.'

The wreckage was spread for hundreds of yards. It was Paul Galland's 17th victory, and his last, for just 5 hours later he was killed when he was shot down into the sea by a Spitfire while returning from an escort mission for the bombers to Canterbury. Edman, who then dispatched the Spitfire, was himself shot down and killed on 21 March 1944, by which time he had five victories.

At the end of October 1942 the Battle of Alamein resulted in a victory for the Eighth Army over Rommel's Afrika Korps, and then it was announced that on 8 November Allied Forces had landed in North Africa. At last it seemed that the tide had turned in the Allies' favour. Better times for 2 Group, too, were anticipated. The North American Mitchell II had begun to equip 98 Squadron (which had disbanded in Coastal Command in July 1941), and 180 Squadron, which both reformed at West Raynham in September, though the squadrons would not begin flying operations until they

moved to Foulsham on 15 October. Even then, problems with turrets, guns and other systems would delay them further.

In October 1942 the Lockheed Vega Ventura entered the picture. Crews sardonically named it the 'Flying Pig' (a reference to its porcine fuselage). When asked what the Ventura could do that the Hudson couldn't, they answered, 'Consume more petrol!' S/L Ray Chance, CO 'A' Flight in 21 Squadron (which had disbanded at Luqa, Malta, on 14 March and re-formed at Bodney the same day), remembers:

'We spent the summer converting to Venturas – a larger version of the Hudson! In fact it was a Lodestar passenger aircraft, converted – its civil origins never deserted it. Venturas came in "penny numbers", sometimes one a week, sometimes two. The manual came with it. As new crews came in (an upper gunner was needed), I taught the young pilots to take off and land and formate, etc. S/L Peter Shand [W/C, killed flying a Mosquito on 20/21 April 1943] did the same with 'B' Flight.'

Venturas carried a crew of four/five, could carry 2,500 lb of bombs and was armed with two .50 and six .303 inch machine guns. Two other Ventura squadrons, 487 RNZAF and 464 RAAF, were formed at Feltwell on 15 August and 9 September respectively, occupying dispersals recently vacated by 75 New Zealand Squadron Wellingtons. 487 was commanded by W/C F. C. 'Frankie' Seavill, who came from a sheep-

Lt Paul Galland of 8./JG26. Collings' Boston, which he shot down on 31 October, was his 17th and last victory, for just 5 hours later he was shot down and killed by a Spitfire while returning from an escort mission for the bombers to Canterbury. (via Nigel Buswell)

farming family at Waingaro, and had left New Zealand in 1930 for a career in the RAF. 21 Squadron remained at Bodney until October 1942, finally moving to nearby Methwold, where it would remain until April 1943.

Ventura operations began on 3 November 1942 when three crews from 21 Squadron, led by the CO, W/C R. J. P. Pritchard AFC, tried to raid a factory at Hengelo but had to bomb railway lines instead. Further sorties were flown on the 6th for the loss of three Venturas. S/L Ray Chance remembers:

'I lost two close friends on that foray. F/O A. E. K. Perry was killed in action, and F/O Brown did not return, but later we heard that he was a PoW. Another close friend was pilot W/O2 V. R. "Hank" Henry

RCAF, a boy of 20 who had come all the way from Vancouver. He died on his first trip, on 7 November, and is now buried at Flushing.

My crew of "S-Sugar" on 7 November were Sgt "Steve" Stephens, WOP/AG, Sgt "Robbie" Robinson, navigator, and F/Sgt Edinborough DFM, upper gunner. We took off around midday for Terneuzen to attack oil installations there. The flight over the North Sea at about 100–200 feet was uneventful. It was also called a cloud-cover raid, the met forecast being that there would be a front over the Dutch coast with cloud base at about 800 feet. We saw the Dutch coast approaching and flashed over the sand dunes at 50 feet, to keep below enemy radar. We had been going some while when Robbie called me up on the R/T and said, "Sorry, sir, but I'm lost."

I said, "OK, Robbie, stay on this course for a while and see what turns up."

Silence, and we skimmed along for another 10 minutes when up pops Robbie again and says, "Sorry, sir, but I'm still lost."

We were somewhere near the Dutch/Belgian border and could have been heading for Bruges or even Antwerp. As this was totally unsatisfactory I decided, rightly or wrongly, to pull up to 250–300 feet to see if I could pick up a pin-point position. As soon as we reached that height without warning there was an enormous high-pitched explosion. A shell had gone through the fuselage about 3 feet behind my head and exploded in the fuselage. It should have blown my head off, but I found later that I had one of the Venturas with a 2-inch steel plate behind the seat. This saved me, but unfortunately it caught my wireless operator. I kept a straight face and a straight course. I couldn't see behind me. Then Robbie came through from the navigation section in the nose and looked down the fuselage. In his slow, unemotional Lancashire voice, he said, "Steve's been hit, sir."

I said, "Then bring him alongside me."

The crew, including a F/O who had "come along for the ride", dragged him and laid him down at the side of me. He was covered in blood from head to foot. I later discovered that he had been blinded by phosphorous burns to the eyes, his elbow joint was smashed and he had 30 bits of small shrapnel in him. His lips were moving.

I said, "What's he saying?"

"He wants to know if we're going back."

Two of the crew said, "He's bleeding to death. If you turn back now, sir, you might just save his life."

This calls for very hard decisions when you have

been in the same crew for six months. There is a deep personal friendship and bond that grows up quite regardless of rank. There lay poor Steve in an ever-widening pool of blood. I pulled the "stick" back and shot up into the clouds at 800 feet, levelled off and let them give him such help as they could. Someone tried a morphine injection. They said again, "He wants to know if we're going back."

I shouted to them, "Shout in his ear and say we've turned round and we're going back."

We had not. We were going straight on.

After this I descended through the clouds to ground level again. I calculated that it would be 10 more minutes to the target (and 10 minutes back to at least this point), putting 20 minutes on to Steve's time. When the time was up on that course Robbie and I decided to do a square search of the area, and if the oil installations could not be found I was permitted to look for a secondary target.

I decided to fly NNE, when we should come to the estuaries from the Rhine. Then F/Sgt Edinborough called me up from his top turret and said that firing was coming at us from behind. So up again into the clouds for blind-flying, as one instrument had gone. After a few minutes I decided to come down again. As I broke cloud I saw to my left a broad estuary and three ships sailing out to the sea in line astern. I said, "This is it."

So we did a diving turn to the left and, pulling out above the masts of the rear ship, did an attack on all three from the rear. Having pressed the bomb button on the wheel, I immediately pulled up straight into the low cloud base and climbed to 800 feet in cloud. Steve wasn't taking any part in all this, though as we dived one way and then the other I saw blood run to one side of the cockpit, then the other.

After some time flying blind I felt sure we must be over the sea, so I put the nose down and broke cloud again quite low down. I was slap over a harbour. At once flak guns opened up, so yet again stick back and up into the clouds. This time we kept the course we had chosen for home. After 15 minutes we ran out of

Ventura operations began on 3 November 1942 when three crews from 21 Squadron, led by the CO, W/C R. J. P. Pritchard AFC (third from the right wearing a Mae West) tried to raid a factory at Hengelo but had to bomb railway lines instead. Far left is the Intelligence Officer, 'Jimmy' Grantham. (Wartime Watton Museum)

cloud cover; we had passed through the front and were in clear blue sky at 800 feet. At once the worry was German fighters, so down to sea level and give it all its got.

As we approached Great Yarmouth I pulled up to about 1,000 feet so that we could easily be seen and fire off the identification colours of the day. There were three Royal Navy ships parallel to the coast heading north, but they were quite unimpressed by our activities and at once opened fire on us! I was just beginning to feel that it just was not my day!

Poor Steve was again thrown about the bloody cockpit floor. They didn't hit us but as I headed overland into Norfolk a low November mist had settled in the late afternoon. Finally we admitted that we were lost above this low fog, although there was a perfect blue sky above. We stooged around for over half an hour looking for something. At last by the grace of God I saw Swaffham church tower sticking up through the mist. A cheer went up. I knew where I was and the course to fly to Bodney and Methwold.

One of the crew must have worked the W/T set, for as I came in low over the hedge an ambulance and a fire engine were at the end of the runway and raced down the runway with us. The medics were wonderful. Before the great wheels had stopped they were inside with a stretcher, and by the time I reached the perimeter track Steve was already on his way to RAF Hospital, Ely.

When I got to dispersal I walked slowly over to an elder tree, leaned against it wearily, then bent down and threw up. That evening I stole a gallon of petrol, put it in the Flight Truck and drove to Ely. Steve was propped up and was what is euphemistically called "comfortable". Matron told me of his injuries and the 30 little bits of shrapnel they'd got out of him. Thankfully he lived, regained his sight and later demanded to go back again to 21 Squadron and do some more. It is sad that they do not give medals to young men like Steve who showed such quiet but indomitable courage.'

Losses in 2 Group generally were high. For instance, in November 107 Boston Squadron flew 11 sorties for the loss of four Bostons and 16 aircrew killed – an almost 40% loss rate! On a raid on the marshalling yards at Courtrai on 7 November S/L Philip Rex Barr DFC hit high-tension cables and crashed near Wevelgem; he and his observer, F/O Walter Barfod DFC, were

On 6 November 21 Squadron lost three Venturas, including AE784, which crashed at Waddenzee, 5 kms east of Den Helder. (Otto Keller collection)

Bombs dropped from 8,000 feet by 226 Squadron Bostons, led by W/C Surplice DSO DFC, fall on Caen-Carpiquet aerodrome on 6 November. (RAF)

killed. Two 107 Squadron Bostons collided near Le Havre on the 10th with no survivors. There was not even the consolation that the 'tip and run' raids by 2 Group on airfields, power stations and docks, flying low over the sea, so reminiscent of the shipping strikes, were accomplishing much material damage. Then, in December 1942, 2 Group at last had an opportunity to really make a significant contribution to the bomber offensive.

Chapter Six

Operation *Oyster*

'Ki te mutunga' – *'Through to the end'*

Motto of 487 Squadron RNZAF

Preparations for Operation *Oyster*, the most ambitious daylight raid conceived by 2 Group, had been given the green light on 9 November 1942. It would involve a daylight precision strike on the Philips radio and valve works in Eindhoven, 60 miles from the coast of Holland and 50 miles from the Ruhr. Philips was the largest manufacturer of its type in Europe, producing over one-third of the German supply of valves and certain radar equipment. Although some industrial processes had been dispersed to other sites, Eindhoven was still the main centre, especially for research into electronic countermeasures and radar, and its destruction was of vital importance. Production was centred in two factories, both in built-up areas within the town, which demanded precision bombing from a very low level to minimise the danger to the local people.

Originally plans called for the Stryp Group main works to be bombed by 24 Venturas, 12 Mitchells and 12 Mosquitos, while 12 Venturas and 36 Bostons would at the same time attack the Emmasingel valve and lamp factory. The slower Venturas would lead the way at low level with HE and 30 lb incendiaries before surprise was lost. On 17 November a full-scale practice was held on a route similar to the one to be used, with the St Neots power station as the 'target'. Many

basic lessons were learned, while other problems associated with a mixed force, such as the differences in bombing techniques and cruising speeds, were exposed. The Mitchells fared particularly badly on this first practice, but even worse were the Venturas. Next day their crews tried again on their own on the same route. They finally perfected their performance on the third practice, on 20 November, when all four aircraft types took part.

These simulated attacks revealed deficiencies that led to the two Mitchell squadrons, 98 and 180, being withdrawn from the starting line-up for the raid, scheduled for Wednesday 3 December. In any event, since converting to Mitchells both squadrons had been plagued with turret and gun, intercom and oxygen problems, and were far from operational. It was also anticipated that smoke and fires from the Venturas' incendiaries would obscure the target for the succeeding waves, so they would have to go in last behind the Bostons and Mosquitos. Consequently, the routes and timings differed between the aircraft, the fastest, the Mosquito, being followed by the Boston, then the slowest, the Ventura. Obviously, it was vital for each squadron to arrive over the targets separately, to avoid confusion, yet it was imperative that the whole attack be completed in the shortest possible time. Therefore it was finally decided that the Bostons would, after all, attack both plants, and with 11-second delayed action bombs. These would hopefully divert attention from the Venturas as they climbed to bombing height.

By 2 December preparations were complete. Jim 'Dinty' Moore recalls:

'At 2030 hours at Oulton our presence was requested in the briefing room with 11 other crews from the squadron. [The same procedure was being carried out in the operations rooms of the other seven squadrons at five other 2 Group stations: Marham (105 and 139 Squadron Mosquitos), Swanton Morley (226), Great Massingham (107), Feltwell (464 and 487 Squadrons, who were flying their first full-scale Ventura operation); and Methwold (21 Squadron Venturas)]. There was a great deal of animated discussion, various characters claiming to be "in the know", telling us what the target was going to be, followed by an expectant silence when our CO, W/C Pelly-Fry [who would lead the operation] stepped on the dais, the cover being removed from the large target map.

The operation would involve 84 aircraft from the Group: 36 Bostons, 36 Venturas, and 12 Mosquitos. In addition, our withdrawal was to be covered by four fighter squadrons of Spitfires, Mustangs and Typhoons, who would meet us at the coast, while the Americans were to launch a high-level attack with [36] Flying Fortresses on Lille as a diversion.

After the briefing we were confined to camp, the telephone was put out of bounds, so we settled down for a disturbed night. The following morning we climbed into the flight trucks and made our way up to the 'drome all keyed up for this special operation. We collected our parachutes with the usual comments from the packers such as "Bring it back if it doesn't work", and made our way out to the aircraft. It was then that the unforgivable happened and we were informed that the operation had been postponed [because of bad weather on the Continent]. It is difficult to describe your emotions at a time like that, for although you might feel a sense of relief you know that you will eventually fly on this operation so the overriding reaction is one of frustration.

Having been briefed for the operation there was no way that the authorities were going to let us loose on the community in case word got out about our plans. They dreamed up a variety of service-type devices to

W/C Hugh Pelly-Fry (second from left), leader of the operation to Eindhoven on 6 December 1942, pictured at Oulton with (far left) S/L D. Griffiths, Jerry Baker, S/L Dickie England, F/L Jim Lee, and an unknown sergeant. (via Jim Moore)

keep us occupied, for which we displayed little enthusiasm.

Thankfully, the morning of Sunday 6 December dawned and we were told that "it was on", so we were driven up to the 'drome with the predominant feeling being to get it over with. At 1115 hours we took off, forming up as No 3 to our "Wingco" [Pelly-Fry, who would open the attack, with F/L "Jock" Campbell flying as his No 2], and setting off on a course that took us directly over Norwich on our way to the coast. The noise of this large force of low-flying aircraft brought many of the citizens to their doors to see what was going on.'

Altogether, 12 Bostons in 88 Squadron, 12 of 226 Squadron and 17 Venturas of 21 Squadron were to bomb the Emmasingel valve factory. Twelve Bostons of 107 Squadron, 14 Venturas of 464 and 16 of 487 Squadron, plus eight Mosquitos of 105 Squadron, led by W/C Hughie Edwards VC DFC (with F/O 'Bladder' Cairns), and two of 139 Squadron were to attack the Stryp Group main works, while S/L J. E. Houlston AFC DFC of 139 Squadron would take off at noon to carry out damage assessment.

F/Sgt Bill Lee in Ventura 'L' of 487 Squadron, with a Maori tiki called KIA-ORA painted on its side, taxied out at Feltwell. Peter Mallinson, his air gunner, was flying his first operation, no more than eight weeks after his 18th birthday.

AIRCRAFT & CREW STATES AT 1800 HRS. 5 DEC	SQDN.	TIME ON TARGET	TASK	EFFORT	R.T. S.A.C.S.	TAKE OFF TIME EST	ACTUAL	CALL SIGN	W.T. S.A.C.S.	SERIAL	E.T.R. BASE	TIME LANDED	CAPT. OF A/C
MITCHELL AIRCRAFT 41 CREWS 51 Sec J Sgt Waterlog SERVICEABLE 22 AVAILABLE Nil	107	1230		6	Roamer	1113		BC1	AH5		1336		
				6									
VENTURA AIRCRAFT 67 CREWS 83 SERVICEABLE 53 AVAILABLE 49	226	1230		6	Illingworth	1125		8UT	FD9		1345		
				6									
BOSTON AIRCRAFT 58 CREWS 84 Wallisham SERVICEABLE 42 AVAILABLE 53	88	1230		6	Holtby	1133		IWT	T1K		1345		
			Z21 Eindhoven	6									
MOSQUITO AIRCRAFT 32 CREWS 52 Sec G SERVICEABLE 16 AVAILABLE 26	21	1236		9	Fogey	1133		BJ8	30L		1354		
			AIRBORNE	8									
BLENHEIM AIRCRAFT 29 CREWS SERVICEABLE 14 Nil	464 Swanton 2nd	1236		7	Eclipse	1133		N7G	8BT		1354		
				7									
SQUADRON CODE LETTERS 139 XD 180 EV 21 YH 88 RH 226 MQ 98 VO 320 NO 105 GB 464 SB 107 OM 487 EG	487 Swanton MC	1236		8	Organ	1133		UD5	K6R		1354		
				8									
	105 Taila SecG	1232		8	Reveille	1132		7PM	6FQ				
	139 Tamarisk	1232		2	Earthquake	1132		7PM	LW1		1330		
	139	1250	Damage Assessment	1		1200		7PM	LW1 F		1342		S/C Houlston
			Total -	94									

The operations board at Bylaugh Hall, 2 Group HQ, showing aircraft and crew states at 1800 hours on 5 December 1942, eve of the famous Operation Oyster *to Eindhoven. (RAF)*

'Much to our relief the secret had been kept, and after another hurried briefing, and having been issued with rations and escape kits, etc, we were in the air at about 1140. We manoeuvred in to our formation along with 464 Australian Squadron who shared our airfield. Before we reached our coast, we were joined by many other aircraft. I think there were about 100 in all. It was a very impressive sight, I can tell you. We were all flying very low over the sea – it seemed about 10 feet to me!'

'Dinty' Moore continues:

'The instructions to fly at no more than 50 feet over the sea to avoid detection by German radar were

Aircrews and aircraft of 464 Squadron RAAF, one of the three Ventura squadrons that participated in the raid on the Philips works at Eindhoven. (IWM)

Mosquito IVs of 105 Squadron at Marham on 11 December 1942. DZ360 'A' failed to return from Termonde on 22 December 1942, and F/Sgt J. E. Cloutier and Sgt A. C. Foxley were both killed in action. DZ353 'E' later served with 139 Squadron, becoming AZ-B of 627 Squadron, but failed to return from Rennes on 8 June 1944 when F/L H. Steere DFM and F/O K. W. 'Windy' Gale DFC RAAF were killed in action. DZ367 'J', flown on the Eindhoven raid by F/O W. C. S. 'Bill' Blessing, failed to return from Berlin on 30 January 1943 and S/L D. F. W. Darling DFC and F/O W. Wright were both killed in action. DK336 'P' lost its starboard engine returning from a raid on Copenhagen on 27 January 1943, struck a balloon cable and a tree, and crashed at Yaxham, Norfolk, killing Sgt R. Clare and F/O E. Doyle. DZ378 'K' was damaged on 20 December 1942 after two sorties. DZ379 'H' later joined 139 Squadron at Wyton, and on 17 August 1943, the diversion for the Peenemünde raid, failed to return from Berlin when it was shot down by a night-fighter and crashed at Berge, Germany. F/O Cook, the American pilot, from Wichita Falls, Texas, and his navigator, Sgt D. A. H. Dixon, were killed (via Phillip J. Birtles)

strictly adhered to as we careered across the North Sea. The "Wingco" had the good fortune to have an excellent navigator, "Jock" Cairns, who guided us to our correct landfall.'

What of the rest of the formation? Two Bostons had aborted, while the Mosquito formation, which had departed the coast at Cromer and had flown further north of the main force, had unfortunately got ahead of schedule, Edwards and "Bladder" Cairns having successfully navigated their way through a 200-foot cloud base over the sea. The Mosquitos were supposed to rendezvous

with the rest of the formation at the target, but they now made landfall with the Bostons and Venturas at the Scheldt Estuary. Edwards had to slow the Mosquitos to just 150 mph and fly at 50 feet in order to stay behind the others when they should have been flying to the Stryp Works at 270 mph, before climbing to 1,500 feet, diving and releasing their bombs from 500 feet.

Peter Mallinson recalls: 'Bert Lowe, our navigator, said, "Dutch coast ahead." No sooner had he said this than we were greeted with a small amount of ack-ack, which increased as we approached the coast.'

Boston AL693 'U' flown by F/L Johnny Reeve and his crew on the Eindhoven raid. This photograph, taken during a practice flight just prior to the raid, shows WOP/AG Jim 'Dinty' Moore in the rear gun turret with F/O 'Skeets' Kelly, who took photos of the raid from this aircraft. AL693 flew 31 sorties in 88 Squadron between 23 March 1942 and 3 January 1943 before going to North Africa. It later served with 114 Squadron and was lost in a crash landing on 17 September 1943. (IWM)

Air gunners in 487 RNZAF Squadron. Left to right: Dennis Potter; Arthur Sharp; G. W. Trenery (KIA 3.5.43); unknown; Pat Stokes (KIA 6.12.42); D. L. Rowland (KIA 3.5.43); and Peter Mallinson, gunner in AE811 flown by F/Sgt Bill Lee on the Eindhoven raid. (via Peter Mallinson)

Over Walcheren, Ventura AJ213 'N' of 464 Squadron, flown by Sgt S. C. Moss RAAF, was shot down; it crashed at Vrouwenpolder and all the crew were made PoW. AE701 'F' of 487 Squadron, flown by F/Sgt Alex Paterson, was hit and crashed off Oostkapelle with the loss of the whole crew. The remainder of the formation headed inland, where 23 Bostons and Venturas failed to avoid a huge flock of ducks that smashed windscreens, splattered the cockpits with blood and feathers and damaged wing surfaces. Two gulls came through the nose of F/O Philip Burley's aircraft, injuring his navigator, F/O Herbert Besford, in the legs, while at the same time the draught whisked his maps away. Besford directed his pilot from then on by memory.

'Dinty' Moore continues:

'It was a pleasant sunny day and as we skimmed over the flat countryside we saw some of the Dutch men and women bedecked in their Sunday best. Many of them gave us a friendly wave. Despite the occasion and the obvious risks, the sense of speed, flying at about 20 feet, was truly exhilarating. On our way to the target I saw a lone Fw 190 fighter, whose pilot must have had quite a shock on seeing the approaching aerial armada and sheered off.'

P/O Jack Peppiatt, in 'B' Flight, behind F/L Johnny Reeve, had the same sense of excitement.

'Flying on the deck was always thrilling and we watched each other from aircraft to aircraft. Crossing the coast was a bit tense for two reasons. One, you were anxiously looking to identify a landfall and, two, the ack-ack gunners had a head-on view of you; for this reason we came in firing our guns to make them keep their heads down.'

Peter Mallinson adds:

'The first thing that struck me were the sandhills and pine forests, which looked like those at home – I soon found out the difference, though: these forests were full of machine gun nests and the sky was filled with tracer. Little blobs of light were whizzing all round our plane, some very fast and others seemed to appear as a slow curve. Bill Lee excelled himself with violent evasive action. We were soon out of this area, though, and by dropping over the treetops this made a screen that gave us some protection behind.

When I had read about other aircrew reporting people waving to them while low-flying over occupied countries, I found it hard to believe – I didn't *now*! As we hopped over trees and roofs there were people waving like mad, handkerchiefs, even flags. I suppose, with the leading aircraft having already passed over, it gave time for them to run out of their homes.'

Jack Peppiatt continues:

'The journey cross-country was a *Circus*, really. We slid about, keeping sight of our leader and watching to avoid airfields. The other hazard was overhead cables, etc, and the trick was to look out to the sides ahead so that you could spot the lines of pylons, which could reveal where the invisible cables might be. Although there was a lot of apprehension, there was also a great thrill in it. Talk over the intercom went on the whole time between the navigator and myself, discussing where we were, where the leader was going, and did you see that railway or canal, etc? I saw the landscape flying by with brief flashes of recognition; a house, some people, vehicles and every now and then a blink as I thought we had gone too near an airfield.'

As the bombers passed near to Woensdrecht airfield Fw 190s and Bf 109s of 4th and 6th Staffeln JG1, could be seen taking off, and the formation was also bracketed by heavy flak from the airfield defences. A 20 mm shell from the airfield flak defences hit the starboard engine of a 464 Squadron Ventura, flown by S/L Tony Carlisle, but he continued to the target, and Sgt Smock RCAF had more than 5 feet of his wing torn away when he hit a chimney; however, he was able to nurse the aircraft back to Norfolk safely. AT196 'C', flown by W/C Frankie Seavill, 487 Squadron CO, was hit by flak and crashed at Schaapskooi on the airfield at Woensdrecht; all four crew were killed. Like almost everyone else in the Venturas, Seavill was flying his first operational sortie, and he had refused a Group Captain post to stay with 487. S/L Len Trent, the 'B' Flight Commander, pressed the firing button on his control column and sprayed a flak gun position with .50 and .303 machine gun fire. A 21 Squadron Ventura flown by P/O H. T. Bichard was attacked by Uffz Rudolf Rauhaus, one of the pilots in II./JG1 returning from combat with the American attacks in France, and was shot down. He crashed at Rilland, but he and two of his crew survived and were made PoW.

Jack Peppiatt takes up the story:

'As we neared the turning point near Eindhoven [at Oostmalle, SSW of Turnhout] it did get taut. We all knew that if the target was missed there would be no way of recovering. In front I had glimpses of the leading Bostons and we began to pack in as we saw the buildings of the factory way ahead. The first two went in low and we then sailed up to 1,500 feet – that felt very vulnerable! We seemed to suddenly stand still and hang about waiting to be shot at.'

'Dinty' Moore says:

'Finally, I heard Freddy saying the target was straight ahead of us and, turning around, I could see the factory towering above the surrounding houses. 88 Squadron approached the main site at the lamp and valve factory from the south side at roof-top height and immediately began climbing to 2,000 feet in order to make shallow dives on to the factory.

The leading pair, whose bombs had 11-second delay fuses, ploughed straight in at low level, while Johnny led the remainder of the formation up to our bombing height of 1,500 feet. By now the Germans had opened up with light flak from batteries around the town, and one that was on the top of the factory itself. We dropped our bombs on the target, returning to nought feet without delay, and looking back I could see heavy explosions in the building, so it was evident that the bombs had landed in the right place.'

'By the time we were over the factory,' says Jack Peppiatt,

'it was all smoke and explosions, with Bostons all around at different angles and at that point there was a bang. "R for Robert" turned several degrees to port like a weather-vane, while I heard Len Dellow telling me that there was a big hole in the fin just above his head, but the aircraft seemed to handle all right and at that stage I was more concerned with where we were to go next.'

Twelve Bostons of 107 Squadron dropped their loads on the Stryp Group main works. First over the target was S/L R. J. N. MacLachlan's crew. They encountered a flak gun on one of the factory buildings and one of his gunners opened fire on it, forcing the German crew to abandon their exposed gun position and flee into the factory building just as MacLachlan's bombs scored a direct hit and destroyed the structure. This feat would earn MacLachlan the DFC.

107 Squadron Bostons in formation. The leading aircraft, W8337, being flown here by F/L A. F. 'Tony' Carlisle, who as a S/L flew a 464 Squadron Ventura on the Eindhoven raid, was coded 'H' at the time of the Oyster *operation when it was flown by F/L Don Smith in 226 Squadron. (RAF)*

Meanwhile, the Bostons of 226 Squadron, led by S/L J. S. Kennedy and S/L G. R. 'Digger' Magill, released their delayed-action bombs on the Emmasingel valve factory before the Mosquitos came in behind at 1,000 feet with high-explosive and incendiary bombs. W/O A. R. Noseda DFC and Sgt J. W. Urquhart (both KIA 9.1.43) bombed the target, but were intercepted on the return in the Overflakee area by two Fw 190s; although damaged by cannon fire, they managed to return safely.

F/O 'Jack' Rutherford RNZAF, S/L J. S. Kennedy and F/Sgt Eric Lee of 226 Squadron, who crewed Z2234 'X' on the Eindhoven raid. (George Casey)

F/O Kimmel and F/O Kirkland, F/L Patterson and F/O Mills, and F/Sgt Monaghan and F/Sgt Dean, also bombed the target from 1,000 feet. Mosquito DZ371 'A' of 139 Squadron, flown by F/O J. E. 'Junior' O'Grady and Sgt G. W. Lewis, was hit in the engine and, trailing smoke and flames, pulled away to head back towards England. They made it only as far as 30 miles off Den Helder, where they crashed into the sea at 1300 hours. The crew were never found. Two other Mosquitos, crewed by F/L Bill Blessing RAAF and Sgt Lawson, and P/O Bruce and P/O Carreck, were forced to abort. S/L George Parry DSO DFC, in his Mosquito with F/O 'Robbie' Robson, decoyed an Fw 190 away from the bombers, then returned and bombed the target at 1,000 feet.

A Boston turns away after bombing the Emmasingel valve and lamp factory, about 1 mile south of the main works, and the target for 88 and 226 Boston Squadrons and 21 Ventura Squadron. The leading aircraft of 88 Squadron attacked at rooftop height with 11-second delay bombs, and the remaining aircraft bombed at 1,000–1,500 feet with HE and incendiary bombs. (RAF)

Last in were the Venturas, flying 4 minutes behind the Bostons and carrying their incendiaries and delayed-action bombs. In the space of just 7 minutes, 1232–1239 hours, four of the Venturas were shot down by flak. The first two to go down over Eindhoven were AE945 'E' of 464 Squadron, piloted by Sgt Beverly M. Harvey RCAF, which crashed in Schoolstreet with the loss of all the crew, and AE940 'T', a 21 Squadron Ventura flown by F/L Kenneth S. Smith. All four crew, including F/L Wallace Martin RAAF DFC, who was Squadron Bombing Leader of 464 Squadron, and who had volunteered to navigate for 21 Squadron, were killed. They were quickly followed by another 464 Squadron machine, AE702 'Q', piloted by F/O Maurice G. Moor, which crashed on the Philips factory. AE902 'F' of 487 Squadron, flown by F/Sgt John L. Greening, cleared the rooftops and crashed at Woensel on the northern outskirts of Eindhoven. Both crews were killed.

Peter Mallinson, in the 487 Squadron formation, continues:

Top *Smoke rises from several sections of the Philips Emmasingel valve and lamp factory.* (British Official)

Middle *The Stryp Group main works on fire as seen from a 487 Squadron Ventura.* (via Peter Mallinson)

Bottom *Sgt Ted Leaver DFM, F/L 'Yogi' Yates-Earl DFC and F/O Ken Houghton DFC of 226 Squadron, who crewed AL678 'R' on the Eindhoven raid, examine a seagull's head that completely penetrated the leading edge of their Boston wing during the operation.* (RAF)

'As far as we were concerned the terrific barrage proved ineffective. Bill rose from about 20 feet to about 60 feet. I heard the navigator say "Bomb doors open". Then we flew into clouds of smoke. "Bombs gone." I saw lots of flashes and sparks rise into the centre of the target – what a blaze! As I looked back from my turret I saw two German machine gunners still on the roof. I should think it must have been impossible for them to get down and they were most likely blown up by other planes behind us. [Len Trent also noticed the gunners as he climbed to clear the parapets and launched his stick of bombs into the building, holing it from basement to rooftop. He could not help admiring him, saying that 'in his book' he was 'a damn good soldier'.] S/L "Digger" Wheeler, our ['A'] Flight Commander, was in front of us, so one by one we formated on him again, dived down low and belted as fast as we could for home.'

After the bombing the aircraft streaked for home at low level, desperately avoiding high-tension cables, flak, flocks of birds again, and fighters, before they reached the sanctuary of the open sea.

'We headed after the gaggle of aircraft heading north-west,' remembers Jack Peppiatt of 88 Squadron, 'until both I and my navigator, Sgt Kirk, began to wonder why they didn't turn west toward the coast. By now we were all down hugging the ground for comfort. We made a joint decision what to do and some of the aircraft made the turn; we went with them (they later proved to be 107 Squadron) but we were also joined and passed by Mosquitos as time went on.'

'Dinty' Moore continues:

'We headed for home although the "Wingco's" aircraft had been damaged by flak, so he was having difficulty in keeping it under control, which put us off course. [W/C Pelly-Fry's aircraft was hit just after he released his delayed-action bombs. With much-reduced hydraulic pressure, a large hole in the starboard wing and a coughing and spluttering starboard engine, he avoided the rooftops, but could not climb above 800 feet or keep up with the others on the way home. He came back alone after two Fw 190s were beaten off.]

We were encouraged on our way to the coast by the efforts of German anti-aircraft gunners. The remainder of our formation reached the coast without the attention of any German fighters, which may have been due to the fact that we were not returning by our intended route. We must have been well off course for we saw no sign of the fighter escort with whom we should have rendezvoused at the coast. Other squadrons who did return by the planned route were less fortunate, not only being harried by flak, as we were, but also by the unwelcome attention of German fighters.'

Fw 190s of 5./JG1, which had been summoned from Schiphol, now arrived on the scene. Jack Peppiatt's Boston was one of those singled out.

'After a few minutes settling down it all went up with a bang as Fw 190s appeared. Without doubt the next 20 minutes or so were full of action and not a little confusion. Some 10 or 20 aircraft were screaming along, full throttle, in a loose mass; no one wanted to be at the back where the Focke-Wulfs were coming in to attack and wheeling away for another go. They had one problem, which I think was that, as they dived,

P/O Jack Peppiatt of 88 Squadron, seen here at his wedding to Freddie, a WAAF. (Jack & Freddie Peppiatt)

they had to pull out early to avoid hitting the ground because we were all at zero feet. I distinctly saw cannon shells hitting ploughed fields in front of me and moving on ahead as the Focke-Wulf began to pull out.

At one point a fighter slid past us and sat just to my right as he slowed – so close I could stare at the pilot and admire the yellow spinner. Meanwhile, Len was calling for me to jink and then shouted that he had got one. If he did I really don't know how he did it as I was sliding and diving constantly. The astonishing

AL749 'R-Robert' of 88 Squadron flown by P/O Jack Peppiatt of 'B' Flight behind F/L Johnny Reeve on the Eindhoven raid. (Jack Peppiatt)

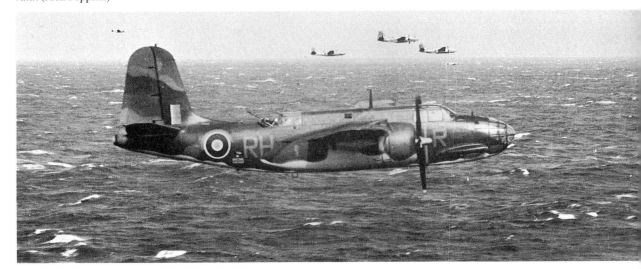

Ventura AE692 YH-K of 21 Squadron, which was flown by P/O Smith on the Eindhoven raid. AE692 was shot down on 21 April 1943. (Wartime Watton Museum)

thing was that we didn't collide, as aircraft constantly criss-crossed in front of each other.

Over the Dutch islands the attacks petered out and we flew steadily just off the water until Len quietly told me that there was an aircraft sliding over us from the side, obviously unaware that we were under him. It all went dark as a big black shadow arrived, and I sat rigid hoping that he wouldn't come lower, then throttled back gently to get behind him. If you know the height of a Boston fin you will know how we felt. Soon after this incident a Boston [AL737, flown by Sgt Cecil A. Maw of 107 Squadron, which was shot down by 5./JG1 at 1250 hours] just exploded in front of us and we flew through the debris; it was so completely destroyed that there was nothing big enough to hurt us. I may say that this occurrence really hit us. We looked down and back to see just the yellow stain of the marker from the dinghy, all that was left in just those few seconds. As we left the coast of Holland yet another Boston went in on our starboard side, possibly the pilot who had been wounded earlier [W/O Alan J. Reid of 107 Squadron, who crashed in the River Scheldt at 1252 hours]. These two events perhaps weighed on us more than anything else.'

Another Boston, Z2295, a 226 Squadron machine flown by F/O Norman J. A. Paton DFM, crashed at 1255 in the sea west of De Beer after being hit by Marine flak. The fourth Boston lost was AH740, flown by the CO of 107 Squadron, W/C Peter H. Dutton, who was shot down at 1259 into the sea 6 kms west of Katwijk aan Zee. Ofw Ernst Heeson, Uffz Günther Kirchner, Uffz Stellgeld and Fw Reitshofen of 5./JG1 each claimed a Boston destroyed.

Just before they reached the Zeider Zee the Venturas were bracketed by flak. Peter Mallinson recalls:

'This followed us right over the water. I noticed big splashes of water in front and behind us – boy, was I scared – I thought it was aircraft crashing, but we later learned that it was German heavy ack-ack shells bursting on the water in the hope of us running into one of these "spouts". It was about this time that I saw a tug-boat, towing a string of barges. I let go a few rounds at it but we were soon out of range. I'll bet the tug captain was as scared as I was because he was being shot at from both sides! Anyway, after using more violent evasive action we were soon over the open sea, heading as fast as we could for home.

I kept a good look out, especially in the sun. We gunners were told time and time again "Watch out for the Hun in the sun". All this time we were very thankful not to be attacked by enemy fighters, but we were told later that our own fighter escort was having a good time somewhere above us. We eventually sighted England and there were four loud cheers, one after the other, then altogether. Another 40 minutes and we were back at our dispersal, carefully examining our plane for damage. There wasn't a scratch. The only casualty was the remains of a stork, which was stuck in the port engine air-cooler. I only hope it wasn't carrying a baby cargo at the time. Birds are a menace when flying at low level and many other aircraft had broken perspex in turrets and nose cones. My pal Pat Stokes and his crew did not return from this trip. [Sgt P. J. Stokes, his pilot, F/Sgt Alex Paterson, and the two other crew members, were killed in action]. They said that about 11 aircraft didn't return from this trip, but if this is an overall estimate, then it's not too bad out of a hundred.'

Sgt A. V. Ricketts' Ventura in 21 Squadron, the ninth and last overall, ditched 7 miles off Bawdsey after a piece of flak severed a fuel pipe and he finally ran out of fuel; all four crew were rescued by ASR from Felixstowe. P/O Gordon Park of 487 Squadron crash-landed in the Fens.

Boston AL754, 'D-Donald', piloted by F/Sgt G. E. T. 'Nick' Nicholls of 107 Squadron, crash-landed at Great Massingham on one engine and his wheels up, and overshot the airfield. The aircraft went through a gun position and a hedge and finally came to rest in a slit trench. 'D-Donald' was written off, but the crew escaped relatively unharmed; Nicholls was awarded the DFM for his exploits. Sgt Burns, meanwhile, put down at Ipswich.

Sgt Chas Tyler's Boston in 88 Squadron had been hit in the starboard engine, and they had a very anxious flight across the North Sea, as Bob Gallup, the observer, recalls:

'Shortly after we had released the bombs we were hit by flak in the starboard engine. We lost contact with the rest of the squadron as we began to slow down. We were unable to gain height and the prospect of covering the 150-mile North Sea return flight looked remote, so it was decided to force-land in Holland and give ourselves up. After turning back inland, however, we conferred once more and decided to "have another go". We turned for the Dutch coast once more, and as we crossed out again every gun in Holland seemed to be firing at us. The tracers seemed to be like hailstones in reverse. Over the sea we tried to gain a little height but were unable to do so.

After about 50 minutes we recognised Lowestoft

Boston III AL754 'D-Donald' of 107 Squadron, which F/Sgt G. E. T. Nicholls crash-landed at Great Massingham on one engine and with wheels up on his return from Eindhoven. (Aeroplane)

ahead. We crossed the coast and force-landed immediately, finishing wheels-up in a ploughed field at Carlton Colville. My feet were buried in soil and I had a problem getting out through the top escape hatch. As we hit the ground the strap of Chas Tyler's seat harness broke and he hit his head on the gun sight. Apart from that we were unhurt. Chas was taken to Lowestoft hospital while Stuart and I were taken home by the farmer for a lovely meal. After we had been to see Chas in hospital, we were taken to the local pub, where we were allowed to win every game of darts. We spent that night at the farm near the aircraft, with clean sheets and pillow. Life was great until next morning, when transport arrived to take us back to camp.'

'We landed back at Oulton,' 'Dinty' Moore remembers,

'after an exciting and memorable operation, which had taken us 2 hours and 20 minutes without a scratch, my only excuse to use my guns being to fire at some of the flak positions. The "Wingco", in the meantime, found his way home with difficulty, having attracted the attentions of a German fighter; without hydraulic power he had to come in with his wheels up, making a safe if bumpy landing. The aircraft looked in a sad

F/L Charles Patterson, pilot of DZ414 'O-Orange', the Film Photographic Unit Mosquito, signs the Form 700 prior to taking off from Marham with F/Sgt Jimmy Hill, the FPU cameraman, for the Eindhoven raid. Patterson's faithful spaniel, Jamie, who flew low-level exercises with his master, will wait for his safe return. (Charles Patterson)

way but the crew walked out, though "Jock" Cairns later found out that he had suffered a cracked vertebra.'

As he approached Oulton Jack Peppiatt thought about the damage to his fin.

'Len tried to assess what might happen as we landed, as he could see to some extent. I realised that the hole was through the pitot head and as a result I had no altimeter or ASI, which meant that I would be coming in faster than usual. When we reached the airfield and flew over I could see Pelly-Fry's aircraft belly-flopped on the grass in the middle of the longest run, and I felt that I needed all the 1,100 yards for my performance, so it was off to Attlebridge where there was a long concrete runway. We plopped in with a sigh of relief and waited patiently for transport to Blickling, where we found that they had all gone to Swanton for a party . . . which we missed. The episode over Holland had resulted in me sweating profusely, so much so that my battle-dress tunic was saturated and my bar of chocolate had melted into the fabric.'

Over 60 tons of bombs hit the factory buildings, which were devastated, essential supplies destroyed and the rail network disrupted, but 14 aircraft – nine Venturas, one Mosquito, and four Bostons – had been shot down. Photographs taken after the raid showed that both factories had been very badly damaged, fully justifying the decision to make the attack in daylight from low level. The Germans reported that 'Damage was caused to nearly all the work buildings'. The factory was in the middle of Eindhoven, so a considerable number of homes were also destroyed or damaged, yet the loyal Dutch patriots' spirits were bolstered and they praised the RAF crews for their precision bombing, which resulted in little loss of life on the ground. In fact, 107 houses and 96 shops were completely destroyed, and 138 Dutch workers and civilians living around the factory were killed and 161 wounded. Seven German soldiers were killed and 18 wounded.

'Dinty' Moore concludes:

'The following day the national newspapers carried the story of the raid with several photographs. The heading in the *Daily Mail* read "Heaviest Day Bombing Raid of the War" – "Big Dutch Radio Works Smashed". It did

226 Squadron veterans of the Eindhoven operation of 6 December 1942. Left to right: F/Sgt W. H. C. Leavitt RCAF, who flew W8287 'F'; F/O L. P. Frizzle, who flew Z2261 'W'; F/O Hoskins; and F/L Don Smith, who flew W8337 'H'. Leavitt received the DFC for the Eindhoven raid. (RAF)

W/C Hughie Edwards (centre, facing camera) pictured with his navigator F/O H. H. Cairns (left). Edwards led the Mosquitos of 105 and 139 Squadron at Eindhoven. (via Philip Birtles)

W/C R. J. P. Pritchard AFC of 21 Squadron, pictured beside his Ventura II, AE856 'Z-Zebra', in which he led his squadron over Eindhoven. He received the DFC for his action, one of eight awarded to aircrew who took part on the operation. The cartoon duck is entitled 'HELL'S A-POPPIN!'. (via Wilf Clutton)

me, so she was easily persuaded to take the afternoon off work so we could go and buy our engagement rings. The film of the Eindhoven raid was taken by F/O "Skeets" Kelly, who flew with us, and F/L Charlie Peace. I always remember sitting in a cinema when one of their productions was included in the newsreel and the audience applauded enthusiastically.'

W/C Hughie Edwards VC DFC, W/C Pelly-Fry and W/C R. H. Young AFC of 464 Squadron were awarded the DSO. Also bestowed on crews who took part were eight DFCs, including awards to W/C R. J. P. Pritchard AFC of 21 Squadron, P/O J. M. Rankin of 107 Squadron, F/L E. F. Hart of 464 Squadron, F/L 'Jock' Cairns and P/O C. A. Evans DFM of 88 Squadron, and two DFMs, including one to F/Sgt W. H. C. Leavitt RCAF of 226 Squadron. On 10 February 1943 Edwards was promoted to Group Captain and he became Station Commander of Binbrook. By the end of the year he had taken up an appointment in Air Command, Far East Asia, and held the rank of Senior Air Staff Officer until the end of 1945. He remained in the post-war RAF and was awarded the OBE in 1947. In 1958 he was promoted to Air Commodore and finally retired from the service in 1963. He returned to Australia, was knighted, and in 1974 became Governor of West Australia.

What of the others who took part in the Eindhoven raid? S/L J. E. Houlston AFC DFC of 139 Squadron was killed in action on 20 December. Four of the pilots in 487 Squadron (which was taken over by W/C Grindell following the loss of Seavill) – P/O S. Coshall, F/O S. B. 'Rusty' Perryman, F/Sgt T. J. Baynton and F/Sgt A. E. Coutts – were killed on 3 May 1943. Others, like Hugh Pelly-Fry, who was surprised to be appointed, in 1943, Air Equerry to HM King George VI, survived the war. He later commanded a Halifax bomber station and in 1945 was posted to Australia to command RAF Camden, near Sydney.

much to raise the morale of the British people, who up to the end of 1942 had had little to cheer about. As for me, as soon as I had been de-briefed I found a telephone to let Norma know all was well. She had been looking in vain for us to return over Norwich, so she was beginning to worry. Next day I met her during her lunch-break and proposed. She agreed to marry

Chapter Seven

Victors
and the Vanquished

'A souped-up version of the Hudson, the Ventura wasn't exactly popular with the operational squadrons . . . "Fine aeroplane," I heard one pilot comment, "for carrying mail, but as an operational aircraft I don't rate it."'

From Air Gunner *by Mike Henry, Boston observer*

Early in January 1943 Jim 'Dinty' Moore returned to Norfolk with his fiancée Norma from leave 'to get on with the war'. 2 Group was now commanded, since 29 December 1942, by AVM J. H. d'Albiac. Operations continued much the same, as 'Dinty' recalls:

'During January we were briefed to take part in four *Circus* operations with varying degrees of success due to the weather. It should not be forgotten that a method of identifying a target through cloud had not, so far, been fitted to our aircraft, although there would be a system known as "Gee H" brought into service within the next 12 months.

On 9 January our target was Abbeville, so we took off "into the wild blue yonder", everything going according to plan, meeting our escorting fighters on schedule and crossing the French coast, where we were met with the usual hostile reception. We flew on until we were only 40 miles from the target, only to find a thick layer of cloud that made it impossible for us to complete our mission. The risks were exactly the same as if we had actually bombed, so I'll make no comment as to our feelings as we landed after a trip lasting 2 hours 20 minutes.

On the 18th the story was exactly the same, the only difference being that our target was to be Cherbourg, which, of course was screened by cloud, our flight lasting 2¹/2 hours. On the 21st we had better

luck, the Met man having got his forecast right. The target was the Dutch port of Flushing, which I had last visited on 25 April 1941 with George and Ron. On this occasion, however, we did not take off alone, nor were we to fly at low level. This was to be a *Circus* involving 12 Bostons, flying in two boxes of six aircraft accompanied by our usual fighter escort. It

Some 36 500 lb bombs and 48 250 lb bombs dropped by 12 Venturas of 21 Squadron burst among the docks at Cherbourg on 15 April 1943. One bomb scored a near-miss on the whale-oil ship Solglimt, *which is seen in dry dock. All the Venturas returned safely.* (RAF)

In January 1943 Bostons of 2 Group, shortly to be reinforced by Mitchells and Ventura squadrons, carried the war to the Continent when weather permitted with Circus *raids like this one, which shows a IIIA bombing a target in France.* (IWM)

was a pleasant day with excellent visibility, so much so that I could see the Dutch coast long before we reached it.

We were obviously not welcome as large and menacing black balls of flak appeared in the sky ahead of us. The formation manoeuvred gently to avoid the threat, until we actually got on to the bomb run to the target, that anxious period when we flew straight and level. Finally, I felt the aircraft lift as our bombs left us on their way to the target. We now turned out to sea without any sign of the Luftwaffe, leaving the flak behind us, and returned to Oulton after a flight lasting just 2 hours. Flushing was of special significance to we members of 2 Group as one of our squadrons in a *Circus* attack there was attacked by an overwhelming number of German fighters, every one of our 12 being lost.'

On 22 January six Mitchells of 98 Squadron, led by W/C Lewer, and six of 180 Squadron, led by W/C C. C. Hodder AFC, flew their inaugural bombing operation, an attack on oil targets at Terneuzen (Ghent) in Belgium. It went ahead 24

hours late because the necessary bombs were not forthcoming on the 21st. Flying at wave-top height all the way, an unlikely hazard was encountered by S/L Slocombe, in a 98 Squadron Mitchell, who was injured in the face when a seagull shattered his canopy. The attack was made from 1,500 feet amid heavy flak and fighter attack, which were responsible for the loss of two 180 Squadron aircraft, one of them being flown by W/C Hodder.

On 25 January 226 Squadron returned to action with a raid on the docks at Flushing, when F/Sgt Wilson's aircraft was shot down by flak. On 27 January Hughie Edwards VC DFC led nine Mosquitos of 105 Squadron in a daring low-level raid on the Burmeister & Wain diesel engine works at Copenhagen, and on the 31st Mosquitos of 105 and 139 Squadrons bombed Berlin for the first time. (The final large-scale daylight raid by 105 and 139 Squadrons took place on 27 May 1943, on the Zeiss Optical factory and the Schott glassworks at Jena.)

In France, meanwhile, dislocation of the

supply route to the Atlantic U-boat bases was uppermost in the minds of the War Cabinet, and a directive issued for bombing operations in January–March 1943 called for round-the-clock attacks on U-boat bases on the west coast of France. This meant that while the heavies attacked at night, the mediums would support them with raids on railways and docks by day.

One of the prime targets in the campaign was the railway viaduct at Morlaix, on the north Brittany coast, a masonry structure more than 900 feet long and over 200 feet high that carried the main railway line to the U-boat base at Brest. If it could be destroyed, the Germans would have no alternative but to re-route supplies via Lorient, and this would add an additional 100 km to the journey. However, is destruction called for pin-point accuracy because of the risk to the French population in the heavily built-up area around the viaduct. On 26 January 12 Venturas of 21 Squadron at RAF Feltwell, supported by fighters of 10 Group, set out to destroy the viaduct, but the operation was aborted because 2/10 cloud in the target area prevented accurate bombing.

'Dinty' Moore in 88 Squadron went on a *Circus* to Abbeville.

'Everything was going according to plan, meeting the escort, climbing rapidly over the sea to our operational height before crossing the French coast, where we made our correct landfall. We then turned on to the course to the target, when we found it screened by a layer of cloud. Someone up there must have been looking after the interests of the good people of this town. The operation lasted 2 hours 45 minutes and involved the same risks as if we had actually bombed the target.'

Next day crews were kept at fine pitch with a low-level exercise on the iron and steel works at Corby by 89 aircraft from eight squadrons.

On 29 January 12 Bostons of 88 Squadron, led by S/L Gunning DFM, took off at 1353 hours on a *Circus* operation to attack the locomotive works at St Omer, but they were recalled at 1400 hours. Twelve Venturas of 21 Squadron, with fighter escort, crossed the North Sea to attack blast furnaces and steelworks at Ijmuiden, but thick cloud ruled out bombing by all but two of them.

On the same day, meanwhile, a force of 12 Bostons from 226 Squadron was once more dispatched to bomb the Morlaix viaduct, taking off from Swanton Morley at midday. At 1320 hours they rendezvoused with 35 Spitfire VBs of 310, 312 and 313 Squadrons of the Czech Wing over Exeter at 500 feet, and the formation set course at 1330 hours. They flew across the Channel accompanied by their escorts, then dived to bomb the target from 8,000 feet, dropping approximately 11 tons of high explosive. Visibility was good with little cloud, and the bomb-aimers had no difficulty seeing the target, though flak was heavy and accurate. The bombs from the first box fell in a built-up area to the north-east of and adjacent to the viaduct, with one or two hits on the railway line between the

The final large-scale daylight raid by 105 and 139 Mosquito Squadrons in 2 Group was on 27 May 1943, to the Zeiss Optical factory and the Schott glassworks at Jena. Mosquito DZ467 GB-P of 105 Squadron failed to return. (RAF)

On 29 January 1943 11 tons of bombs dropped from 8,000 feet by Bostons of 226 Squadron led by F/L Don Smith DFC rain down on the French town of Morlaix, the target being the viaduct, a masonry structure 958 feet long and 207 feet high, built in two tiers of nine and 14 spans, on the main Paris–Brest railway line used to supply U-boat pens on the Atlantic coast. Stray bombs from the second box of Bostons hit a school, killing 39 children and one teacher. (RAF)

viaduct and a cutting to the east. Several bombs from the second box fell on the railway line on the eastern edge of the viaduct. Stray bombs had also hit a school and 39 children and one teacher lay dead in the rubble.

After leaving the target the Bostons came under attack by Fw 190s, in all probability from III./JG2, who pressed home their attacks with great determination and skill and shot down F/O Clifford Thomas's Boston. As he attempted to ditch the aircraft, the starboard wing-tip hit the sea and the Boston cartwheeled and sank in a cloud of spray. Lost with Thomas were F/O the Hon Richard L. G. Bowyer, the 22-year-old son of the 1st Baron Denham and Lady Denham of Weston Underwood in Buckinghamshire, Sgt Robert Morton, aged 22, and Sgt George Currah. F/Sgt Leavitt's Boston limped back to England very badly damaged and was left at Exeter pending repairs. The remaining ten returned to Swanton Morley. The breaching of the Morlaix viaduct closed the main line used for naval supplies to Brest for almost two months, but at a high price.

Bad weather during January and February curtailed much of 2 Group's operations, but on 11 February heavy cloud cover enabled low-level *Circus* raids to be made by pairs of Bostons on French targets, and on the 13th five raids were mounted by the Group. 107 Squadron attempted to bomb the lock-gates at St Malo, but their bombs missed and they hit the docks instead. It would be two months before they would again operate Bostons on operations.

On 15 February all three Boston squadrons, 88, 107 and 226, were stood down, most of their crews being dispatched to North Africa where the Blenheim V, or 'Bisley', had suddenly been

F/O Cliff Thomas, pilot, 226 Squadron (KIA 29.1.43 on the Morlaix raid) pictured here with his son Derek. (Derek Thomas)

replaced by the Boston III. Blenheim losses had become untenable, especially after W/C H. G. Malcolm of 18 Squadron had his formation virtually wiped out in a daylight raid on Chouigui on 4 December 1942, an operation for which he won a posthumous VC. Daylight raids were then abandoned in favour of night raids, but the Blenheim was outdated and lacked suitable defensive armament. All Boston Mk IIIs were therefore ordered to the Maintenance Unit at Burtonwood to be prepared for modification for service by the light bomber squadrons in North Africa. All that now remained in 2 Group were Mosquitos of 105 and 139 Squadrons and the Venturas of 21, 464 and 487 Squadrons. There was further disruption in 2 Group at the end of the month when the Venturas, the Mitchells of 98 Squadron and a few 88 and 226 Squadron Boston crews participated in a large-scale tactical exercise aptly named *Spartan*. Thus for more than two weeks the Mosquitos were the only aircraft operational in 2 Group.

On 18 February 'Dinty' Moore married Norma in the beautiful St Peter Mancroft Church in Norwich, with his brother Peter as best man. Peter had served at Oulton for a time as an electrician before having been accepted for aircrew; when he returned to 218 Squadron at Waterbeach he found that his first crew had

Brothers in arms: Peter (left) and Jim 'Dinty' Moore. Peter joined 218 Squadron at Waterbeach, where his first and second crews were lost on operations. Friends to whom he spoke formed the impression that he did not expect to survive his tour of operations, and on 28 May 1943 he was lost when his Stirling was shot down off the Dutch coast with no survivors. (Jim Moore)

gone, having already been lost on operations, and the second crew to which he was allocated had also failed to return from an operation. Friends to whom he spoke got the impression that he did not expect to survive his tour of operations; sadly

Ventura II AE854 EG-J 'Joybelle' of 487 RNZAF Squadron with a bomb log showing 18 operations completed. On 28 March 1943 Venturas of 464 and 487 Squadrons damaged six ships in a raid on Rotterdam-Wilton and scored direct hits on three more. (Central Press)

he was lost on 28 May when his Stirling was shot down off the Dutch coast. There were no survivors.

'Dinty' Moore's return from honeymoon coincided with the beginning of a period of non-operational flying, which was spent mainly in adapting to the Boston IIIAs now being modified for gas-spraying and smoke-laying operations for frequent Army Co-Operation exercises.

'During my absence from Oulton, 88 Squadron completed a number of operations, but at this time our morale was pretty low as we had been declared non-operational. We still had a few Bostons left, but until we received some more from the USA (which took until 28 June) we were to remain in the non-operational category.'

While the Boston squadrons were working up with new aircraft, much of the bombing burden fell on the Ventura squadrons. On 15 March 11 Venturas of 21 Squadron bombed St Brieuc airfield in Brittany in a 10 Group *Circus*. On the 28th at Rotterdam-Wilton 24 Venturas of 464 and 487 Squadrons damaged six ships and scored direct hits on three more. All three Ventura squadrons flew two *Circus* operations on the 29th when in the morning S/L Len Trent DFC RNZAF led a formation and followed an attack by 21 Squadron Venturas on warehouses at

Dordrecht, and in the afternoon he led a large formation to bomb the docks at Rotterdam.

At the end of March 320 (Dutch) Squadron, which had been formed in June 1940 from Dutch Naval personnel, moved from Methwold to Attlebridge to await re-equipment with the Mitchell II. The 'Flying Dutchmen' had been operating a motley collection of Ansons and Hudsons, mainly on convoy protection and rescue duties from Northern Ireland, until they were transferred to 2 Group on 15 March.

On 3 April 464 and 487 Squadrons moved to the grass airfield at Methwold, a satellite of Feltwell (which returned to 3 Group), replacing 21 Squadron's Venturas, which moved to Oulton. There they replaced 88 Squadron, which in turn moved to Swanton Morley, as 'Dinty' Moore recalls:

'During April the "powers that be" decided that we had had the privilege of living in the home of nobility long enough, and moved us from Oulton and Blickling Hall to the purpose-built aerodrome at Swanton Morley. However, there was a marvellous chef in the Officers' Mess and the food was absolutely first class.'

Early in April, 464 and 487 Ventura Squadrons also moved from Feltwell.

On 4 April a formation of 24 Venturas was

At the end of March 1943 320 (Dutch) Squadron moved from Methwold to Attlebridge to await re-equipment with the Mitchell II. They had been operating a motley collection of Ansons and Hudsons, mainly on convoy protection and rescue duties from Northern Ireland, until they were transferred to 2 Group on 15 March. (Jan P. Kloos)

Right *320 (Dutch) Squadron crew members at Lasham in October 1943. Left to right: B. de Haan; C. J. den Tex-Bondt (KIA 20.6.44); A. Hamelink (KIA 29.11.44); E. Bakker (KIA 25.10.43); Loeff; R. W. H. van Pelt (KIA 25.10.43); Breedveld. (Jan P. Kloos)*

Below *Venturas of 487 Squadron. The nearest aircraft is EG-H, taking off from Methwold in the spring of 1943. (Tom Sheehan collection via Theo Boiten)*

Bottom *487 RNZAF Squadron at Feltwell in early 1943. S/L Leonard Trent, who led the fateful Amsterdam operation on 3 May, survived and was awarded the Victoria Cross in 1946 for his heroic action, is seated off centre (hands crossed without gloves) next to W/C Grindel, CO. On Grindel's left after the adjutant is S/L 'Digger' Wheeler. F/O Rusty Perryman (KIA 3.5.43) is second from left, while Gordon Park is first right. (via Peter Mallinson)*

dispatched to bomb Caen/Carpiquet airfield, while another 24 Venturas flew a *Circus* to the shipyards at Rotterdam escorted by five squadrons of Spitfires and one squadron of Typhoons, and 12 Venturas of 21 Squadron headed for Brest and St Brieuc escorted by Spitfires of 10 Group. All the bombers attacking Rotterdam were hit by flak and two ailing Venturas were finished off by Fw 190s. Three more Venturas were shot down on the Brest raid by enemy fighters. Their luck then seemed to change for the better, for on the next four operations, aided by escorting fighters, they beat off fighter attacks to get their bombs on target. However, on 21 April, when Venturas of 21 Squadron headed for the marshalling yards at Abbeville, their frailties were exposed once again.

One of the 12 Venturas that taxied out failed to take off after getting into the slipstream of another aircraft ahead. The 11 remaining aircraft headed for France in two boxes, led by F/L

David Dennis. Pilots of II./JG26 were being inspected at their base at Vitry by Generalfeldmarschall Hugo Sperrle when the Venturas were detected approaching the Somme Estuary at 9,000 feet. Immediately the pilots, led by Kommandeur Oblt Wilhelm-Ferdinand 'Wutz' Galland, broke ranks and ran to their aircraft.

They sighted the Ventura formation north of Abbeville. While Galland and some of his fighters took on the bombers in a ferocious assault, the remainder kept the Spitfire escort occupied. JG26 attacked from head-on, only breaking off at about 50 yards. F/Sgt Wilf Clutton, WOP/AG in Sgt Ionworth 'Ted' Bellis's Ventura, No 3 on the S/L in the first box of six, recalls:

'As we crossed the French coast the leader's aircraft shouted "Bandits!". I got into the astrodome to look around. The fighters were immediately engaged by our Spitfire escort and a ding-dong air-fight began. We weaved all over the sky but kept on course. Before

F/Sgt Wilf Clutton, WOP/AG, who survived the operation to Abbeville on 21 April 1943 when three Venturas in 21 Squadron were shot down. (Wilf Clutton)

Sgt Ionworth 'Ted' Bellis, pilot, 21 Squadron. (Wilf Clutton)

we reached the target another attack on our box was made, and our No 6, Sgt R. H. Wells, was shot down. Our bombing run commenced at the same time as another attack. Naturally it was "steady, steady" all the way until "Bombs away!". F/O G. L. Hicks, our No 4, was hit by cannon shells and his aircraft's nose burst into flame. It was a nerve-racking period made more so by the fact that No 4 did not go down immediately but remained in formation, a flying torch, and still bombed up. However, down she went as we let the bombs go. It was a direct hit. We made for home being attacked all the way to the coast. In the last attack F/O G. B. "Chippy" Chippendale, our No 2, had his tail shot away and went down. I had gone down to the guns but there was nothing I could do. I went back to the astrodome and looked around. There were only three of us left.

At interrogation it appeared obvious that all the attacks were directed at the leading six; the second box got away scot-free. There was no doubt that, but for the leadership of S/L Dennis, it might have been a lot worse, and we did get through to the target and hit it. Shortly afterwards S/L Dennis received the DSO.' (JG26 also shot down a Spitfire, while receiving no losses themselves.)

Worse was to follow on 3 May when *Ramrod* 16 was mounted to encourage Dutch workmen to resist German pressure in Holland. Six Boston IIIas of 107 Squadron (which had resumed operations on 1 May under W/C Dickie England, who had taken over the squadron on 10 April) and 12 Venturas of 487 Squadron were involved. The Bostons were assigned the Royal Dutch steelworks at Ijmuiden, while the Venturas, led by 28-year-old S/L Leonard Trent DFC RNZAF, 'B' Flight Commander, were sent on a diversion to bomb the Amsterdam power station, escorted by three Spitfire squadrons. Trent won the right to lead this *Ramrod* ahead of S/L Jack Meakin, 'A' Flight Commander, on the toss of a coin. Before their departure from Methwold Trent told his deputy, F/L A. V. Duffill, that whatever happened he was going over the target. P/O Monty Shapiro, 30-year-old observer in P/O T. L. B. 'Terry' Taylor's aircraft, said of Trent:

'He was an outstanding leader in air combat. He really cared for his crews and was a brilliant leader of formation flying. He was the complete antithesis of what you'd expect of an outstanding combat flier. He

On 21 April 1943 the Venturas of 21 Squadron were attacked by II./JG26, led by Kommandeur Oblt Wilhelm-Ferdinand 'Wutz' Galland (right), younger brother of Adolph, and they shot down three of the Venturas and a Spitfire escort without loss to themselves. 'Wutz' was the second brother to die (Paul having died on 31 October 1942), when he was killed in action on 17 August in combat with 56th Fighter Group P-47s during the disastrous 8th Air Force raid on Schweinfurt. (Bundesarchiv)

didn't take part in any drinking parties. Every evening he went home to his wife. But he was an exceptional squadron leader.'

En route to Amsterdam 'Q', piloted by Sgt A. G. Barker, aborted after losing the escape hatch. Tragically for the Venturas, a mistimed 11 Group *Rodeo* 212 sweep had already alerted the enemy defences and they ran headlong into a Schwarm of 2./JG27, and 28 Fw 109A-4s of II./JG1 from Woensdrecht, led by Gruppenkommandeur Hptm Dietrich Wickop. While several pilots of all three Staffeln from JG1 kept the escorting Spitfires at bay, others went after the Venturas. F/L Viv Phillips, Trent's observer, yelled, 'Here's a whole shower of fighters coming down on us out of the sun; they may be Spits – 20, 30, 40 . . . Hell's teeth, they're 109s and Fw 190s!'

They picked off the Venturas in just a matter of minutes. Among the first was Duffill's, which turned for home trailing smoke, to land safely back at Feltwell.

F/O Stanley Coshall's observer, F/O Rupert North, who was on his seventh sortie, recalls:

'Tracer bullets were whizzing around, enemy fighters were flashing past and our planes were going down in pieces or flames. It was plain that we would soon be hit and the tension and suspense were paralysing.'

Two Fw 190s attacked at 11,000 feet and the air gunner, Sgt G. H. Sparkes, was killed. A fierce fire was burning inside the fuselage. Coshall was

last seen reaching for the cockpit escape hatch. This had the effect of sucking the flames into the cockpit and North jumped clear through this exit via the back of the pilot's seat. He managed to get one clip in place before opening his canopy and landing on his feet, but was quickly captured. He spent three months in hospital recovering from multiple burns. The WOP/AG, Sgt W. Stannard, who was on his 21st sortie, lost his parachute in the blaze. He saw North jump clear and was trying to reach his burning parachute pack when the flames drove him back right into the tail-cone. An explosion then cleanly severed the tail unit, and Stannard came down trapped inside, landing near the village of Bennebroek. He had a badly burned left hand and forehead, two flesh wounds in the leg where he had been hit by exploding .303 ammunition, slight concussion and a cut on the head, the latter two sustained in the actual descent.

Hptm Dietrich Wickop (right), Gruppenkommandeur II./JG1, whose Fw 190A-4s were credited with seven of the ten 487 Squadron Venturas lost on 3 May 1943. Wickop claimed one as his 11th victory (he was killed in action by P-47 Thunderbolts on 16 May), and his wingman, Uffz Rudolf Rauhaus, claimed another. Rauhaus is seen in the first photograph getting out of the cockpit of his Fw 190A 'Yellow 3' of 6th Staffel, which shows the coat of arms of his home city, Neuss. (Eric Mombeek)

A few seconds and a few miles apart, 'O-Orange', Taylor's Ventura, shuddered from the shock of deadly accurate cannon fire. The first thing Monty Shapiro was aware of 'was cannon fire passing through the front of the aircraft and the order to bail out. I thought it was the end. We appeared to be falling to earth with no engines. The rear gunner was dead. I had no idea what was happening to the others.' Shapiro had been wounded in the arm by the same burst of fire that had killed the gunner and wounded the WOP/AG, Sgt T. S. Tattam.

Inside the cockpit the badly burned pilot had decided to make a quick end to his suffering, but incredibly, as the Ventura dived earthwards at 350 mph, the fire diminished and he was able to gain some measure of control, enough to attempt a crash-landing. Amazingly Taylor managed to belly-land 'O-Orange' with his bombs and two wounded crew members still aboard. It hit the ground at 250 mph, leapt into the air and crashed down again, eventually coming to rest in marshland near the village of Vijthuizen, on the outskirts of Haarlem, 5 miles from Amsterdam. After clambering out of the wreckage, Taylor was surprised to hear cries for help from the rear of the aircraft.

'He had no idea that we were still aboard,' explains Shapiro. 'He thought we'd all bailed out!'

Eight Venturas had been shot down before they reached the power station, and that of F/O S. B. 'Rusty' Perryman, which was badly damaged, went down at 1753. Only Trent's and F/O T. L. Baynton's aircraft remained. As Trent saw his bombs overshoot the power station Baynton was shot down and then Trent too came under intense fire from both flak and fighters. Hptm Wickop (his 11th victory) and his wingman, Uffz Rudolf Rauhaus, both claimed a Ventura, and five more were credited to II./JG1. Finally, Trent's Ventura went into a spin and broke up. Two crew died trapped inside, but Trent and Viv Phillips were hurled out to survive and become PoWs. It was only after they were repatriated that the full story became known, and on 1 March 1946 Trent was awarded the Victoria Cross for his leadership and gallantry. Boston BZ227 of 107 Squadron from the Ijmuiden force, flown by F/Sgt Frank S. Harrop, and a 118 Squadron

Spitfire flown by W/C 'Cowboy' Blatchford, were also lost.

On 11 May the Mitchells of 180 Squadron resumed operations when railway communications at Boulogne were attacked, one aircraft being lost. By then 107 was the only squadron still using Bostons on *Circus* operations. Meanwhile 88 and 226 Squadrons were flying almost daily exercises. On 15 May 12 Bostons of 107 Squadron, led by W/C Dickie England, flew a *Circus* to Abbeville-Drucat airfield. They were met in strength by Bf 109Gs and Fw 190s of JG54 'Grünherz' ('Greenhearts'), who made repeated attacks on the formation between Poix and Le Touquet. F/Sgt Kindell, England's air gunner, damaged two fighters while two were shot down by the escorting Spitfires. Oblt Horst Hannig, who had 30 victories, was killed when his parachute failed to open. None of the Bostons was lost, although F/Sgt Noble had to crash-land at Detling and F/Sgt Truxler force-landed in a Kent hop-field near East Peckham.

On 23 May 487 Squadron resumed operations with an attack on a power station and coking plant at Zeebrugge. They came through safely. Five days later it was the turn of 21 Squadron to attack Zeebrugge. F/O David Pratt led the two boxes of six Venturas; Sgt Bellis was his No 3. Wilf Clutton, his WOP/AG, recalls:

'There was no flak and no fighters and we got our bombs away. Upon diving away from the target Davy Pratt's aircraft side-slipped into ours. His wing caught ours and immediately crumpled. His tail fins then hit us underneath. I shouted on the intercom "Davy's hit us!", but Bellis could not hear me; the Ventura made a terrible row in the dive. He had not even felt the jolt. The last we saw of Pratt's aircraft was hitting the sea off Zeebrugge – an unforgettable memory.'

The day before, 27 May, AVM Basil Embry replaced AVM J. H. d'Albiac at 2 Group HQ, Bylaugh Hall, with the task of preparing the Group for invasion support in the run-up to Operation *Overlord*. Embry had lost none of his fire and determination, which he now brought to bear in all echelons of his new command. Morale was low and was not helped by the transfer, to 8 Group Bomber Command, of his two Mosquito Squadrons; 105 became the second *Oboe*

A Mitchell II of 180 Squadron in July 1943. (Aeroplane)

On 27 May 1943 AVM Basil Embry assumed command of 2 Group at Bylaugh Hall with the task of preparing the Group for invasion support in the run-up to Operation Overlord. (via Paul McCue)

squadron, and 139 high-level 'nuisance' raiders. Boston aircraft were slow to arrive, so 88 and 226 Squadrons re-equipped with the North American Mitchell II and III, while 107 Squadron was on gas-spray and ASR duties.

On 1 June 2 Group was transferred first to Fighter Command then, when this divided to form Air Defence of Great Britain (ADGB), into 2nd Tactical Air Force. Meanwhile, 98 and 180 Mitchell Squadrons at Foulsham, Norfolk, had finally cured their turret, gun, oxygen and intercom problems, while 342 (Lorraine) Squadron was working up on the Boston IIIA at Sculthorpe. The Free French, which re-formed at West Raynham, Norfolk, on 1 April, was commanded by W/C A. C. P. Carver, with W/C Henri de Rancourt as French Commandant. 'A' Flight was known as Metz Flight and 'B' Flight was called Nancy Flight. Boston IIIas were in short supply so training was carried out on early Bostons and some Havoc Is and IIs. The need to lay concrete runways at West Raynham in May led to the French having to move to Sculthorpe.

180 Squadron Mitchells at Foulsham, Norfolk, in May 1943. 180 and 98 Squadrons flew their first operation on 22 January 1943 when six from each squadron bombed oil targets in Belgium. (John Smith-Covington via Theo Boiten)

342 Squadron would fly its first Boston operation on 12 June, with an attack on the power station at Rouen.

Another of Embry's immediate concerns, after dismissing suggestions that 2 Group should re-

equip with Vultee Vengeance dive-bombers, was to replace the Venturas in 21, 464 RAAF and 487 RNZAF squadrons with fast, well-armed Mosquito MK VIs, but these too were in short supply, and would be denied him until

464 Squadron at last converted from the Ventura to the Mosquito Mk VI in August 1943. These squadron Mosquitos were photographed at Hatfield on 2 June 1944. (de Havilland via Philip J. Birtles)

August/September. As if to emphasise the urgent need to replace the Ventura, on 22 June W/C R. H. S. King, CO 21 Squadron, was killed when his Ventura was hit by flak on a raid on a gun position near Abbeville-Drucat airfield in France. G/C W. V. L. Spendlove DSO, who had only taken over as the new Station Commander at Swanton Morley on the 13th, P/O Henry Gatticker, navigator, F/Sgt J. Koller, P/O

On 22 June 1943 Ventura AE910 of 21 Squadron was shot down by flak north-east of Abbeville-Drucat. It was flown by W/C R. H. S. King, CO, with P/O Henry Gattiker, F/Sgt J. Koller and P/O Kinglake, plus G/C W. V. L. Spendlove DSO, Station Commander, Swanton Morley for just two weeks; they were all killed. King's faithful bull terrier Fiddle, who was carried on all operations, also perished. (RAF)

Kinglake, and King's bull-terrier, Fiddle, who always flew with his master, were lost.

Sgt Wilf Clutton, WOP/AG in Sgt 'Ted' Bellis's Ventura, in the second box of six, recalls:

'One of the crew said the W/C had gone down. We'd only had one burst of flak. We had also been hit. Ted Bellis said, "I can't hold it!" I looked at him. He had both feet on the steering column. The trim tab wires had been snapped by a piece of flak and he was having trouble keeping the aircraft level. He said we might have to jump. Denny Denton, the top turret gunner, and I got down and saw that the wire was hanging loose.

"What do we do now, Ted?' we asked.

He said, "Pull on it!"

We pulled. I don't know how, but we levelled out. By now we were alone. The rest of the formation had gone. Then we sighted two fighters. They were Spitfires! One came up on the right side, the other on our left, and escorted us home. We had a long, low run into the airfield and Ted landed perfectly.'

Sgt Eric Bateson's Ventura was severely damaged by flak but he managed to get the aircraft back as far as Lympne, where he attempted to lower the undercarriage, but found that the starboard wheel would not lock down. Bateson proceeded to fly around the airfield for 1¼ hours trying to get the wheel locked down with the crew even using urine to top up the hydraulic tank, but this was to no avail and he was forced to make a belly-landing. On inspection the aircraft had 21 flak holes in the fuselage.

On 20/21 July 464 and 487 Squadrons discarded their Venturas and left Methwold for Sculthorpe, where they began training on Mosquito FB VIs in August. 21 Squadron continued Ventura operations, on a few occasions, until September, when the squadron joined them at Sculthorpe, also to commence training on the Mosquito.

In July 2 Group operated on 18 days of the month, sending mainly pairs of Bostons to bomb rail targets in France. On 12 July 88 Squadron was assigned power stations at Swevenghasm, Grand Quevilly, Langerbrugge and Yainville. 'Dinty' Moore recalls:

'Johnny Reeve not being on the Battle Order, I

Explosions from bombs dropped by 21 Squadron Venturas explode on the airfield at Tricqueville on 18 August 1943. (RAF)

volunteered to fly with F/O Jack Peppiatt. We attended the briefing to find that we were detailed to attack a power station at Ghent, using cloud cover, with a number of other Bostons. We took off at 1015 hours, soon finding ourselves belting across the North Sea, skipping over the waves.'

The weather was not really suitable, and as they came into the coast Jack Peppiatt and others had to judge how much cover there was. Peppiatt remembers that it was:

'very much a guess as we were at sea level, but clearly there was nowhere near the 7/10 we were told to look for. In another aircraft was a friend of mine. He chose to go in and was the only one to do so. His photographs showed he had bombed a civilian target in error and he was removed from the squadron overnight.'

On 23 July Johnny Reeve was back on the Battle Order, as 'Dinty Moore' recalls:

'We were detailed to carry out a nine-aircraft attack

from low level on a target at Alost. On this occasion we were briefed not to rely on cloud cover. We taxied out, taking off at 1040 hours, the remainder of the formation following us, as we were to lead the attack. We headed off, yet again, across the North Sea, meeting the usual enthusiastic reception as we crossed the coast. The pilots had become experts at flying low level so it was the usual exhilarating experience of madly dashing along hopping over telegraph lines and so on. Navigating at low level was an extremely difficult task, at the speed at which we flew, giving the observer little time to identify landmarks.

We were all tearing along, as the estimated time for the target to come into view arrived, when Freddy saw that we were slightly to the west of Alost. He pointed this out to Johnny, expecting him to lead the formation around to make the attack for which we had been briefed. However, Johnny in his wisdom decided not to, leading our formation back to Swanton Morley. Having risked our necks in a flight lasting 2 hours, we were less than pleased to land back at base still carrying our bombs. It is always easy to stand in judgement, but whatever decision Johnny made, it had to be instant, so it may well be that his was the right one, for the defenders in Alost must surely have been more than ready for our arrival.

Two days later Johnny was not on the Battle Order, so I volunteered to fly with F/O Johnny Wilson, the New Zealander. During the briefing I suddenly had the very real premonition that this was going to be an operation from which I was not to return. It was a strange sensation. I seemed to be a spectator of all that was going on around me, having no control over the events. I automatically put on my flying gear, collected my parachute and walked out to the aircraft, climbing in and getting ready for take off. The engines had been started and we were preparing to taxi out when a message came to say that the operation had been cancelled. It was just like waking up from a nightmare. It was as if I had been mesmerised, barely aware of what had been said in the briefing, almost as if I were under the control of some strange force.

The following day, 26 July, Johnny was back on the Battle Order, so another WOP/AG [the squadron gunnery leader, F/L Francis J. G. Partridge] took my place in Wilson's crew. At our briefing we were informed that 11 of our aircraft were to carry out a *Circus* attack on the Luftwaffe base at Courtrai. [Three large-scale *Ramrod* operations were taking place, each one involving more than 100 aircraft. While the RAF Bostons attacked Courtrai, home of

F/O 'Dinty' Moore (far right) with the rest of his crew in 88 Squadron: F/O Freddy Deeks, observer (who was responsible for painting the 'Excreta Thermo' design on the nose of their Boston, F/L Johnny Reeve, and Newfoundlander Sgt Johnny Legge, air gunner. (via Jim Moore)

JG26, 18 USAAF B-26 Marauders, covered by 11 squadrons of Spitfires and one squadron of Typhoons, would attack St Omer airfield, and eight squadrons of P-47 Thunderbolts would attack Rotterdam.]

We took off at 0940 hours, forming up, as had become our normal practice, in two formations, setting course for our rendezvous with our fighter escort. On crossing the English coast we climbed rapidly to our normal operational height of about 12,000 feet. It was obvious on our arrival over the French coast that the Germans were determined to make life difficult for us, the flak barrage being even heavier than usual. As if this wasn't enough, we were attacked by a number of determined Focke-Wulf 190 fighters which had broken through our escort, so battle was joined in earnest. Whenever the enemy fighters came within range we fired at them with some success, for we WOP/AGs claimed to have damaged three of them between us.

One of our aircraft was obviously in difficulties and eventually crashed, the pilot being F/O Wilson [who was shot down by Johannes Naumann of II./JG26. Naumann had fought during the Battle of Britain, defended the German battlecruisers against Swordfish on 12 February 1942, and served with distinction in the Home defence for the rest of the war. He claimed 34 victories and was awarded the Knight's Cross.] Wilson managed to release his canopy so he and the navigator, P/O "Jock" McDonald, F/L Partridge, my replacement, and Sgt T. T. "Terry" Hunt of the RAF Film Production Unit [a Pathé-Gazette cameraman] were able to get out. We were very relieved to hear that they had survived, though they had become PoWs. It would seem that my premonition had some substance. It really had been one of our more hectic operations, actually lasting for 3 hours, though I imagine it seemed a lot longer.

During any operation my feelings were a strange mixture of fear and excitement, although on low levels there was always the exhilaration of our speed in relation to the ground. During attacks by enemy fighters there was no time for fear, as you were fully occupied in fighting back in order to survive. However, the worst moments were on *Circuses*, when there was no sense of speed, no fighter attack but anti-aircraft shells bursting around you about which you could do nothing but pray, when you felt terribly vulnerable.'

During August 2 Group continued low-level daylight raids on targets in France. On 8 August

During a Circus to the Luftwaffe base at Courtrai on 26 July 1943 F/O Johnny Wilson's Boston in 88 Squadron was shot down by Hptm Johannes Naumann, Staffelkapitän of II./JG26 from Lille-Nord airfield, home of 6./JG26. Wilson belly-landed BZ399 on the airfield perimeter, as this photograph, with Naumann perched on the fuselage, shows. Wilson, his observer P/O 'Jock' McDonald, WOP/AG and squadron gunnery leader F/L Francis J. G. Partridge, and Sgt T. T. 'Terry' Hunt, a Pathé-Gazette cameraman, all scrambled out alive.

14 Bostons from 107 Squadron, led by Dickie England, 12 Bostons from 342 Squadron, and bringing up the rear 12 Bostons from 88 Squadron, carried out a low-level raid on the Naval Stores Depot at Rennes. The target was well hit and the main section was set on fire. There were no fighters and later it was learned that they had been up in strength some 40 miles to the rear. However, intense flak over the target area brought down P/O W. P. Angus of 88 Squadron, and S/L Spencer of 107 Squadron was forced to crash-land at Hurn after receiving a shell burst on the nose of his Boston. P/O Allison had flown so low near the target that he had left behind his pitot tube hanging on a high-tension cable, and Dickie England returned with 5 yards of cable trapped in his bomb doors. He was heard later to remark that he had always wanted a tow rope for his car!

On 16 August the Bostons tried a repeat of

their success at Rennes, with a raid on the armament and steel works at Denain, a target not previously attacked. Dickie England again led, with 13 Bostons, followed by 12 each from 342 and 88 Squadrons. Take-off was made in the late afternoon and the Bostons flew in loose units of six abreast at low level to Pevensey Bay, where they headed across the Channel. On arrival over France they were joined by Typhoons for their escort 50 miles inland. 'Dinty' Moore wrote:

'The attack was very successful. However, the withdrawal was another matter, made worse by a multitude of flies smearing the perspex.'

The first Boston to crash did so immediately after the attack, and as they passed close to Douai another collided with high-tension cables and crashed in flames. By the time they reached Tournai, despite meeting their fighter escort, they

Boston IIIs of 107 Squadron in formation. During August the Boston squadrons (and others in 2 Group) began transferring from Norfolk airfields to bases in the south of England. (Aeroplane)

On 8 August 1943 38 Bostons from 88, 107 and 342 Squadrons carried out a low-level raid on the Naval Stores Depot at Rennes. The first six aircraft of 107 Squadron, led by W/C England, attacked from 50 feet and the remainder from 1,200–1,500 feet, dropping 5,800 lb of bombs. The target was well hit and the main section was set on fire. Intense flak brought down P/O W. P. Angus in 88 Squadron, and S/L Spencer of 107 Squadron was forced to crash-land at Hurn. (RAF)

The Denain steel and armament works under attack by 12 Bostons of 88 Squadron, led by S/L Cunningham, on 16 August 1943. (RAF)

were attacked by enemy fighters. Six Bostons were shot down on the raid, four of them from 88 Squadron. F/Ls Brinn and Arthur 'Rufus' Riseley evaded and eventually returned to England.

On 16 August 98 and 180 Mitchell Squadrons at Foulsham moved to Dunsfold, and on the 19th 88 Squadron left Swanton Morley and flew to a new aerodrome at Hartford Bridge, near Camberley. They were joined the following day by 107 Squadron from Great Massingham, and shortly after by 342 (Lorraine) Squadron, to form 137 Wing, 226 Squadron making its debut using Mitchells on 17 August when an abortive attack was made on the marshalling yards at Dunkirk. 2 Group was now something of a 'United Nations force', with 464 RAAF and 487 RNZAF Squadrons; 320 (Dutch) Squadron (which in August moved from Attlebridge to Lasham); and 305 Polish Squadron. The Poles had suffered appalling casualties on Wellingtons, and on 5 September they began re-equipment on the Mitchell II, while early in September 21 Squadron at Hartford Bridge at last began

conversion from the Ventura to the sleek Mosquito FB VI.

'Dinty' Moore remembers 342 Squadron:

'They were a lively crowd, easily identified by their navy blue uniforms. They had one fault, which was when they were airborne there would persist in using their radios to chatter to one another despite repeated warnings to comply with radio discipline. They could also boast the only female Intelligence Officer in the Air Force, the attractive Section Officer Massias.

Our arrival at Hartford Bridge sparked off many rumours and a great deal of speculation, our aircraft being painted with new markings to indicate that we were part of the Allied Air Force, so we became convinced that the invasion of Europe was about to take place.

The beginning of September was an opportunity for us to put into practice the time we had spent in laying down smoke screens for the Army, though in this case it was to be the Navy, which was carrying out mine-sweeping operations to within 7 miles of Boulogne, where they were threatened by batteries of heavy coastal artillery. Canisters were loaded into our bomb bay and we took off, flying low over the sea in pairs until we sighted the mine-sweeping flotilla, which was chugging its way towards the French coast. We flew between the ships and the coast, laying down a smoke screen that was then extended by our partner. The screen was, of course, replaced by the next pair of aircraft from the squadron. It was a very satisfactory feeling to lay a smoke screen "for real" after the number of times we had done it in practice.

On 4 September we led one of the formations of six Bostons in a *Circus* attack on the marshalling yards at Amiens, and the next day we were part of a force of 23 Bostons detailed to carry out a *Ramrod* attack on the Luftwaffe base at Woensdrecht. The flak barrage was particularly heavy over the coast and the target, though the Luftwaffe once again declined to get airborne. Despite the attentions of the anti-aircraft gunners we were able to bomb the target and return to Hartford Bridge.

The climax to these combined operations, known as *Starkey*, which was obviously a rehearsal for the invasion, came on the 9th when we laid down another smoke screen for a naval flotilla 8 miles off Boulogne. Johnny was then promoted to the rank of Squadron

Leader and we were posted to 107 Squadron on the other side of the aerodrome.'

One of the other new arrivals in 107 Squadron was a crew composed of F/O George Bernard 'Johnny' Slip, pilot, Frank Thomas, navigator, and P/O John Bateman, the WOP/AG, who had 'crewed up' at 13 OTU, Bicester, that summer. John Bateman recalls:

'We felt privileged to join the famous 107 Squadron, which was commanded by the equally famous Dickie England DFC. He was about 27 years old and a born leader. It was a very happy squadron with a terrific feeling of "esprit de corps", due principally to Dickie's superb qualities and personality, and that of his two Flight Commanders, S/L W. "Paddy" Maher and H. G. Britten, who welcomed us with great enthusiasm; not once were we referred to or made to feel like "new boys".'

On Sunday 3 October operations were flown against a series of transformer stations between Paris and Brittany. Every squadron in 2 Group was involved, each being allocated one in the

Boston 'G-Joan' of 107 Squadron. Left to right: Frank Thomas, navigator; Arthur Bullen (spare gunner used to man the belly gun position on Ramrods *and* Circuses*); F/O 'Johnny' Slip, pilot; P/O John Bateman, WOP/AG; and ground crew, just before take-off from Hartford Bridge in September 1943.* (John Bateman)

series, which were to be attacked from low level. For the first time the Mosquitos of 464 and 487 Squadrons at Sculthorpe took part, the latter being led by the Station Commander, G/C Percy Pickard, the former by W/C H. J. Meakin. Their targets were power stations at Pont Chateau and Mur de Bretange, and to reach them the two squadrons flew to Exeter before setting out across the Channel.

Meanwhile, soon after midday, W/C I. J. Spencer led the Bostons of 88 Squadron off to attack the Distre transformer station, while Dickie England led 107 Squadron's Bostons to another transformer station at Chaingy, on the outskirts of Orleans.

It was 'Dinty' Moore's 69th operation:

'It was a beautiful sunny day as the engines of the 36 Bostons of the three squadrons were being warmed up prior to take off. At 1240 hours we were airborne, forming up on W/C Dickie England and setting course over the south of England, coming down, as usual, to nought feet as soon as we were over the sea. I felt a sense of occasion, as if we were taking part in something special, my excitement easily overcoming my fear. We made a perfect landfall, crossing the coast without opposition and speeding low across the French countryside towards Paris.

Finally the outskirts of the capital city came into view with the Eiffel Tower dominant on the skyline. We had still not been challenged as we changed course for Orleans, although we saw first a Do 217 flying overhead, and later a tiny Fiesler Storch spotter aircraft, which were both too far away for us to engage. Indeed, our camouflage was so good that I doubt if the crews of either aircraft were aware of our presence.

On our arrival at the target the two leading aircraft with delayed-action fuses on the bombs remained at low level while we led the rest of the formation up to 1,500 feet as we had done on the raid on Eindhoven. Every one of the 12 aircraft dropped its bomb load and as we turned away I could see the bombs exploding, completely destroying the transformer station. During the attack there was no enemy interference from any source, which was a pleasant change.

On the return journey the only target that presented itself to me was a railway goods train, peacefully plodding its way across the countryside, at which I fired a few rounds as we flashed past. As we crossed the coast on our way home the Germans opened up with some light flak, one of our aircraft being slightly damaged, the first and only aggressive act we

Bostons of 88 Squadron in formation in September 1943. 'A' is 'Excreta Thermo' piloted by S/L Johnny Reeve. (IWM)

encountered during our flight, which lasted for 3 hours.

This was one of those occasions which must have been the answer to a planner's dream – effective navigation, avoidance of flak concentrations and the finding and bombing of an undefended target that was destroyed, the whole operation passing without a single hiccup. It was later established that this series of attacks had caused maximum disruption to the French electrical system and the railways, which were electrified from Paris to Brittany. [Also, 342 Squadron bombed the Chevilly transformer station near Paris, and the finale was provided by 320 Squadron's Mitchells, which flew a *Ramrod* operation against the Grand Quevilly power station at Rouen.] On this occasion one of the pilots of a Mosquito attacking another transformer station was AVM Embry, using his pseudonym 'W/C Smith', who simply had to be involved.'

If this operation had been a planner's dream, that on 22 October, by three squadrons of Bostons, was his nightmare. P/O John Bateman, WOP/AG in F/O Johnny Slip's crew in 107 Squadron, whose first operation this was, explains:

'On the evening of 21 October we looked at the notice board after dinner and saw that we were on the Battle Order for ops the following day. At last the moment had arrived after months and months of training, and I suddenly found that I had acquired a colony of butterflies, which happily soon dispersed. As briefing was scheduled for quite early the next morning, we decided to forgo our usual after-dinner drinking and go back to our quarters, which was a small Nissen hut shared with John Brice and Dougie George. Sleep at first was elusive and we chatted on quite late into the night with much speculation as to what the target was to be, but that would be revealed at the briefing.

We arranged for an early call, and after bathing and shaving I got dressed and filled the cigarette case that my father had given me, making sure my lighter was filled with petrol. The lighter and cigarette case filling became a routine before each op as I had a dread of not having a cigarette in the event of being shot down! We then walked over to the Mess for the traditional breakfast of bacon and eggs, then on to the briefing room in the back of an uncomfortable Bedford truck. The briefing room was a large Nissen hut with a platform at the far end, behind which was a map board nearly the whole width of the platform. The furniture consisted of hard wooden folding chairs, which would

seat 130 bods. This morning it was full as the three squadrons were participating in a "maximum effort" – 38 aircraft.

As was usual the Station Commander opened the proceedings with a "Good Morning, gentlemen" to the crews of 107, 342 (Lorraine), led by W/C Henri de Rancourt, and 88, led by W/C (later AVM) I. J. Spencer. The destination was an aircraft and aero engine repair works at Courcelles in Belgium, a target of sufficient importance to warrant a "maximum effort".

The briefing was then handed over to Dickie England, who was to lead the op. He described the target and surrounding pin-points in some detail; the route chosen would take us away from known flak positions and near Colijnsplatt on the island of Walcheren off the Dutch coast, and at some point we would turn south for Courcelles. Our bomb load was 250 lb HE with 11-second delay fuses that would give us adequate time to clear the target. We would fly six abreast with approximately 20 seconds between flights, and on the approach to the target we would fly in as tight a formation as possible. After bombing we would head for Knocke-sur-Mer on the Belgian coast and en route would be met by a Typhoon fighter escort. Under no conditions were bombs to be dropped other than on the target; if it was not located they were to be brought home or ditched in the sea if individual captains thought this action necessary for any reason.

Dickie England was a highly professional officer who carried out the briefing in a quiet and authoritative voice, all the while pointing to the map and occasionally indicating possible hazards. After he had finished the Met Officer gave his forecast of the wind, cloud and weather conditions we were likely to encounter. Dickie then detailed off the pilots to their individual briefing, the navigators to theirs and the gunners to theirs, then wished us all "Good Hunting".

At the aircraft I climbed into the gunner's cockpit. I closed the hatch that formed the centre part of the floor and stowed my 'chute in the rack on the starboard side together with a spare packet of Martins cigarettes; as a non-smoker Frank always carried a bar of chocolate and a can of orange juice. I then set the radio transmitter to the allocated frequency, and what a super little radio it was compared with the antediluvian 1083/1084 on the Blenheim. As I had synchronised my guns only the day before I knew that they were OK, as were the ammo belts to each gun. Meanwhile Johnny was walking round the aircraft with the rigger, visually checking all the moving surfaces, and making sure that the pitot head cover had been removed. By this time Frank had settled himself at his little table with the maps, instruments and the rest of the paraphernalia that all navigators seemed to carry, which was a complete mystery to me. Eventually Johnny climbed up on to the port wing on his way to the cockpit, just pausing for a few seconds to have a quick word with me, and we wished each other good luck. I put on my helmet with the mike hanging loose to one side and plugged into the intercom socket. After a while, "Pilot to navigator – do you hear me?"

Frank's reply: "Navigator to pilot, I hear you OK."

Then, "Pilot to gunner. Do you hear me?"

"Gunner to pilot. Hear you OK."

Johnny then signalled to the fitter on the trolley-acc raising his left hand and started the port engine, similarly with the starboard engine, then ran them up gently. In a few minutes Dickie England moved away from his dispersal towards the perimeter track, followed by the rest of 'A' Flight, then 'B' Flight. Take-off time was scheduled at 1345 and at the precise moment the first two Bostons took off in echelon. Dickie led the procession in 'A-Apple', which beneath the cockpit had the inscription 'ENGLAND EXPECTS', followed by F/O John Brice, F/Sgt Teddy Hoeg, F/L R. C. McCullough, ourselves, and F/L H. G. "Brit" Brittain. These six aircraft comprised 'A' Flight of 107, plus six more, who were to lead the operation. The remaining aircraft took off in pairs, the last two taking off at 1349. When all aircraft were airborne and at about 1,000 feet, they formed up into six flights of six aircraft abreast with about 150 yards separating each flight.

Our three ground crew – fitter, armourer and rigger – stood at the edge of the dispersal point and waved the "thumbs up" sign. Like all ground crews, they were the backbone of all aircrews, who without their expertise would have been absolutely useless. They worked all hours and in all weathers and very rarely grumbled, and on the odd occasions they did we fully sympathised with them. The "chiefy" was an older man with years of service and was always helpful and encouraging to his lads. One evening each week we would take them to the local pub at Yateley. I think they appreciated our gesture and we certainly appreciated their interest and what one could almost call devotion to what they considered *their* aircraft.

Having reached the runway the two leading aircraft formed up in echelon, then the next pair, then us. With

the brakes full on the engines were run up, and at the "green" from Flying Control the first pair rolled down the runway followed by the rest of us, until all 36 aircraft were airborne. When we had gained sufficient height we formed up in a line abreast and circled the airfield until all three squadrons were formed up at about 1,000 feet, then set course for Orfordness where we were to cross the coast. When we were somewhere near Stowmarket, "Gunner to pilot, Brit's broken off and heading for home – must have a problem." Brit had aborted with what we found later to be an engine malfunction (he was replaced by W/O T. V. Glynn).

After a while, "Pilot to navigator, coast coming up. Are we on course?"

As we passed over Orfordness, "Navigator to pilot – on course."

We were always formal in our communications with one another over the intercom, which was really a matter of discipline and eliminated idle nattering – very rarely did we use Christian names.

We had descended a bit and crossed the coast at something under 500 feet. "Pilot to gunner. Test guns."

"Gunner to pilot. Testing."

I swung the guns over the side and fired a short burst. "Gunner to pilot – guns OK."

At this time we were flying at about 50 feet above the water on a beautiful, clear autumn day that made it so much easier to scan the skies for possible bandits – no cloud cover for them. "This is a piece of cake," I thought. "Just like an exercise."

"Navigator to pilot – we appear to be about 5 degrees off course."

"Pilot to navigator. Check again."

Two minutes later, "Navigator to pilot – confirm, 5 degrees off planned course."

"Pilot to navigator, either Dickie has changed the plan or you have boobed. In any case, we follow the leader."

As strict W/T silence was to be observed, as we had been told at briefing, it wasn't broken now, but if we had really been off course we felt that a more senior crew would have broken silence, so we assumed we were OK.

"Pilot to navigator. Enemy coast ahead."

"Navigator to pilot. OK, but I'm convinced we are still off course, miles off course."

"Pilot to gunner. Keep you eyes skinned. It's possible we're making a duff landfall."

Within a minute we were over the Dutch coast flying over flat silt land when all hell was suddenly let loose. Without warning the whole flak battery must have opened up and the sky around us was full of flak bursts. They had got our altitude absolutely spot on. It was just like going through a wall, and how we escaped must remain one of life's mysteries.

As Brit had gone home we were on the right of our flight, and as the flak continued to come up I saw the four aircraft on our left take the full punishment. Dickie's plane took a direct hit in the starboard engine, which fell from the nacelle and rolled along the ground like a gigantic ball of fire. His aircraft pitched sideways, cartwheeling into the ground at 280 mph. The other three must have been hit almost instantaneously, and all hit the ground in a complete shambles of fire, smoke and scattered pieces of metal. I couldn't see exactly where the flak was coming from and just fired my guns in the general direction without taking any sort of aim. Johnny had his finger on the button and exhausted nearly all his ammo. What seemed like an eternity probably lasted only a couple of minutes or so, then we were out of range. I could see the following aircraft getting a fairish dose, but they were jinking all over the sky and not flying straight into the stuff as we had done. I saw only two of them go down. This was my first trip and it was the only time in all my operational experience that I had seen such a large formation broken up so completely.

Eventually, "Pilot to navigator, any idea where we are?"

"Navigator to pilot, not a clue. Climb up a bit and I might be able to recognise something."

"Pilot to navigator. Climbing up to 1,500 feet."

But after a few moments Frank had to admit that he was unable to recognise anything and was quite lost. "We could be anywhere," he said. Johnny throttled back a bit and rocked the aircraft to indicate to anyone following that they should take the lead. Another plane came up alongside and we formated on him, but it soon became evident that he was equally as lost as we were. Eventually some sort of leadership evolved and we pressed on towards Courcelles.

Now that the excitement was over I had a moment to take stock, and to my astonishment found that I was almost ankle deep in empty cartridge cases, which I kicked away towards the tail of the aircraft, and although I was standing in an open cockpit I was quite amazed to find that I was overheating, so I took off my battledress top and peeled off two pullovers before putting the top back on again. I would like to have thought that I was sweating through exertion, but the awful feeling came to my mind that it must be fear,

although throughout that short encounter I had been too busy to have had any thoughts about personal safety.

By this time we had got down on the deck again and I was keeping a sharp look-out for bandits as the Hun flak boys must have radioed our course to the Luftwaffe. However, we pressed on weaving this way and that and eventually settled a course that Frank told us was in the direction of Courcelles. However, for one reason or another we failed to pin-point the target and turned for home, meeting some more or less accurate flak.

Thirty miles off the coast, "Navigator to pilot – unidentified fighters ahead and above."

I craned my neck round as far as I could to see forward and about 1,000 feet above us was the welcome sight of our Typhoon escort. They turned and, still flying above and behind, escorted us out of the coast. We were going home! Our chums kept a steady course with us and I then knew that there were no snappers about and could relax a little. As we crossed the water I could smell cigarette smoke, which could only have come from Johnny's cockpit, so I lit one, then another, and another.

When we landed 3 hours and 20 minutes later and taxied to our dispersal, there was our faithful ground crew waiting for us, and when we told them of our experiences their expressions had to be seen to be believed. But they just got on with their jobs in silence, which was unusual, and when Frank opened the bomb doors they pushed the empty bomb trolleys under the fuselage to unload the bombs that should have been left behind at Courcelles.

De-briefing was a solemn affair. Several of the crews confirmed that they were 5 degrees off our planned course as we crossed the Dutch coast, and we wondered why the more experienced crews had not broken W/T silence to query the change of course. I don't remember Frank expressing any satisfaction at being proved correct. It was later concluded that this disastrous navigational error could only be attributed to the fact that Dickie's compass was showing an error, though it had been swung only a day or two before by his navigator, F/O P. Anderson. The crews of F/O Brice, F/O R. C. McCullough and F/Sgt Teddy Hoeg were the others lost (Hoeg's commission had been promulgated that day). F/O Stolloff and F/Sgt Chappell and their crews in 342 and 88 Squadrons respectively were also lost. W/C England's award of the DSO was announced on the day after his death in the *London Gazette*.

W/C Richard Geoffrey 'Dickie' England DSO DFC, CO 107 Squadron, killed in action on 22 October 1943. (John Bateman)

AVM Basil Embry, a former commander of 107 Squadron, wrote of England, 'He was a great leader who commanded universal respect and admiration', a sentiment echoed by everyone who was privileged to have served with him.

Thus ended our first operation.'

Chapter Eight

Hitting Back

'Il le fallait' – *'It had to be done'*

On 5 November 1943 24 Bostons of 88 (under a new squadron commander, W/C Mike Pollard) and 107 Squadrons, 24 Mitchells of 98 and 180 Squadrons, 14 Mitchells of 226 with four of 305 and six of 320 squadrons, were scheduled to attack a secret German weapons site at Mimoyecques. However, the proposed *Circus* attack was scrubbed in the morning because of bad weather, and another attempt in mid-afternoon only got as far as Guildford before W/C Spencer decided that conditions were too bad and turned the formation round for a return home. The operation finally went ahead on 8 November, and follow-up *Ramrod* attacks were made on the 9th and 25th, while Typhoons of 2 Group hit a back-up site at Audignhen.

A few days after the 5 November abort Johnny Reeve's crew were greatly surprised to hear that they had been 'screened' and were sent on rest. 'Dinty' Moore recalls:

'My feelings were completely different from those I had experienced at the end of my extended first tour. I had only taken part in 18 operational sorties and we had been involved in so much training in preparation for the invasion that the news came as a sort of anti-climax.'

John Bateman also found himself on the move:

'After a further 16 or so ops with 107 (motto "Nous y serons" – "We shall be there"),' some of them "fairly hairy",' he recalls, 'I was posted to 98 Squadron (motto 'Never failing') at Dunsfold near Guildford. The CO of 98 was W/C R. K. F. Bell-Irving, known to everyone as 'B.I.'. After a bit of a party the night before, Johnny [Slip] insisted on flying me to my new airfield.'

(Slip stayed with 107 on conversion to Mosquitos and was eventually posted to India, when he joined 84 Squadron. In December 1945, when the squadron was detached to help out the Dutch who were having trouble with the Indonesians, he was killed in Java.)

During January–February 1944 the Mitchells of 226 Squadron were used to make bombing strikes on flying-bomb sites in the Pas de Calais. On 1 February 107 Squadron moved to Lasham near Alton in Hampshire and re-equipped with the Mosquito VI. On the 14th 226 Squadron's Bostons flew from Swanton Morley for the last time, when they took off for Hartford Bridge to train for their role in the forthcoming invasion of France. 2nd TAF would be tasked to destroy tactical rather than strategic targets as and when D-Day arrived, so to be near the invasion front all squadrons were moved further south. On 18 November 1943 305 Polish Squadron transferred from Swanton Morley to Lasham, Hampshire,

Above *Mosquito FB VI LR297 of 613 Squadron at Lasham, Hampshire, in January 1944. 613, 107 and 305 (Polish) Squadrons together formed 138 Wing, 2nd TAF.* (de Havilland via Philip J. Birtles)

Right *Sgt H. J. 'Appie' Otten, pilot; Jan P. Kloos, observer-bomb aimer; Wally Baumann, gunner; and Sgt J. J. C. 'Jack' Lub, gunner, of 320 Squadron. On 18 March 1944, after ditching in the sea following a raid on Gorenflos, Sgt Jan Ot, Lub, Sgt H. F. Gans and Cpl F. I. Posthumus were rescued by a Sea Otter, which taxied all the way across the Channel when it could not take off! Posthumus was killed in action on 8 June 1944, but the others survived the war. Jack Lub, for instance, flew 26 operations on Hudsons and 75 more on Mitchells.* (Jan P. Kloos)

Below *A 320 (Dutch) Squadron crew at Dunsfold in the summer of 1944. Left to right: Almekinders, Fransen, Vos, and de Groot.* (via Jan P. Kloos)

A stick of bombs dropped from a 98 Squadron Mitchell aimed at a harbour installation on the French coast explode along the shoreline. (via John Bateman)

Targets in France: in the first photograph a VI site is well and truly 'pranged', while an airfield also comes in for attention by Mitchells of 98 Squadron. (via John Bateman)

joining 107 and 613 Mosquito Squadrons to become part of 138 Wing. (In December 305 Squadron converted to Mosquito FB VIs after just five operations with Mitchells.) It will be remembered that 88 and 342 Boston Squadrons and 226 Mitchell Squadron, all in 137 Wing, were at Hartford Bridge with 139 Wing, comprising 98, 180 and 320 Mitchell Squadrons at Dunsfold. On 31 December 1943 21, 464 and 487 Squadrons of 140 Wing took off from Sculthorpe for the last time, bombed Le Ploy, France, then landed at their new base at Hunsdon. Early in 1944 2 Group HQ left Bylaugh Hall in Norfolk for Mongewell Park in Berkshire.

Meanwhile, targets were nominally the V1 sites in the Pas de Calais. On 8 February nine Mitchells attacked targets at Pois de la Justice. Thirty miles inside France, W/O Storey's Mitchell took a flak hit in the port engine, but he was able to re-cross the Channel and make an emergency landing at West Malling. On the same day 3 Squadron Typhoons twice made attacks on

shipping off Den Helder. During the second sortie F/Sgt N. J. Cook in JR684 crashed into the sea 30 miles off Lowestoft and failed to return. On 14 February 3 Squadron's Typhoons began returning to Manston, and Swanton Morley geared up for the build-up to the invasion of Europe.

On 15 February F/L J. L. 'Les' Bulmer, navigator, and his pilot, F/L Ed McQuarrie RCAF, joined 21 Squadron, 140 Wing, at Hunsdon, having completed the Night Intruder course at 60 OTU High Ercall. Les Bulmer remembers the move:

'We, together with George Murray and Harry Batt, and Gordon Bell-Irving [a cousin of W/C Bell-Irving] and Bert Holt, were a bit surprised to find ourselves in 21 Squadron in 2nd TAF instead of one of the three Intruder squadrons, 418, 605 (both in the UK) and 23 in Malta, for which we had been trained. When we joined, 21 Squadron's principal occupation was attacking V1 (*Noball*) sites at low level. We had no experience of low-level navigation so we spent all of

F/L J. L. 'Les' Bulmer (back row, third from left) and his pilot, F/L Ed McQuarrie RCAF (front row, third from left), pictured at No 3 Mosquito Course, 36 OTU, Greenwood, Nova Scotia, in 1943. They joined 21 Squadron, 140 Wing, at Hunsdon on 15 February 1944. (Les Bulmer)

Mosquito FB VI LR356 YH-Y of 21 Squadron flown by S/L 'Tony' Carlisle on a Noball *operation in early 1944.* (via Les Bulmer)

February practising low-level cross-country and formation flying.

On 18 February we watched all three squadrons of the wing take off in a snowstorm for what we later discovered was the Amiens prison raid. This was led by the 140 Wing CO, G/C Charles Pickard. The only time I saw him was in the Mess the night before the raid. The whole squadron was sworn to secrecy when we heard he was missing in case he had got away, but it was not long before we received news that he was dead. He was replaced by Peter Wykeham-Barnes.

Our first operation was a Night Intruder to the airfield at Montdidier on 2 March. Although we were new boys, because we'd been trained as Night Intruders we had more night-flying experience on Mosquitos than the old hands. We took off at 1955 and returned at 2155. It was uneventful. I was not sure what to expect as we crossed the French coast, but I rather imagined it would be flak and searchlight all the way in and all the way out. Instead there was just total darkness, with the odd glimmer of a light, and nobody seemed to be interested in us at all – or was a night-fighter creeping up on us? I kept a constant look-out rearwards. The night was very dark and *Gee* was jammed once we crossed the coast, so navigation had to be by dead-reckoning. We were somewhere in the area but could not locate the airfield and the Germans would not co-operate and put on the lights for us, so we returned home somewhat disappointed.

Mosquito FB VI MM417 EG-T of 487 RNZAF Squadron with a 500 lb bomb carried under each wing. 487 was one of three Mosquito squadrons that took part in the raid on Amiens prison on 18 February 1944, the others being 21 and 464 RAAF. (via Philip J. Birtles)

2 Group Mosquitos tried various techniques in attacking *Noball* sites. The normal method was to go low-level all the way, but this had resulted in aircraft sustaining damage by 20 mm flak when crossing the coast. On 4 March we were one of four aircraft to attack two sites. Our target was near Esclavelles, and we took off at 0810. *Noball* targets were far too small to get four aircraft over them within 11 seconds, which was the delay we had on the 500 lb bombs. The squadron CO, W/C 'Daddy' Dale, led with "A" Flight Commander S/L Joe Bodien as his No 2. As a "sprog" crew we were to stick with F/L Mike Benn, who was one of the squadron's most experienced pilots. [The Hon Michael J. Benn DFC, at 22, was the eldest of three sons of William Wedgwood Benn, the prominent politician who was created Viscount Stansgate on 22 December 1940.]

We crossed the Channel at low level and climbed as we reached the coast to about 3,000 feet to avoid the flak. There we split into pairs for our respective targets and got down on the deck. Not long afterwards I noticed a red glow on the edge of a wood on the starboard side. This became several red balls that travelled rapidly towards us, and it was then that I realised what flak looked like from the wrong end. The stream of 20 mm appeared to be heading along the wing and into the cockpit, so Mac and I instinctively ducked. Luckily it passed overhead and we went thankfully on our way.

At briefing we had arranged to fly beyond the target, turn and attack on the way out. We arrived at the turning point but nothing happened. There was strict radio silence so we couldn't ask Mike and his navigator, F/O W. A. Roe, what they were doing. We just had to stick with them and hope that they knew where they were. Eventually they did start to turn and all hell broke loose. In fact, Roe had missed the turning point, and when he did eventually start to turn he led us into a real hornet's nest. Everything happened so fast, but we suddenly found ourselves in a valley with a railway in the bottom and rows of huts up the valley sides. I don't know what the area was but they obviously objected to our presence and the sky erupted in 20 mm flak from all directions.

Mike Benn started to climb out of harm's way and we followed behind, but were surrounded by streams of tracer and we had an uncomfortable few seconds when flak intended for Mike was crossing in front of our nose, while that for us was crossing just behind the tail. Mac said, "Sod this, I'm going down", and shoved the stick forward. As he did so there was a

F/L The Hon Michael J. Benn DFC, one of 21 Squadron's most experienced pilots, with whom F/Ls Ed McQuarrie and Les Bulmer flew an operation against V1 targets on 4 March 1944. (via Tony Benn)

loud bang. I checked to see if we were on fire or losing fuel, but everything was normal.

By this time we had lost sight of Mike Benn and were somewhere south-east of the target. If we tried to make the target on our own we might arrive just as his bombs were due to explode, so we headed for a secondary target in a wood. We duly dropped our four 500-pounders on a hut in the wood and fled at high speed towards the coast. We flew low over a large chateau outside which German troops were milling around, then I told Ed to climb before we hit the coast. Unfortunately I left it too late, and we were on top of the coast as we started to climb. Up came the flak, hosing around us, and down went the nose as we sped out to sea, weaving like mad and followed by the now all too familiar tracer. Soon we were clear and heading for home, somewhat relieved to find ourselves still in one piece.

When we got back to Hunsdon we found that a 20 mm shell had come up underneath us from the port and entered the starboard nacelle. It blew a large hole in the inboard side of the nacelle and a smaller one in the outboard side. Shell splinters had knocked chunks out of the starboard flap and out of the fuselage side just about where I was sitting. I was thankful that a Mosquito had a thick skin; if it had been metal I would probably have had a sore bum. The shell struck in the only part of the nacelle where it couldn't do any damage – in the rear fairing. Any further forward and it would have smashed the undercarriage.

For another *Noball*, on 7 March, to near Les Essarts, our leader was D. A. "Buck" Taylor, with Philippe Livry as his navigator. We decided to stay high after crossing the coast, identify the target, dive on it, then climb back up to 3,000–4,000 feet until clear of the coast on the way back. There was a flak position on the right of our approach to the target, so we arranged that we would both fire our cannons as we dived, hoping that this would make them keep their heads down until we were clear. Everything went according to plan, and we arrived over the target and went into a steep dive, both of us firing cannons on the way down. There was no problem from the flak position, but as we pulled out of the dive and released the bombs a burst of 20 mm shot up vertically in front of us. Buck was clear, but we had no choice but to fly through it. As we climbed away I looked back to see the whole site erupt as 4000 lb of high explosive went off. I must say that I've always had a grudging admiration for the guy who shot at us. To be blasted with eight cannons, and yet have the nerve to jump up and let fly at us, presumably aware that he was about to get eight 500 lb bombs around his earholes, took some courage.

Ed said, "Check around. I think we've been hit."

There was so much racket from the cannons as we dived that I hadn't heard any bang, but I checked for fire and loss of fuel. The fuel gauges were reading normal, so we joined up with Buck for the return trip. We climbed to 4,000 feet and stayed there until clear of the coast, then dropped down to sea-level over the Channel. Soon after we were clear of the French coast Buck's aircraft fired off a Very cartridge, and he was obviously in trouble. I checked the list of the colours of the day, but the one he'd used wasn't on it. We were puzzled and expected him to ditch at any moment, but nothing happened. I tackled Philippe at debriefing and he explained that he had to have a smoke – he used a long cigarette holder – and since the designers of the Mosquito had forgotten to include an ash tray in the specification, he was forced to improvise. An empty

F/L D. A. 'Buck' Taylor and S/L Philippe Livry, who led a 21 Squadron operation to a V1 site near Les Essarts on 7 March 1944. (Les Bulmer via Colin Waugh collection)

Very cartridge case would fill his requirements, so he emptied one! Smoking in or near an aircraft was strictly forbidden, but Philippe was a law unto himself.

Ed had been right in thinking that we'd been hit – a 20 mm shell had exploded in the port spinner. It appeared that bits of it had gone rearwards through the engine, because the bottom cowling had a number of carbuncles that weren't there when we started. And yet the engine and propeller pitch mechanism had functioned perfectly, which gave me a great deal of confidence in the Merlin.

I was beginning, though, to think that if these sort of trips were the norm, then sooner of later a shell would find a vital spot and our chances of completing a tour of ops looked none too promising. In the event these were the only times that we sustained damage, although they weren't the only times the enemy took a dislike to us and let fly.

Our next two ops were also against V1 sites, but employed a very different technique. Six aircraft, in two vics of three, joined up with two Pathfinder Mosquitos, fitted with *Oboe*, at the coast. We followed the lead *Oboe* aircraft up to 20,000 feet, while the second *Oboe* aircraft tagged along behind in case of equipment failure in the lead aircraft. We had an escort of six Spits, which was some comfort. The idea was that we would maintain close formation on the *Oboe* aircraft. His four bombs were set to drop in a stick, and the boffins had calculated that, by the time the third bomb appeared out of the bomb bay, we would have woken up and released our bombs also. So the leader's third bomb was supposed to be on target, with the first two undershooting and the last one overshooting.

The only snag with this system was that *Oboe* required that we fly in tight formation, straight and level for 10 minutes until bomb release. This was not exactly amusing, since the Germans were somewhat hostile and slung a lot of heavy flak at us as we

approached the target east of Abbeville. It was a long 10 minutes, sitting there at 20,000 feet, having to take everything that was thrown at us and not being able to take avoiding action. You just prayed that your name was not on any of the bits of metal that were being flung into the sky. The Spits, wisely, kept well clear of the formation at this time, as did the stand-in *Oboe* aircraft, who only closed in tight at the last minute.

With bombs gone we turned for home. From that height Dungeness looked so close. The rest of the formation had adopted a "last man home's a sissy" attitude and were hell bent for the English coast. With wartime camouflage it was difficult to see an aircraft from above; it merged very effectively with the ground below. So suddenly Ed and I found ourselves all alone in the sky and, reckoning that we'd outstayed our welcome, stuck the nose down and went, hell for leather, for Dungeness and safety. We were travelling so fast that, even with the throttles right back and the undercarriage warning horn blowing continuously, the

Gen Dwight D. Eisenhower, Supreme Allied Commander, flanked by ACM Sir Trafford Leigh-Mallory and G/C Larry Dunlap RCAF, station commander, with W/C Alan Lynn and AVM Basil Embry behind, during a visit to Dunsfold on 18 April 1944. (via John Bateman)

ASI was indicating well over 300 mph. And I was wondering at what speed the wings came off.

Part way across the Channel we caught up with another Mosquito and tried to maintain some form of decorum by flying in formation with him. One of the Spit escort managed to catch us up in mid-Channel and stayed with us until we crossed the Kent coast, when he did a victory roll and headed for his base, wherever that was.

At de-briefing the flight leader, S/L Ritchie, issued a rocket. He said we'd behaved like naughty schoolboys who'd been breaking windows and then run away. I don't think we cared that much, as long as we'd broken the right windows. Sadly, we hadn't. The much-vaunted *Oboe* had caused us to drop our bombs several miles, I believe, from the target. So, as a penance for our sins, we had to go out next day and do it all over again, and this time we did all come back together.

For the rest of March, and the first half of April, our ops were all Night Intruders on airfields in Holland and France. We never spotted any aircraft, but we did bomb and strafe the runways and dispersals. At Evreux the Germans were most co-operative and switched the lights on for us. We made what we thought was a bombing attack – that is, until we got

Mitchell FV914 VO-A of 98 Squadron over northern France on 19 April 1944. (IWM)

back to base and I got out to find a dark object hanging under each wing which shouldn't have been there. Ed had forgotten to select the bombs.'

Moves were now afoot to prepare 2nd TAF squadrons for operations from French airfields, which, it was anticipated, would be largely derelict following a retreat by the Luftwaffe and the German Army if the invasion went as planned. John Bateman recalls:

'In accordance with our role in support of the ground forces, we were supposed to be a mobile force capable of moving from airfield to airfield at a moment's notice. And when we moved out of the comparative comfort of our sleeping quarters at Stovolds Farm and into tents erected in a rise just beyond the perimeter of the airfield it was a bit of a shock to the system. But we soon adjusted and settled into our new way of life. We were fortunate in retaining the use of the Mess and all the other amenities previously available. We also gained a slight financial advantage in that we were paid a "hard living" allowance of a few bob a day, but in gaining this we lost the services of our batmen and batwomen who had previously made our beds, cleaned our shoes and buttons and provided us with early morning tea!'

More discomfort followed in March–April. To simulate the type of tactical targets against which 2 Group would be employed in the run-up to D-Day, Boston, Mitchell and Mosquito crews arrived at 2 GSU (Group Support Unit) at Swanton Morley to take part in two-week training exercises in full field conditions. All crews lived under canvas and life was distinctly uncomfortable, while night interdictor training (bombing and strafing the enemy's communications by night), bombing of illuminated targets and convoys, and runs on a 'spoof' V1 rocket site and a four-gun flak battery installation were carried out.

During their sojourn at Swanton, on 11 April, six Mosquitos of 613 Squadron, led by W/C R. N. Bateson, succeeded in destroying the Gestapo records of the Dutch Resistance in the Kunstzaal Kleizkamp (the Kleizkamp Art Galleries), a 90-foot-high five-storey building situated close to the Peace Palace in The Hague.

On 12 April F/L J. L. 'Les' Bulmer and F/L Ed McQuarrie of 21 Squadron were intruding over

Prior to D-Day, Boston, Mitchell and Mosquito crews in 2nd TAF spent two-week stints under canvas at Swanton Morley to experience the kind of field conditions that were anticipated in France! (John Bateman)

the airfield at St Dizier when a searchlight was turned on them.

'We took exception to that,' recalls Les Bulmer, 'so we flew right down the beam, firing our cannons as we went. That soon put it out. Didn't do our night vision a lot of good, though – we were almost blinded for a while. On our return journey we ran into searchlights near Abbeville, and there were so many that we were in and out of them for about 10 minutes. There was no sign of flak so I kept a sharp eye out for night-fighters but didn't see any. I was beginning to wonder where I'd taken us, because a concentration of searchlights such as this was normally reserved for large cities, and I was convinced that we were nowhere near a town, let alone a city.

All was revealed when we got back to de-briefing. While we'd been away the flak map had been changed, and where before there had been no flak position, there was now a large green area with 800 marked against it. This meant that we had just flown through a large defended area with 800 light AA guns in it. It seems that the Germans, in a bid to stop the destruction of their individual V1 sites, had concentrated a number of them into one large area heavily defended against low-level attack. I think

someone might have told us before we took off.

For the second half of April Ed and I were on a *Gee-H* course at Swanton Morley. This was to be our precision blind-bombing aid. Although I got good results in practice raids on Boston Stump and the central tower of Ely Cathedral, on operations it – and sometimes I – was something of a failure, so this piece of equipment was not much used. In fact I only carried out three *Gee-H* sorties. On the first the equipment packed up. On the second we dropped our bombs from 20,000 feet on the Seine crossing at Duclair – at least that was where they were supposed to go. I have a feeling that they were nowhere near. The third, and last, I put down in my log-book as *Gee-H* trouble, but some unkind person came along afterwards, crossed out '*Gee-H*' and inserted 'finger' and drew a small picture of Percy Prune's award of the highly Derogatory Order of the Irremovable Digit.'

John Bateman returned from Swanton Morley to Dunsfold to find a pleasant surprise:

'I suppose W/C Bell-Irving must have felt a bit sorry for me, as he asked me if I would care to fly with him temporarily as a supernumerary crew as he already had a full crew. I was very happy with this offer and operated with him four times as a tail gunner and once as course winder, where I sat next to him in the jump seat and had an entirely new view of everything. Our targets were flying-bomb sites in northern France.

On 8 May I was due to fly with "B.I." on ops, but the night before Nick Carter asked me if I could take him to London as he had an appointment at the Air Ministry and couldn't get station transport. After dinner I asked "B.I." if this would be OK and he readily agreed, and in any case I was only a spare bod. Nick and I duly went to London and returned latish in the evening, having stopped for a noggin at the "Jolly Farmers" in Guildford and at the "Three Compasses". When we called in at the guard room we were told that "B.I." had been shot down and was reported missing.

In the morning he had led the squadron to Charleroi marshalling yards but 10/10 cloud prevailed and the formation did not bomb. In the evening he had led the formation to attack a *Noball* at Bois Coquerel from a bombing height of 13,000 feet. Flak was extremely accurate, and just after bombing "B.I.'s" machine had received a direct hit in the nose. It broke away from the formation and went into a spin before crashing. No chutes had been seen to leave the aircraft. He was 24 and is buried at the cemetery at Abbeville. F/Sgt Winter, the navigator aboard F/Sgt Anstey's Mitchell, was hit in the head by shrapnel and died without regaining consciousness just after the Mitchell landed at Friston.

The next morning a Mosquito flew into Dunsfold flown by Johnny Slip who knew that I was flying with "B.I." and heard that he had bought it and assumed that I had too. He had come to collect my belongings to take to my parents and just couldn't believe that it was me he saw in the Mess. It was very touching of him to have bothered, but just typical of him. We rather overdid the celebrating that evening, so he stayed the night at Dunsfold before flying back the next day. Nick, of course, joined the party and it was through him that I lived to enjoy another day.

Then for the second time I was crewless, and a few days later I was posted to the Central Gunnery School at Catfoss to take a Gunnery Leaders course. After about a week I phoned W/C Alan Lynn, who had assumed temporary command of 98 Squadron, to ask him if I could come back, but he would not let me, and to cap it all I received a telegram from Keith Cudlipp with the message, "Get some D-Day hours in!"'

'Dinty' Moore was on an Air Gunnery Instructors

W/C Alan Lynn, who assumed temporary command of 98 Squadron after the death in action on 8 May 1944 of W/C Roderick Keith-Falconer Bell-Irving. Lynn always stuck a piece of chewing gum behind the tail skid before taking off on ops, and retrieved it on landing! (John Bateman)

Course at Manby, Lincolnshire, during which they were informed that Allied forces had, at long last, landed in France.

'I remember sitting back and thinking that here I was in the safety of a classroom while my old friends were involved in a truly historic event for which we had worked so hard and risked so much. I also wished Peter and so many others I had known could have lived to see this day. I later learned how 2 Group's two remaining Boston squadrons, 88 and 342, had, in addition to bombing the enemy, laid smoke to screen the invasion force at one beach-head from the German coastal guns. Further, all of the squadrons, Bostons, Mitchells and Mosquitos, had been heavily engaged in bombing troop concentrations, railways, Panzer divisions, indeed any target requested by the Army, with considerable success.'

All six of 2nd TAF's Mosquito fighter squadrons performed defensive operations (264 Squadron flew jamming patrols before they went looking for enemy fighters) over the invasion coast on 5/6 June. (In the spring of 1944 29, 264, 409, 410, 488 RNZAF and 604 Squadrons had formed in 85 Group, and 219 joined 147 Wing on 26 August.) Fewer than 50 plots were made on 5/6 June and only F/O Pearce of 409 Squadron claimed a kill. Then things hotted up. 604 Squadron alone destroyed ten aircraft on 7 and 8 June (on 6 August 604 became the first fighter squadron to move to France.) On 7 June 456 Squadron destroyed four He 177s and three more on the 8th. (On 5 July 456 claimed three enemy aircraft to bring its score to 30 victories since 1 March.)

'When D-Day arrived', recalls Les Bulmer, '21 Squadron was out whenever weather permitted patrolling behind the battlefront looking for anything that moved. The night of D-Day, the 6th, we were briefed to patrol the Caen–Lisieux–Boisney road to stop German reinforcements reaching the beach-head. We were told that there was a corridor across the Channel in which every aircraft must stay on outward and return flights. Our night-fighters were patrolling on either side of the corridor and were likely to regard any plane that was found outside the designated area as hostile.

As we left the English coast a hail of flak went up from a ship in mid-Channel right where we were headed. Pretty shortly down went an aircraft in flames – it looked like one of our four-engined bombers. It seemed that one of our own ships (the Royal Navy got the blame) had parked itself right on the path that every aircraft going to and from the Continent that night would be following. And, in true naval fashion, it let fly at everything that went over. We decided to risk the night-fighters rather than fly through that lot and did a wide detour.'

In night operations on 7/8 June 1944 70 Mosquitos of 107, 305 and 613 Squadrons operating to the west on rail targets at Argentan, Domfort and Lisieux, sealed approaches to the bridgehead.

'The scene over France,' continues Les Bulmer, 'had changed completely. Whereas before D-Day there had been almost total darkness, now there were lights

Boston IIIs of 88 Squadron fitted with smoke installation pipes below the fuselage for smoke-screening the beach-heads on D-Day, pictured at Hartford Bridge in June 1944. (IWM)

everywhere and most of the Normandy towns burned for several nights. Navigation was much easier; you just flew from one fire to the next.'

The opportunity for break-out and the eventual invasion of Germany was now within reach, and 2nd TAF would go all the way with the ground forces. On 11 June 12 Mosquitos of 107, 464 and 487 Squadrons attacked petrol tankers in a railway marshalling yard at Chaterault at the

Below *Mitchell IIs of 226 Squadron, May 1944.* (IWM)

Bottom *The crew of Mitchell VO-A of 98 Squadron, June 1944.* (Bush)

request of the Army. W/C Mike Pollard and five other Mosquitos of 107 Squadron arrived at 2244 hours to find fires burning in a large area, with smoke rising to 4,000 feet. Attacks continued on railway targets on the night of 11/12 June when 50 aircraft from 88, 98, 107, 180, 226 and 320 Squadrons bombed the railway junction at Le Haye, west of Carentan. Two nights later 42 Mosquitos of 107, 305, 464 and 613 Squadrons strafed and bombed troop movements between

Below *Mitchell 'W' of 98 Squadron flown by F/O Nevin Philby RAAF operating from Dunsfold in June 1944.* (National Archives of Canada via Paul McCue)

Bottom *Pilots in 107 (Jamaica) Squadron in 1944. Left to right: W/C Mike Pollard, CO; F/O De Rosier (USA); F/O J. Ballachey (Can); F/O Sanderson (Can); F/O Karl Aiken (Jamaica); F/O Taylor (Can); and F/L McLure (Can).* (J. Ballachey via Paul McCue)

Tours and Angers-Vire, Dreux and Falaise, and Evreux and Lisieux.

On 22 June Mike Benn DFC was killed. He had taken off with his navigator, F/O W. A. Roe, on a Night Ranger operation from Thorney Island in a Mosquito FB VI. On becoming airborne he found that his airspeed indicator was not working so he returned to base. Another aircraft led them into the approach to ensure that they were at the right speed, but they were too

Below *This crew of Boston IIIA 'L' in 88 Squadron have just returned to Hartford Bridge after an operation on 20 June 1944. Left to right: Ray Moule WOP/AG; Jock Niven, pilot; George Louden, navigator; and Les 'Ginger' Walker, WOP/AG (his 50th operation).*

Bottom *A Mitchell II of 180 Squadron taking off from Dunsfold in mid-1944.* (Paul McCue)

Mosquito NS837 YH-G crewed by F/L Mike Benn DFC and F/O W. A. Roe, which overshot the runway at Thorney Island on the night of 22/23 June 1944. The aircraft was led in to the approach by another Mosquito, but touched down too far along the runway and went through the sea wall. Benn died of his injuries. Roe, who was slightly injured, later crewed up with F/L Lloyd and they were shot down and taken prisoner on 7 August 1944. (Les Bulmer via F. R. Lucas)

fast and Benn overshot the runway, went through the sea wall and crashed in the sea. Roe survived but the armour plate behind the pilot's seat moved forward and broke Mike Benn's back.

They were in shallow water and Roe managed to keep Benn's head above water until the rescue team arrived, which took some time because nobody knew where they were. Benn was taken to sick quarters, but died the following day. (His younger brother, Tony, who was training as a pilot in Rhodesia at the time, became a Sublieutenant in the RNVR but the war ended before he could see action. De-mobbed in 1946, he became Viscount Stansgate upon the death of his father but later renounced the title to become the well-known Labour politician.)

On 14 July, Bastille Day, the Mosquitos of 2nd TAF were called upon for an important task in France, as Gordon Bell-Irving explains:

'AVM Basil Embry came to Thorney Island to brief us for a daylight low-level attack on a special target at Bonneuil Matours, near Poitiers. He was a formidable presence. We were told that the raid was on a Gestapo barracks and was to punish those responsible for the murder of some British prisoners of war who had been clubbed to death with rifle butts in a nearby village square.'

In fact, the soldiers clubbed to death were a reconnaissance party of the SAS, code-named 'Bulbasket', who were dropped south-west of Chateauroux on 5 June to harass the 2nd SS Panzer Division on its move from Toulouse to Normandy. The main party was dropped on 11/12 June and joined up with the Maquis. On 3 July their main camp in the Foret de Verrieres was attacked by German troops. Nine SAS members got away, but 31 SAS and Lt Tom Stevens, a USAAF evader, who had joined them, were taken prisoner. One officer was wounded before capture and was tied to a tree and publicly beaten to death in Verrieres. Three SAS prisoners were also wounded and taken to hospital in Poitiers, where they were given lethal injections. The remainder, including the American and two other SAS captured previous to this engagement, were shot in the Foret de Saint Sauvant near the village of Rom. The German unit responsible for this atrocity was believed to be the 158th Security Regiment from Poitiers. The SAS survivors signalled the UK with the information of their disaster and that the unit responsible was billeted at Bonneuil Matours.

Bell-Irving continues:

'There was no model of the target for us – there hadn't

S/L Gordon 'Peter' Panitz of Queensland, CO 464 Squadron RAAF, and F/O Richard Williams of NSW, who led the raid on Bonneuil Matours on 14 July 1944. (IWM)

been time to prepare one. Basil's final words before sending us on our way were, "If you get shot down and taken prisoner don't shoot your mouth off about retaliation. You can't out-piss a skunk!" This struck me as being colourful but anatomically incorrect. I expect he'd heard it from a Texan.

The raid went quite smoothly. We took off in the late afternoon to hit the target at dusk, when the occupants of the barracks would be having dinner. There were 18 aircraft with crews from 21, 464 and 487 Squadrons led by G/C Wykeham-Barnes. At about 2,000 feet we skirted the Cherbourg Peninsula, and on passing a little too close to the Channel Island of Alderney our tidy formation was fired on by a heavy shore battery. Considering our altitude and range this came as a surprise. We scattered in a relatively disciplined way and reformed as soon as we were out of range.

I think we made our landfall near St Malo and went down to about 50 feet from there until just short of the target, where we climbed to bombing height; our

bombs were fused for a 25-second delay. Bert Holt, my navigator, and I were among the first to bomb, and as we dived on the target I noticed a 20 mm gun firing tracer rather wildly from the roof of the target building. Looking back after bombing there was a lot of smoke and no sign of tracer. We did not re-formate after bombing; it soon became dark and we returned to base independently. The rest of the trip was uneventful and all crews returned safely. Whoever was in the barracks, we were told that 150 had been killed in our raid.'

On 30 July the SAS learned that 2,000–3,000 Germans were massing for an anti-Maquis/SAS sweep, and the majority were billeted in the Caserne des Dunes barracks at Poitiers. This resulted in a raid by 487 and 21 Squadron aircraft on 1 August. Meanwhile, the SAS learned that the survivors of the 158th Regiment were now in the Chateau de Fou, south of Chatellerault, and this was attacked by 107

Squadron on 2 August (305 Squadron attacked Maulny, a saboteur school, on 2 August also). It is estimated that 80 per cent of the regiment were killed, so that unit paid dearly for its actions.

John Bateman returned to 98 Squadron in July.

'On the 24th we bombed German troop concentrations in a wood 5 miles south-east of Caen and met some intense and accurate flak that severely damaged our aircraft. It was on this trip that Keith Lynch and I decided to change places in the top turret. I tugged at his trouser leg to indicate that he should come down, and just after he came out a chunk of flak penetrated the seat, which would have caused him severe discomfort if he had still been in position, not to mention his marital chances.

At 0600 the next morning we were off again to the same target, and again we met with heavy opposition, but no damage this time. We returned after 2 hours and later that day led another attack on a fuel dump near Chateaudun, again meeting opposition en route. We led two further trips on 26 July, again in two different aircraft. The first attack was on a fuel dump at Alencon, and the second on another at Fontainebleau near Paris. On both occasions we ran into heavy opposition, but at Fontainebleau it was extremely accurate, and we lost one aircraft from our

Bombs away from a Mosquito during the raid on the German barracks at Caserne des Dunes, Poitiers, on 1 August 1944. (via Paul McCue)

flight at Dreux. All these ops were carried out at about 16,000 feet, but we did not see a single snapper.

Our navigator was Kees Vandenbergh, who had completed 100 ops. He was a lieutenant in the Dutch Naval Air Service and had completed a tour of ops

The bombed barracks soon after the Mosquito attack. (via Paul McCue)

This reconnaissance photo of the Caserne des Dunes barracks, taken on 2 August 1944, the day after the successful attack by Mosquitos, shows clearly the superb precision bombing carried out by the aircraft of 2nd TAF. (via Paul McCue)

The attack on the Chateau de Fou by Mosquitos of 107 Squadron on 2 August 1944. (IWM)

with 320 Squadron when Alan asked him to join his crew. He spoke excellent English with only a very faint accent. He was also a qualified pilot, which would have been useful if Alan had been incapacitated. As the Dutch were paid extra for each hour of non-operational flying, and even more for operational flying, he would take the aircraft up at every opportunity for air tests and so forth.

One day in the late summer of 1944, with a new F/O gunner who had just joined us, he did an air test in 'O-Orange', which had a new engine fitted. Alan asked Keith and me if we wanted to go with them, but we both declined as we wanted to listen to a radio serial that we had been following; Alan, too, stayed to listen to it as Kees took off. The air test should have taken about 20 minutes, but after half an hour when they hadn't returned we all went up to Flying Control to see if they had any information, but they had heard nothing since take-off. After another 30 minutes there was a telephone call from the police at Guildford to report that a Mitchell had crashed near Chidingford, and as it was the only Mitchell airborne from Dunsfold it had to be Kees.

We were all a bit shattered, but within a few days we were flying again, this time with S/L Bunny Reece, the Wing Navigation Officer, as our navigator. On our first trip with Bunny we were heading for France at about 10,000 feet and had just crossed the coast and tested our guns when Keith and I looked up and saw a very large formation of Liberators of the USAAF about 15,000 feet above us. They were silver and looked very impressive against our rather drab colours. While we were watching with admiration one of them burst into flames and within a minute or so we counted five or six parachutes heading for the drink. We never found out the cause, but concluded that a gunner in the formation had put a burst into one of his chums while testing his guns. Bad show!'

The heavier components of 2nd TAF were expected to follow soon after the outbreak from the beaches, including 2 Group's Mosquito bomber and fighter wings. In the meantime they flew from airfields such as Thorney Island and Lasham. Most of 2 Group's flying, for the Mosquito anyway, took the form of night interdiction, while some of the 2 Group squadrons also interfered with German night flying. Mosquitos from these squadrons would join the circuit of Luftwaffe airfields and shoot German aircraft down as they came in to land or just as they took off. In addition to these night expeditions, there were occasional daylight operations, which included spectacular pin-point attacks on specific buildings.

'August was a very busy month', wrote Les Bulmer. 'With the breakout from the beach-head things moved very swiftly and we harried the Germans in retreat. Sometimes it was sheer slaughter as we found roads

The crew of 'O-Orange' of 98 Squadron. Left to right: John Bateman, Keith Cudlipp, Kees Vandenbergh, W/C Alan Lynn and a sergeant cameraman who took photos on the trip. (John Bateman)

jammed with enemy transport just waiting to be set on fire. Ed and I flew 18 sorties that month, sometimes two in one night. On the 18th we took off at 0010 for our 39th op and were back at Thorney Island by 0145. We re-fuelled and re-armed and were off again at 0350, landing again at 0530. After de-briefing and a meal, we snatched a few hours sleep before attending briefing for the next night's raids. We were off at 2310 that night and back at 0110 on the 19th. Once again we re-fuelled and re-armed and were off at 0415, returning at 0550. So in less than 30 hours we had carried out four operations. Coming back over the Channel on the last one I must have dozed off because I awoke with a start when the aircraft gave a violent lurch. Ed had also fallen asleep and woke just in time to stop us spiralling into the sea.

On 26 August we had a change from beating up transport. The Army wanted the railway bridge at Rouen destroyed to impede the German retreat. It was too small a target for the heavies, so 21 Squadron was asked to have a go. It had to be a night attack because the enemy was bound to defend it with everything he had. Four aircraft, working in pairs, were allotted to the task. One of the pair would fly at around 3,000 feet and drop flares for the other one, which would be waiting underneath. After dropping his bombs the two would change places. Since we were carrying flares in the bomb bay, we could only carry two bombs each under the wings.

F/L Swaine and another crew took off first. We, together with our partner F/L Winder, left at 2235, some 30 minutes or so later. On the way over to France Swaine called up on the R/T to say that it was pretty hot in the target area, that he'd been hit and he

recommended that we abort. Ed and Winder had a brief conversation and decided to give it a whirl – I was more than happy to call it a day but I wasn't consulted.

We had been selected to do the first flare drop, so went in at about 3,000 feet. The enemy took a dislike to us at Cap d'Antifer as we crossed the coast, then we settled down for a straight run in to Rouen. I had my head stuck in the *Gee* set following a *Gee* line that should take us over the bridge from the north-west. Ed was concentrating on following my instructions to stay on the line and waiting for me to give him the order to drop the flares. Thus neither of us was aware of what was going on around us. This was just as well, because afterwards Winder said that he could see exactly where we were above him because of the flak that was following us in. Ignorance is a wonderful thing at times.

Our three flares went down right on target, but by the time we had turned to watch Winder attack, two flares had gone out – presumably shot out – and another had its parachute damaged and fell to the ground on the east bank of the river. However, this remaining flare gave enough light for us to see Winder's bombs burst on the south-west end of the bridge. Ed stuck the nose down and we dived on the bridge before our one remaining flare expired. We let go the bombs just as the flare went out so I couldn't see the results, then called up Winder to tell him that he needn't bother to drop his flares. I think he was as relieved as we were to get the hell out of it. I don't suppose we did much damage to the bridge – if any. But at least we tried.'

Chapter Nine

Rangers on the Rampage

'Train-busting on a dark night was pretty much a cat's-eyes thing. Sometimes a plume of steam might be just discernible, sometimes the glow of a firebox moving along rails.'

Les Bulmer

At 5 am on 31 August 1944, pilot S/L Stanislaw Grodzicki and F/L Adam Szajdzicki, navigator, in 305 (Polish) Squadron, had just landed back at Lasham after a 4-hour patrol over north-east France when they were one of six Mosquito crews put on the Battle Order for the day's operation.

'I had got up late from bed,' remembers Adam, 'and was in rather a hurry to get to the Mess for lunch. I collected my bicycle from behind the tent.

"Adam," I heard the voice of S/L Grodzicki, my pilot, say. "Where are you going?"

"To lunch," I said.

"Forget it. Take your things and come quickly for the briefing. We are flying with five Mosquitos. Orlinski is leading." W/C B. Orlinski was our CO at the time.

"Hard luck," I said. "There goes my lunch."

But the news excited me because it could be an interesting operation. I went back and collected my bag, which was lying under my bed where I had left it earlier in the morning. The ops tent was not very far away, and arriving there I found that some of our crews were already there, and others were arriving. Everybody was asking the same question: "Where? What?"

The map on the wall was marked with a red thread for our track. The route out was over Portland Bill,

F/L Adam Szajdzicki, navigator, 305 (Polish) Squadron. (Adam Szajdzicki)

Mosquito LR366 of 613 Squadron undergoing an operational turn-around at Lasham in 1944. (via Philip Birtles)

Guernsey, Arromanches, then south of Auxerre, north of Langre, ending just north of Epinol. A US flag was pinned in Auxerre indicating that there were American

A Mitchell II braves the flak bursts over the Doullens area of France. (Jan P. Kloos)

forces. The flight plan was already written on the board for us to copy. To the briefing came the Group Captain, our CO and two assistant officers. One of them I knew from previous briefings. The other, a "new face", held a big roll of papers under his arm.

W/C Orlinski called the briefing to order and began: "Gentlemen, our destination is Nomexy where there are reservoirs estimated to hold more than 3 million gallons of German petrol, which must be destroyed. We will fly six aircraft, and not five as stated in the order."

He named the sixth pilot, F/L Smith. Smith had only recently joined our squadron, and was known among us as 'Matilda' because he used to sing or whistle the song, which had a Central American rhythm – 'Matilda, Matilda, took your money and went to Venezuela'. He was the only Bahamian crew member among us. He appeared, beaming with pleasure. It was his second or third operation.

Orlinski said that we were flying in pairs stacked to the rear, but before the last check-point we would separate and increase the distance between the aircraft to 4 miles apart because we would be attacking our target from low level, one by one, and our bombs were fitted with 11-second delay fuses. He added, "I don't want any of you getting blown up by our own bombs. The navigation to the target will be done by my navigator and I will tell you about the start later."

Now the "new face" stepped forward. "Well, gentlemen, here is your target."

With those words he opened the papers. These were the photographs of our destination. He passed them around, saying, "Please have a good look at them, and memorise them well to make sure that you will find your target." After a while he continued. "The photos were taken on the same track as you will be heading for the target. There is also a photo of the last check-point. That is the photo with four large buildings beside the loop in the river bend. Now from that check-point, which we will call zero point, you will have to take a course of 022 for 4 minutes, then – 'Bang!' – you will be over your target. I am afraid that the target will not be too visible from the zero point.' He was finished.

The zero point was very good indeed and could not be mistaken. I tried to memorise the details that were not shown on the map. The three big petrol reservoirs stood on the eastern side of a railway line running north from Epinol to Nancy on an azimuth of about 35–170 degrees. Beyond was the river lined with high trees. I was impressed with the preparations that had been made for this raid. Drawing our track through the target I thought that it had been well chosen. On that approach we probably would not see the light between the tanks and it would present a more certain target for our bombs. The navigation officer gave us the exact run-in time from the zero point, and Orlinski assigned each crew a position in the formation. We were No 2.

He continued, "At 1500 hours proceed to your aircraft, start engines on my signal. We will start rolling right away to avoid overheating the engines as it is very hot today. The start will be in pairs with the second pair accelerating when the first is at the end of the runway. After take-off, turn left. Remember to empty the drop tanks as soon as possible. In the bomb bay are two bombs with 11-second delay fuses. Remember you will be dropping them from low level so don't get too close behind one another. Over the UK and the Channel we will fly at 2,000 feet and later over France we will come down to 200 feet. At this time we have had no reports of German fighter activity along our route, but you never know – so watch it! Keep total radio silence. Only break it in an emergency. Any questions? Oh yes," he added. "There will be the usual man with the Aldis lamp at your dispersal point. Signal him when you are ready and obey his signals." For the benefit of the CO and Matilda, the briefing had been conducted in English.

"We are ready, sir," said Orlinski, saluting the CO.

The CO returned the salute and said to us, "Good luck, boys. Let's go to our aircraft."

I checked the contents of my navigation bag, collected the flares of the day, and put one of them into the top of my left boot. I stuffed my pistol into the top of the right boot. Then, from the box, I collected a 'chute and the harness with the dinghy attached to it, and the bag. This made a very heavy load and it was not easy to carry it the 100 or so yards across the clearing, where our aircraft was standing. Just before leaving the briefing tent, I snatched up the photo of the target and pushed it inside my battledress blouse.

At 'Z-Zebra' the ground crew were waiting, and reported that the aircraft was OK. Stan, my pilot, went to check the aircraft log book and I dropped my gear on the ground and went to check the suspension of the bombs. I gave them a friendly tap, and wished them a good journey and a good landing.'

Stan and Adam went through their take-off checks and finally, at 1535, taxied out to the runway. Adam looked back at the 'wonderful line of Mosquitos' and one by one they took off.

'It was quieter in the cockpit now as the aircraft climbed in a wide left turn. There was only the noise of the wind outside, and the hiss of the fresh air in the ventilators. After one circuit No 1 waggled his wings and we set course for Winchester, levelling off at Angels Two [2,000 feet]. Then we changed course south for Portland Bill, and Portsmouth, full of all sorts of shipping, slipped by on the port side. Craft of all sorts were heading to and from Normandy, some of them towing barrage balloons.

We followed No 1 to Arromanches. I spotted three Dakotas heading north-west, probably flying home the wounded. I watched the sky for bandits and noted the course and height changes in my log. Dropping to 300 feet and increasing speed, we passed Auxerre on the port beam and the ground whistled by. We were keeping well clear of the built-up areas because the Germans could still be there, even though the briefing map showed that the area had been captured by the Americans. We also knew that our own ack-ack chaps were a bit "trigger-happy".

I pushed the safety switch to arm the bombs, logged the time and shouted to Stan to tell him. The loop in the River Marne came in sight and Chaumont was visible on the port beam. Up to now everything was going fine and quietly – we were 2 minutes early. The ground sped by beneath us as I searched the sky for

Cpl Jan Pronk and Piet den Haajer of 320 Squadron arming Mitchell II 'Owe Jongens'. (Jan P. Kloos)

bandits – thank God none were visible. I pulled out the photograph of the target and tried to sort out the details in my mind. This was my last chance to do it. We just had to find the bloody target! I kept repeating this over and over again. I checked my watch again – in 3 minutes we should be at the zero point. Ahead appeared the four buildings, then the bend in the river, just as the photo showed.

"We are coming to point zero, dead ahead. Can you see it?" I said to Stan.

"OK," he said, steering the aircraft slightly to the right and increasing the distance from No 1 to make sure that we were making 022 degrees over the zero point.

"OK," said Stan again. "On course."

I opened the bomb doors as we flew over the zero point and noted the time. But we could not see the target ahead. Instead there was a hill. Orlinski changed course to about 060 degrees and headed towards Epinal on our starboard. Stan spotted him and shouted, "Where is No 1 going? Are you sure we are on the right track?"

"Check that you are on 022 degrees," I replied. I gave a quick glance at the photo and saw that there were vineyards on the slope of the hill between the zero point and the target. I saw vineyards on the hill in front of us. I suddenly realised that French farmers, logically, had probably planted the vineyard on the south slopes of the hill facing the sun.

"Another 2½ minutes to go," I said. "The target must be over the hill."

"Are you sure?" asked Stan.

"That's the course they told us to steer. One and a half minutes to go. There is some flak on the far right."

I had a feeling that soon our Mosquito would start chopping up the vines, we were flying so low. We were going parallel to the slope of the hill.

"Forty-five seconds to go," I called.

Stan pulled up the Mossie over the top of the hill. "Oh Santa Madonna! What a sight!"

Straight ahead and below were the reservoirs, standing at an angle to our course, just like the photo. Stan pushed the stick sharply forward and I shot out of my seat, my head hitting the canopy.

"Bombs gone!" called Stan, putting the starboard wing down and pulling the aircraft up. I spotted the bombs. The right one was slightly ahead of the others and seemed to be going for a break between the tanks. Damn! The second one was heading directly into the middle tank. I held my breath. Is it going to be a direct hit? Oh no! God! It's gone over the tank. Damn! I realised that when we were over the hill and climbing that we had not enough time and distance to put the aircraft into a steeper dive; therefore the bombs had been released too high. One had exploded in the river, one in a field behind it. I was absolutely disgusted. All that way for nothing!

"They missed the tanks," I told Stan.

"Look out for our Mosquitos and their whereabouts," requested Stan, pulling the aircraft up into a very tight left turn. The G-force was pushing me into my seat. I felt a pain in my bottom; the dinghy was not very comfortable as a seat cushion. I wanted to stand up to have a better look around. I was worried about our starboard side because aircraft could be coming from that quarter. Looking over the port wing I saw the river approaching, and through the canopy I saw the burning tanks. We passed over the river, then over the railway, and at that moment a Mosquito passed right under us. Bombs were bursting in the railway yard as we climbed, always in that sharp turn. We flew over the town's houses, then some trees and a hill, while another Mosquito was pulling away from the yard.

The tanks were coming up at 10 o'clock. The G-forces became less tormenting. Stan put the Mossie into a dive and the turn became gentler but steeper. The tanks were at 12 o'clock when Stan opened fire with the cannons. Suddenly the aircraft started to shake and the airspeed dropped by 40 mph. Tracers hit the ground in front of the tanks on the far left, and slowly rose until they pierced the tanks. A red tongue of fire burst from the lower part of the tank, and as the aircraft slid further to the right the tracer hit the central tank. This also burst into flames, as did the third tank, which blew up sending a great cloud of black smoke into the air. We were heading straight for it.

"Oh God! That smoke will cover us."

The Mosquito stopped shaking and the next instant we ran into the dark cloud. The cockpit became dark and smelly for a few seconds before we came out into the clean fresh air beyond. The smell persisted as we made a wide left circle, while happily admiring the fire and looking to see if there was anything else that we could destroy. At that moment a Mosquito passed over the yard.

"Hey, Blue chaps," came a voice on the radio, "there is smoke towards the north."

Before we had finished the circle I spotted another Mosquito passing along the yard. In turn we came in line with the rail line. Stan pushed the stick forward and started diving toward the freight cars standing on the rails, opening fire on them. I noted some flashes on the cars but this time we did not manage to start new fires. Stan was preparing himself for the third run when on the radio came Orlinski's voice.

"Blue, Blue, return to formation over point zero."

Stan immediately set course south. Suddenly, on the radio came the song, "Matilda, Matilda, took your petrol and went to Venezuela. Ha ha!"

I counted six Mosquitos making formation as we set course for home, along the same route as we had taken on the way in. The return flight went quietly and we landed at base at 1955.

At the de-briefing F/L Leimiesozonek, Orlinski's navigator, explained that they had turned eastward after the zero point because he could not see the target ahead. He had turned towards what he thought was a camouflaged target. We found out that the second pair had followed No 1, thinking that we were wrong. The

third pair did not follow us over the hill because they couldn't see the target, so they went around the hill to look for it; these were the Mosquitos I spotted flying over the rail lines. For his efforts Stan was awarded the "Virtuti Militarui" decoration and I was awarded the "Krzyz Walecznych" (Cross of Valour).'

Les Bulmer's final operation in 21 Squadron with Ed McQuarrie (his 52nd and McQuarrie's 50th) took place on 17 September 1944.

'It was to be quite an exciting finish to our tour together,' recalls Bulmer. 'Mosquitos from 138 Wing were detailed to attack the barracks at Arnhem [32 Mosquitos of 107 and 613 Squadron] ahead of the airborne invasion. And 21 Squadron were to do the same to three school buildings in the centre of Nijmegen, which were being used by the German garrison. Both raids were to eliminate the opposition before the airborne forces of *Market Garden* went in later that day.'

F/O Nigel L. Gilson, a navigator in 107 Squadron, had been spending a day's leave in Winchester and was all set for an enjoyable evening to round it off at a dance hall in

F/O Nigel L. Gilson and his pilot, Phil Slayden, of 107 Squadron, at a de-briefing. (Nigel Gilson collection)

Basingstoke, when a friend gave him the news that he had to return to Lasham immediately – they had been looking all day for him – as the squadron was confined to barracks overnight.

'We were met by the usual expectant rumours, but could still learn nothing definite except that we were to be up for briefing at 0530. Ours was a quiet Mess that night, only admin officers were drinking more than lemonade and all air crews were in bed by about 10 – most unusual for us!

Rising before midday was a bit of a strain, but 0530 on Sunday found us all milling around the briefing room with an exceptional complement of "braid and scrambled egg" among us. The tense gaiety and laconic humour of briefing are something one remembers but can't adequately describe. I can recall only two things, the CO's description of the purpose of the Arnhem landing (for that was the cause of the trouble): "If this one comes off the war will be over in 14 days"; and his description of the anticipated reception of the paratroops: "They expect to slide down stocks of 40 millimetre."

A minor flap broke out while navigators struggled with maps, rulers, protractors and computers, working out tracks, courses, winds and other essentials to the successful combat of hostile gremlins, until at last there was a welcome break for a hasty bacon and egg breakfast.

It was a hectic and hilarious meal, then we were back for a final route check and squadron briefing on formation and tactics. Time for take-off was altered twice, but at last we went to our aircraft where tired ground crews, who'd been working half the night, were just finishing bombing and arming up. F/O Phil Slayden, my pilot, and I sat on the grass waiting for the signal to get into our aircraft. In the peace of a brilliant Sunday morning war seemed very far away. Only Dougie, who'd come to the squadron the day before, remarked on the incongruity of it all; the strains of "Abide With Me" from a nearby hangar service sounded too ominous to his unaccustomed ear to pass unnoticed!

The ground crew gave us the usual strict orders to do a good job with their aeroplane and wished us a brief but sincere "Good luck", and we taxied out. We took off into a clear sky already filling with squadrons of ungainly gliders and tugs, took up formation and set course. Soon the English draught-board gave place to a sea of rippled blue, and finally that to the deeply cut green flats of Holland.'

Les Bulmer, meanwhile, was going through the same routine:

'We were still based at Thorney island, so had quite a way to go to reach the target. As a result we had to carry wing tanks, which meant that our bomb load was confined to two 500-pounders in the bomb bay. At briefing we had the usual 2 Group model of the town so that we could familiarise ourselves with the target and the run-in over the town. There would be 15 aircraft, in five sets of three in echelon starboard. W/C D. F. Dennis led, with 'Jock' Murray as his No 2. We led the third echelon, with F/L Bert Willers as our No 2. To ensure that all 15 aircraft would be clear of the target before the bombs exploded, the leading aircraft (the first ten) had 25-second fuses, whereas the rear echelons had the normal 11-second delay.

To stay clear of trouble we planned to fly across the Channel and up to the front line at high level. Once over enemy territory we would drop down to the deck and head for a road that ran north-west from Cleve into Nijmegen. The road would give us an accurate run-up to the target, which consisted of three large buildings forming a semi-circle facing the direction from which we planned to attack, so would be easy to identify.

We took off at 1045 and formed up into tight formation. Somewhere short of the front line we shed our drop tanks – empty tanks could be lethal if hit by flak. Just after crossing the front line we came under heavy ack-ack fire near Weert. There was nothing we could do to avoid it as this would have destroyed the formation. But this didn't stop No 2 in the second echelon from trying to weave – he was a bigger menace than the flak. As far as I know nobody was hit, although a message came over the R/T calling someone by name – which we didn't catch – telling them that they were on fire. I think it probably came from some other formation because there were no signs of fire in ours. But I reckon it caused a mild panic among all our crews.

On the deck it was hard work for the pilots trying to keep one eye on the ground and the other on the rest of the formation. Somewhere along the way there was a cry of "Wires, wires!", and we had to climb to get over an electricity pylon. I was amazed to see that Willers, on our right, seemed to fly underneath! In fact, I found out afterwards that he'd taken advantage of the droop in the cables to stay low.

Our turning point on the Cleve–Nijmegen road came up, which we planned to follow into Nijmegen, but we carried straight on, then circled starboard to come up on Cleve from the east. I had no idea what was going on. Every navigator in the formation, except the leader, must have been wondering what the hell was happening. I could hardly believe my eyes when the leading aircraft opened their bomb doors. Ed followed suit and I yelled at him that this wasn't the target and not to release our bombs. Poor Ed was totally confused, and probably thought I had gone off my head since the leaders were obviously intent on bombing whatever was coming up. After what seemed ages, but was probably only seconds, the leader's bomb doors closed and I breathed a sigh of relief as we shot over Cleve.

On the straight road, with houses on either side and a larger building, which could have been a church or chapel, people were standing watching us go over. I looked back to check that the rear echelons had noticed that bomb doors had been closed and saw, to my dismay, a large cloud of black smoke. Some of the rear six aircraft had let their bombs go. (According to later official reports three aircraft bombed a barrack square in Cleve and machine-gunned troops.)

South-west of Cleve is the Reichwald, a large forest, and we proceeded to career around this. By now there was not much formation left, just a gaggle of aircraft milling around waiting for someone to make a decision. Suddenly I saw two aircraft haring off in the right direction – one of them, I later discovered, was Jock Murray. I told Ed to follow and we chased after them, with everyone else tagging along behind or beside us. We were now 15 aircraft all flying individually towards Nijmegen. And we had no means of knowing whether any of the leading planes were the ones with the short fuses.

We sped up the road to Nijmegen and I could see the bridge over on the right. And then we were over the town looking anxiously for the target. It seemed to be chaos, with Mosquitos going in all directions, flak coming up and Mustangs milling around above us. I noticed one Mosquito climbing away to the north and wondered where the hell he was going. Then another Mosquito shot underneath us almost at right-angles. I shall never know how he found room between us and the rooftops, and I wondered why he was going in that particular direction. Then I realised that he'd seen the target and was heading straight for it. I yelled to Ed to pull round and pointed to the target, by now almost on our port wing-tip. He put us into a tight turn, but we couldn't make it in time.

We shot over the town and I recall the railway station with crowds waiting on the platform and what appeared to be a green-coloured train alongside. In a flash we were clear and out over farmland where we dumped our bombs and fled. On the way in and on the way out the farmers and their families were standing in their doorways waving like made – probably cheering on "the brave RAF" while we were thinking "what the hell are we doing here, let's get the hell out of it."

The element of surprise is essential on low-level attacks and there is no going round again, unless you have suicidal tendencies, so we found a convenient wood and jettisoned our load. In the confusion we forgot to put the arming switches to "OFF", so I just hoped that no one would be passing that way within the next 25 seconds. (We weren't the only ones to blow holes in the countryside. At the subsequent inquest there were several photographs taken by rearward-facing cameras showing jettisoned bombs exploding. There were a few caustic comments from the flight commanders about this. Fortunately, we didn't have a camera on board so we managed to conceal our misdemeanour.)

We found another Mosquito, which seemed to be going in the same direction as us, so we joined him for the journey home. This was uneventful; we didn't even get shot at over Weert this time. Maybe the Germans didn't consider two aircraft to be worth wasting ammunition on. And besides, we were heading for home.'

Arnhem, meanwhile, was being attacked by 107 and 613 Squadrons. Nigel Gilson takes up the story:

'Arnhem identified itself for us – the natives, or their uninvited guests, were distinctly hostile – but we rejoiced in our speed and ploughed in. At first one could watch things quite objectively; one gun team was firing explosive shells, with tantalising persistency, right on our track, and I wondered absent-mindedly by how much they would miss us. Then we dived to attack. I bent to switch on the camera, began to rise, then instinctively ducked again, only to be conscious of an explosion and a shower of perspex splinters. I jerked up, looking anxiously at Phil, and heaved a sigh of relief when I saw that he was OK and that we were climbing again. At least, I think we were climbing – neither of us was quite sure what happened in those 30 seconds. A glance showed that the gun team had been robbed of their prey by the dive, and the shell had burst above us, merely shattering our cockpit cover.

Suddenly Phil called, "Hey, the bomb doors are shut, we couldn't have dropped the bombs!"

I jammed them open and he pressed the tit to drop the bombs; we looked behind for the flash, but there was none, and then we remembered that we'd opened the doors before the dive and must have closed them instinctively during the attack.

But the look behind had shown us one thing – an aircraft with our markings suddenly catching fire in the starboard petrol tank. The flames spread rapidly to the port, covering the cockpit; the aircraft lost height and finally hit a house and overturned into the river. We shall not forget that quickly. Woody and Mac were in that mass of flame.

It was only a matter of minutes before we were over the Zuider Zee again, flying below formations of gliders and tugs. We felt sorry for them – they hadn't our speed, they had to fly straight though the flak, and their occupants had to go down on 'chutes or without engines or guns – no future in that.

The CO called up to check formation; as we called "Here" to our own call-sign we waited anxiously to hear who was missing. Two failed to reply – two out of 14. Woody and Mac, Ted and Griff had bought it – tough luck; we should miss them.'

Les Bulmer returned to Thorney Island (one crew was missing), where the full story of the confusion over their target route unfolded.

'W/C Dennis had a bird hit his windscreen just before reaching the turning point. In retrospect, it might have been wiser for him to pull out and hand over to Jock Murray immediately, but he chose to carry on, not being able to see properly, and hence the mess we finished up in. Only five aircraft claimed to have located and bombed the target. Most of the rest did as we did and dumped them in fields, apart from those who had already got rid of theirs over Cleve.

I've always felt that it was a mistake to have 15 planes in one formation. The usual formation on previous raids of this sort was groups of six in two vics of three. Because each of the following echelons had to be stepped down on the one in front to avoid slip-stream problems, it meant that the leader had to keep a reasonable height above the deck, otherwise the rear echelons would be ploughing a furrow across the countryside. In the event, it was impossible to avoid hitting slip-streams and we were being thrown all over the place, and at tree-top height this is not the healthiest of situations.

It was only later that we learned that the German troops were not in their barracks anyway, so all we succeeded in doing was probably to kill a few innocent Dutchmen and some German civilians. Such is war. In wartime I suppose you can't very well admit to the world that you made a cock-up.

This operation was the last one for Ed McQuarrie and for me – at least, I thought so at the time. He had done the requisite 50 trips and I'd managed 52 because Ed had an argument with a motor cycle early in our tour and finished up in hospital. While he was in there I did two trips with an Irishman, F/O Smith.

Ed and I went on two weeks leave and I expected that we would be sent on rest to an OTU, but I was in for an unpleasant surprise when I returned to pick up my kit and move on. While I was away 2 Group had moved the goal-posts. A tour was now 85 ops, with a month's leave around the halfway mark, 200 operational hours or 12 months on the squadron, whichever came first. I was told to take another fortnight's leave and come back for another 35 trips. It was rather like being given the death sentence. Having survived 52 ops, I couldn't believe that my luck would last for another 35. I never saw Ed McQuarrie again and it is only in recent years that I learned that the RCAF would not go along with the extended tour and Ed was shipped back to Canada.'

Altogether, nine Mosquito bomber squadrons now equipped 2nd TAF. In September 1944, following the outbreak from the Normandy beach-head, plans were in progress to move them to airfields in France. As part of the new-found offensive, Mosquito squadrons outside 2nd TAF also made daylight *Rangers* from France and intruder sorties over the Continent. One of them was 418 (RCAF) Squadron, which in September had flown 100 *Intruder* sorties over France as well as reconnoitring V2 rocket launches. The squadron had re-equipped with Mosquitos in March 1943 and had flown *Flower Intruder* operations out of RAF Ford, Sussex, using AI Mk IV and Mk VIII.

Since January 1944 the Canadians had reaped a rich harvest of victories on day and night *Rangers*, and the high point came in April–May when 418 Squadron shot down 30 aircraft in the air and destroyed a further 38 on the ground. By May the Canadians, based at Holmsley South, had claimed 100 victories. From July to 21 August, based variously at Hurn, Middle Wallop and Hunsdon, 418 Squadron, during the anti-*Diver* offensive, had destroyed no fewer than 123 V1 pilotless bombs. Not surprisingly, therefore, 418 had the distinction of destroying more enemy aircraft both in the air and on the ground than any other Canadian squadron, in both night and daylight operations.

F/L F. A. 'Ted' Johnson DFC RCAF flew 43 operations as a pilot with 418 Squadron. One of the most eventful operations he and his navigator, F/L N. J. 'Jimmy' Gibbons, flew was on 2 October 1944. As their Mosquito streaked close to 300 mph through the night sky a few miles east of Munich, searchlights flicked on to the south-east at Erding airfield and nervously probed the dark clouds above. Johnson said, 'Jim, turn our navigation lights on and off a few times. The natives are getting restless.' A few flashes of the nav lights and the German crews doused their searchlights and waited, and wondered.

It was nearing midnight and the crew had just completed one north-to-south low-level pass over the German airfield intending to strafe Luftwaffe aircraft parked there, but the night was so dark that they had not been able to see a target in time to depress the Mosquito's nose and bring its four .303 machine guns and four 20 mm cannon to bear. However, through the gloom they had seen the shadowy outlines of at least one aircraft on the airfield, so they were now swinging around to the north to set up for a second run at their target.

At this late stage of the war the Luftwaffe had become increasingly wary in its use of its dwindling aircraft resources. Consequently, the Allied air forces had to employ imaginative tactics to find and destroy them. Since the Luftwaffe was doing less and less flying, Johnson and Gibbons had speculated that it should be possible to catch them on the ground at night, and after some experimentation had established that on nights when there was a full moon there was sufficient light to carry out an air-to-ground strafing attack in a shallow dive from about 1,500 feet above ground level. Any

F/L 'Ted' Johnson DFC RCAF (right) with his navigator, F/L N. J. 'Jimmy' Gibbons DFC, of 418 Squadron. (Ted Johnson)

Mosquito TH-H of 418 Squadron crewed by Johnson and Gibbons. (Ted Johnson)

higher and it was difficult to see objects on the ground, while any lower would give insufficient time to aim the Mosquito's nose-mounted weapons, fire a burst and pull out from the dive before striking the ground. Best visibility was obtained by positioning for the attack with the moon on the opposite side of the target.

The Mosquito crew had studied intelligence reports of Luftwaffe flying activity and had noticed that in recent weeks there had been several indications of aircraft flying in the vicinity of Erding airfield. Although it was deep within Germany on the far side of Munich at the limit of the Mosquito's range, they had calculated that if they pre-positioned their aircraft from their operational base at Hunsdon to Ford airfield in Sussex, and re-fuelled and launched from there with full tanks, they could make the round trip.

So at the next full moon phase they re-checked all factors, obtained authorisation for the operation, moved their Mosquito to Ford in the late afternoon, re-fuelled, then took off at 2015 into a hazy autumn night. The moon had not yet risen but it would be up in an hour and the Met forecast had said that although there was a weather front over Germany it should be well east of their target by the time they arrived and the skies should be clear.

The Met man had been wrong. After flying for 3 hours at some 500 feet above ground level, thus hoping to avoid being picked up by German radar, Johnson and Gibbons arrived in the area to find the sky completely obscured by thick, low-hanging clouds. There would be no help from the moon. Determined not to return without trying to attack their target, they flew north of the enemy airfield to a predetermined sharp bend in the Isar River, which could be seen even on this moonless night, and using an accurate course heading, airspeed and time made their first abortive pass. The Germans did not react as they overflew the airfield, so Johnson and Gibbons speculated that no radar alert had been given to the defences and, indeed, they might still be uncertain if this was a hostile aircraft or one of their own with radio communications problems. Hence the ploy to flash the navigation lights when the first German searchlights began their tentative probing.

They again reached their pin-point over the river bend and carefully turned so that when they re-crossed in a southerly direction they would be on the desired course at exactly the selected height and airspeed. The Mosquito passed over the river – precision was essential to success under these adverse visibility conditions.

Gibbons clicked his stopwatch and breathed

into the microphone mounted in his oxygen mask. 'Two minutes 28 seconds to go.'

Ted Johnson grunted acknowledgement and re-checked that the safety guards were off on both the cannons and the machine guns. He tweaked the dimmer control lower on the reflector gunsight to reduce the dim glow of the circle of light with its central dot on the windscreen that was his aiming guide. He needed the gun sight as dim as possible to maximise his chances of seeing something on the ground in the target area. Dim outlines sped under the Mosquito as the two Merlin 25s growled their power across the night sky. Wispy cloud flicked by. Tension in the dimly lit cockpit mounted as the crew strained forward in their safety harnesses, striving to see objects on the ground.

The airfield ahead remained totally blacked out. There was no sign of hostility. Johnson re-checked speed, course and altitude. Gibbons glanced at his stopwatch and said, '30 seconds', then began a countdown at 10-second intervals. As he called out, '10 seconds', Johnson replied, 'Airfield in sight!' and eased forward slightly on the control column, anticipating the need to initiate a quick dive as soon as a target was seen. His right thumb and forefinger tensed over the button and the trigger on the control column that would fire the cannons and machine guns.

Suddenly the vague outline of a single-engine aircraft sitting on the airfield swept under the Mosquito's nose and the pilot made a spasmodic movement to start a dive but in the same second knew it was too late. 'Damn!' was all he said as the airfield continued to race away beneath and the indistinct outlines of hangars on the southern boundary were left behind. Still no reaction from the airfield defences.

The Mosquito made a wide sweeping turn westwards and continued around on to a northerly heading. Gibbons spoke. 'What kind of aircraft was that?'

Johnson replied, 'I'm not sure . . . Could have been an Me 108, an advanced trainer. I couldn't see in time. Let's have one more go.'

A green Aldis-type hand-held signal light directed a series of dots and dashes toward them from the airfield control tower. The Mossie crew were unable to decipher the message since, whatever it was, it was in German.

'Jimmy', said Johnson, 'I think they believe we want to land. Give them a few more flashes on the nav lights, then leave them on steady.' Then, as an afterthought, he added, 'Make damn sure you switch them off the instant I fire the guns!'

Over the kink in the river they commenced their third run. Johnson eased the Mossie down 100 feet hoping to improve the ability to see objects on the ground, and concentrated on holding the air speed and heading. He turned the ultraviolet cockpit instrument lighting a notch dimmer and eased forward on the hard dinghy pack that was numbing his buttocks after 3 hours. The airfield ahead remained in total darkness. A trickle of sweat itched its way down the pilot's back; the navigator's rapid breathing was picked up by his open mike.

'20 seconds to go,' said Gibbons tensely. A moment later Johnson saw the blurred outline of a tree on the airfield perimeter and realised that he had seen it on their second pass. The parked aircraft had to be just ahead! Without waiting to actually see his target he pushed the Mossie's nose down into a shallow dive and at the same moment saw the shadowy outline of the German aircraft. Rapidly he brought the central 'bead' of his reflector gunsight on to it and squeezed both triggers.

The cockpit floor vibrated under their feet from the thunderous bellow of the four 20 mm cannon, each spewing rounds at the rate of 600 a minute. Simultaneously the four .303 machine guns chattered their deadly hail. Streams of glowing tracers lashed forward from the Mosquito's nose and immediately a pattern of strikes from the mixture of ball, incendiary and explosive shells were seen to envelope the German aircraft. The stench of cordite fumes filled the Mossie's cockpit.

On the ground the suspicious anti-aircraft crews were tracking the mysterious intruder in their sights, and instantly the Mosquito fired they loosed a barrage at it. Yellow, white and red fiery streams venomously arced through the darkness, clawing to destroy the attacker. As they pulled from the dive, the Mosquito crew heard a loud bang. Their aircraft shuddered. They had been hit!

Johnson concentrated on controlling his aircraft and keeping as low as he dared without running into the hangars on the edge of the field.

The German flak continued to hose up at them from all sides, but he knew that they could not fire too low lest they strike their own buildings. The volume of incendiary bullets slashing the sky actually provided enough light to see the oncoming hangars well enough to pass over them with minimum clearance. Rapidly they swept away from the hostile area and the ground fire ceased. It as only then that Johnson glanced out toward the left wing-tip and exclaimed, 'My God, Jimmy, you forgot to turn the nav lights out!'

The Mosquito was vibrating badly. The rudder pedals were tramping back and forth so furiously that the pilot could not hold them, and he finally withdrew his feet from the battering. Slowing the aircraft reduced the severity of the vibrations somewhat, but did not stop them. Anxiously the navigator peered toward the tail of the Mosquito, but was unable to see the extent of the damage. Johnson set course to pass south of the heavy defences around Munich, then turned for England while watching the engine temperature gauges for any sign of overheating, and the fuel gauges for loss of fuel. At the reduced speed it would take over 3 hours to reach home base. Would the Mosquito hold together that long?

Knowing that they had thoroughly stirred up the enemy defences, they kept as low as they dared and maintained a watchful eye over their tail for German night-fighters. It was a long flight home. The official maximum endurance of this version of the Mosquito was 6¼ hours. They landed back at Hunsdon after 6 hours 15 minutes! The fuel gauges all read nearly zero.

Upon wearily clambering down from the

The air and ground crew of 'B-Beer', 88 Squadron, W/C I. J. Spencer's former aircraft, at Hartford Bridge. F/O Thompson, navigator (who after being shot down, escaped from France and spent six months in a Spanish jail); S/L Pushman RCAF; F/Sgt Mike Cleary DFM; and Sgt Clarke, undergunner. (Mike Cleary via Paul Lincoln)

The air and ground crew of 'N-Nuts' 'AVI RYMPERE AVI STIRCVS FACIRE' of 88 Squadron at Hartford Bridge in late 1944. Left to right: A. F. W. Valle-Jones; Mike Henry; W/C I. J. Spencer with 'Butch'; and F/O G. E. Ploughman. (Mike Henry via Roy Brookes)

cockpit, Johnson and Gibbons were able to see by the aid of their ground crew's flashlights the damage to their beloved Mosquito. The tailplane and elevators were sieved with shrapnel holes, there was a ragged 1-foot hole in the starboard tailplane, and the rudder was but a skeleton of ribs, but it had brought them home. As they trudged towards the operations room for debriefing by the Intelligence officer, they heard one of the ground crew remark, 'They sure build these Mosquitos tough!'

Also on 2 October, F/O R. Lelong of 605 Squadron took off from his forward base at St Dizier and over the Baltic claimed six enemy aircraft destroyed, plus one 'probable' and five 'damaged'. Lelong returned to base on one engine. Five days later, on 7 October, two Mosquitos of 605 Squadron destroyed ten enemy aircraft near Vienna and damaged six more.

The Mosquitos did not always have it their own way, of course, as the following incident late in September-early October, recalled by Oberfaehnrich Karl-Heinz Jeismann, testifies:

'Because of the Allied air superiority and the consequences from this situation, Hitler ordered on 26 June 1944 to build fighters and nothing but fighters. As a result I was posted to Crailsheim aerodrome for conversion to fighters in the Reichsverteidigung at the end of September or early October 1944, together with other pilots who until that time had only flown heavy aircraft (Ju52, He 111 and Fw 200). As part of our training programme we had to fly a night cross-country sortie (Crailsheim–Leuchtfeuer–Feichtwagen–Ausbach–Crailsheim). We took off in our Arado Ar96s at 10-minute intervals. As I came back to Crailsheim and had just touched down on the runway, I saw in the corner of my right eye a stream of clear tracer fire and immediately after in front of me I saw small yellow and red flames flickering on the runway. I taxied away from the runway, then the flare path was extinguished. With the aid of light signals from a pocket torch I was led to the dispersals.

In front of the air traffic control building I met a group of my comrades. They told me that I had been shot at by a night-fighter. We could still hear the sound of its engines, sometimes closer by, sometimes further away. We kept waiting for the arrival of my comrade who was returning to the airfield. He was a Fahnenjunker Feldwebel, and was my room-mate. Then the moment came when we heard him arriving, and on his final approach my comrade turned away one last time and made a new approach to the runway.

On the eastern boundary of Crailsheim aerodrome was a railway station, and from this direction he flew his final approach. We repeatedly saw his positional lights flashing on and off, but immediately afterwards several rows of tracer fire appeared from behind his aircraft. Also, in the same instant, we spotted a line of tracer coming up from the ground. Both aircraft were clearly on fire. Whereas my comrade turned away over our heads to the left and disappeared behind the buildings on the airfield, the other aircraft turned off to the right, and for quite some time we could see the burning spot reflected against the dark sky.

My comrade had made a desperate attempt to bale out, but his straps had been cut off by the tail unit of the Arado. Next day both Englishmen were delivered to us, one of them bandaged. One man was of slim build and of average height, the other was small and thick set. When one of my comrades offered them a cigarette, we had a discussion among our group if we should make such a gesture, as they had only the night before killed one of our friends.

We soon found out that the British airmen were the crew of a long-distance Mosquito night-fighter, who had flown all the way over France at great height into the southern German area. They had fallen victim to the 2 cm flak guns on a mobile railway truck, which purely by coincidence was positioned at the railway station that night. During the funeral ceremony of my fallen comrade I had ample time to think deeply about it: why he was dead and why I survived. On completion of my training at Crailsheim, I was posted to JG105 to fly Fw 190 fighters in the day-fighter defence of the Reich.'

The funeral of Karl-Heinz Jeismann's comrade in October 1944, killed during a Mosquito intruder attack on Crailsheim airfield. Jeismann is second from left. (Karl-Heinz Jeismann via Dr Theo Boiten)

During the daring low-level attack on the Gestapo HQ building at Aarhus University in Jutland, Denmark, on 31 October 1944, S/L F. H. Denton of 487 Squadron, whose aircraft is seen here, hit the roof of the building, losing his tail wheel and the port half of the tailplane. Denton nursed the Mosquito across the North Sea and managed to land safely. (via Derek Carter)

On 31 October 25 Mosquitos of 21, 464 and 487 Squadrons, 140 Wing, escorted by eight Mustang IIIs of 315 (Polish Squadron), 12 Group, made a daring low-level attack on the Gestapo HQ building at Aarhus, Denmark. The operation was led by G/C Peter Wykeham-Barnes, and AVM Basil Embry, AOC 2 Group, with his navigator Peter Clapham flew the operation in a Mosquito of 2 GSU. Embry wore no medal ribbons and

was known as 'W/C Smith'. The attack was carried out at such a low altitude that one Mosquito hit the roof of the building, losing its tail wheel and the port half of the tailplane, but it limped back across the North Sea and managed to land safely. The University and its incriminating records were destroyed. Among the dead was SS Obersturn Führer Lonechun, Head of the Security Services.

Chapter Ten

Swan Song
of the Panzers

'We are attacked all day and then the Mosquitos harass and bomb us at night.
We cannot "ein Schläfchen machen", or "eine Scheiesse machen"
– we are caught with our pants down!'

Complaint of German prisoners to F/L Eric Atkins DFC* KW*

By November 1944 Nos 107, 305 (Polish) and 613 Squadrons of 138 Wing finally arrived in France, to be based at Epinoy near Cambrai. 137 Wing, with the two Boston Squadrons, 88 and 342, 226 Squadron Mitchells and 107 Squadron Mosquitos, was now stationed at Vitry-en-Artois between Douai and Arras in northern France. On 21 November 136 (Mosquito) Wing was created within 2nd

Tactical Air Force by the arrival from Fighter Command of 418 and 605 Squadrons, which transferred to Hartford Bridge. 418 had scored its 100th victory in May 1944, and in June had flown anti-*Diver* patrols at night, before reverting in September to *Rangers* and abortive *Big Ben* patrols, the latter against V2 rockets. 139 Wing, comprising 98, 180 and 320 (Mitchell) Squadrons, was based at Brussels

Mosquito FB VIs of 613 Squadron at Cambrai-Epinoy in 1945. (Phillip Beck)

The move to the Continent in October–November 1944 enabled 2nd TAF to examine the results of its recent bombing operations in France and Belgium at close quarters. At the invitation of the Canadian 21st Army Group, Alan Lynn, W/C Flying, 139 Wing at Melsbroek near Brussels, takes time out to look over the mass grave of German Chief of Staff, General von Dawans, and his senior staff officers of a Panzer Division HQ, which was bombed on 10 June 1944 in an operation led by Lynn. John Bateman recalled that Lynn, 'an incredibly flamboyant, press-on type', if he could not locate the target on the first run, would inevitably make two or three more until he finally made it. He also had a habit of breaking away from the formation he was leading after bombing, and circle the target to watch the following aircraft on their bombing runs. (via John Bateman)

(Melsbroek). Mosquitos of 21, 464 and 487 Squadrons remained behind at Thorney Island, but in December 1944 the Australian and New Zealand squadrons both sent advance detachments to Rosières-en-Santerre, France, although 21 Squadron would not join them until February 1945.

On 17 November 'Dinty' Moore, now a F/L, should have flown to France to join 226 Squadron to begin his third tour.

'It may seem crazy, but I was terribly unsettled and I became determined to return to 2 Group to complete another tour. I believe the reasons for this were threefold: first of all, my second tour had been less than satisfying, then the loss of Peter and finally hearing the heavy bombers flying over us every night on their way to bomb targets in Germany.'

A Mitchell II of 226 Squadron in France in 1944. (Phillip Beck)

This famous photograph of a 21 Squadron Mosquito jacked up and firing into the butts, taken on 19 December 1944 by James Jarche of Illustrated, *was set up especially for the photographer by F/L Good, Armaments Officer at Thorney Island. Mosquitos of 464 and 487 Squadrons remained at Thorney Island until December 1944, while 21 Squadron did not join them on the Continent until February 1945. (via Les Bulmer)*

Van Strieland, a pilot in 320 (Dutch) Squadron, pictured in the cockpit of his Mitchell 'Blasting Bastard!' at Melsbroek in 1945. (Jan P. Kloos)

He had been delighted to learn that he was to fly as fighter controller on a Mitchell with S/L 'Jock' Campbell, whom he had known and greatly respected when he was on 88 Squadron. However, the weather closed in and it was not until the 19th that 'Dinty' Moore's Anson could fly to Vitry-en-Artois. They crossed at Orfordness, then on to Knocke, Ostend, Nieuport, Ypres and Armentieres, places over which at last they could fly without being shot at.

On landing, 'Dinty' met Jock Campbell and

his crew, but they had just been briefed to take part in an attack in Venlo in support of the Army, so there was little time for conversation, as 'Dinty' recalls:

'I waited until I saw them take off, thinking that I would have plenty to talk about with them when they got back. I then got on with the usual routine of settling into the Mess and finding out the location of the squadron office and so on. While I was doing this Jock was leading his formation in their approach to the target when his aircraft received a direct hit from an anti-aircraft shell and broke up. He and his crew were killed. On the return of the remainder of the squadron I found it difficult to believe the tragic news they brought with them. I suppose, human nature being what it is, that my main reaction would be to thank my lucky stars that bad weather had postponed my arrival.

Vitry-en-Artois had been a Luftwaffe base and was very cleverly camouflaged. It was situated on the main road between Douai and Arras, an industrial area over which many of the battles of the Great War of 1914–18 had been fought. There were many reminders of that horrific conflict, with many memorials to the dead, the most impressive being the enormous Canadian Memorial on Vimy Ridge, which was in our circuit when we were taking off or landing. The Officers' Mess was, for a short while, in hutted accommodation on the aerodrome, then we moved into a rather grand chateau in the little village of Corbehm nearby.

This building stood in its own grounds, surrounded by a dry moat, the most recent occupants having been Luftwaffe officers. The walls of the dining room were completely covered with murals depicting the Battle of Britain. The City of London was being subjected to a bombing raid, numerous German aircraft flying over with Spitfires going down in flames. We were told that some of the local people, who had supported the Germans, were not too keen on our presence, so we were instructed not to go out alone and always to carry a loaded revolver. By contrast, we received invitations and could not have been made more welcome.

This tour turned out to be completely different from my previous ones, for if the weather was fine it was a case of saying, "What time is take-off", and not, "Are we flying today?", as we had previously done. As I did not have a crew, being a Gunnery Leader, I was to fly as fighter controller with whichever pilot was leading a formation. We had no need of an escort. Operating at around 12,000 feet, generally in formations of 24 or 36 aircraft (flying in units of six aircraft), we had sufficient firepower to cope with any isolated fighter attacks. Our role was to act as a form of very long-range artillery in support of the Allied armies engaged in their battle with the Wehrmacht.

I did not have long to wait for my first operation, for two days after my arrival I was detailed to fly with S/L Betts AFC on an attack on troop concentrations at Randerath. There were 36 aircraft, 24 Bostons and 12 Mitchells, taking part, and once we were airborne it was an impressive sight to see six boxes of six aircraft all heading for the same target area. Every aircraft dropped their bombs, meeting little opposition from the enemy, and we were all back on the ground after a flight lasting 2 hours 25 minutes. I couldn't help thinking that if this is what operations were like, this was going to be a "piece of cake". Bombing German troops was so impersonal, one just couldn't visualise what mayhem we were causing on the ground, though as they were troops and not civilians, one felt that it was thoroughly justified.

Even though almost all our targets were on or immediately behind the German lines, it was impossible to see any sign of the land battle that was taking place. On many occasions we could see the vapour trails of the American Fortresses and Liberators on their way to and from targets in Germany some 20,000 feet above us. On one operation a German rocket, on its way to London, narrowly missed the aircraft in one of our formations as it sped upwards.

My next operation took place on 25 November when I was briefed to fly with F/O Parsons, our target being the marshalling yards at Mönchen-Gladbach, some distance behind the enemy lines. The operation called for maximum effort, involving 34 Mitchells and 12 Bostons, flying in the usual boxes of five or six aircraft. I chose to sit in the tail position where, though there were no guns fitted, I had an unimpeded view to direct the fire of all the gunners in our box in case of attack by enemy fighters.

Our force looked a pretty impressive sight. Approaching the target I could see the menacing black balls of heavy flak bursting in the sky as the Germans tried to find our height. I had been leaning forward to get a clear view when something made me sit up straight; at the same instance a piece of shrapnel burst through the perspex cover of my tail position, where my head had been, and my face was cut by fragments of perspex. At that moment the Mitchell flying as our No 3, piloted by P/O Sidney Moore, received a direct hit on the port engine, which burst into flames, the aircraft plunging to the ground below with the loss of all on board.

Despite this tragedy every one of our aircraft, ignoring the barrage, flew on and bombed the target, which was well clobbered. Apart from shooting one aircraft down, the Germans damaged six others, in addition to ours, which had 20 holes in the fuselage. On landing I went into de-briefing not appreciating that my face was smeared with blood. News reached the Officers' Mess before I did that Moore had "bought it", so it was assumed that it was me, not P/O Moore, who had been shot down, so my arrival caused something of a surprise.

Next day my pilot was a very popular and well-known member of 2 Group, S/L Lyle DFC*. We were briefed to bomb a bridge being used by the German Army at a place called Deventer. Our force on this occasion was 18 Mitchells and 18 Bostons, which would represent a total bomb load of 108,000 lb. Perhaps as a result of my last operation, I decided to control from the mid-upper turret, only to find that my view was restricted, so I never used it again. On our approach to the target the anti-aircraft barrage was very heavy, and despite our evasive action it was beginning to find our height.

It was then that the Mitchell flying as No 5 in our second box of six aircraft received a direct hit amidships, breaking in two and hurtling towards the ground below with the loss of all on board. The pilot, I learned later, was F/O Twining. Despite the unwelcome attentions of the anti-aircraft gunners, once again every remaining aircraft bombed the target. The result of our efforts cannot have been particularly successful, however, as this was a target we would visit several times, unless the Germans replaced the bridge after our call. The flight lasted 2 hours 50 minutes, which was rather longer than many in which we were involved.

I had only been with the squadron for seven days, yet during that time we had lost three Mitchells and their crews, so any notion I had that this tour was going to be a "piece of cake" had quickly been dispelled. I couldn't have blamed my colleagues if they had looked upon me as a "Jonah" – you know, someone who brings bad luck – although they never gave any such indication.

On the 29th I returned to Deventer flying with F/L Rimmell, occupying my tail position, as part of a force of 24 Bostons and 18 Mitchells. The anti-aircraft barrage was again heavy, though to our relief it was not concentrated on our formation. The following day, with the same pilot, we bombed Dunkirk, which was still occupied by the Germans, having been by-passed by the advancing Allied Armies. The town was completely surrounded, but the garrison refused to surrender and was a target we bombed without deriving any satisfaction. They were probably low on ammunition, for we found only a very light and inaccurate barrage.'

In 21 Squadron, meanwhile, Les Bulmer began the second half of his tour, flying with F/L Bert Willers.

'It was comparatively quiet compared with the first half. The pace had slowed down quite a lot because of poor weather conditions. Our first sortie took place on 18 November, and by now we were patrolling into Holland and Germany. We only managed three ops in November and just two in December.

On 4 December, as there was not much doing, we were ordered to keep our hand in on low flying, so we did a cross-country over France, which by this time was clear of Germans, apart from the Channel ports. We quite enjoyed ourselves, the French countryside being ideal for low-level flying, especially as we were no longer being shot at. Somewhere along the way we came across a large field that sloped up to a house standing on a ridge. This was just the place to practice a camera gun attack using the house as a target. We tore across the field, just about clipping the grass with our prop tips, then climbed to get over the house between the chimneys at either end of the building. As we did so there was a loud bang and a flash just in front of the windscreen. I thought we'd flown into some power cables that we hadn't seen, or an aerial stretched between the chimneys.

We climbed to about 500 feet and turned to see what damage we'd done to the house. There was nothing we could see, but several figures shot out of the house and gazed skywards. I don't know whether they were shaking their fists or not, but at that moment Bert said, "Oh Christ, look at that." Sticking out of the top surface of the port wing was a large chunk of very solid-looking cable. It was buried into the leading edge right up to the main spar and just outboard of the engine. The rest of the cable trailed back under the wing and was whipping up and down just clear of the tailplane.

F/L Bert Willers (left) and Les Bulmer of 21 Squadron supposedly going over the route while their Mosquito is warmed up behind in this staged photo taken by James Jarche. Les Bulmer recalled that he did not seem to appreciate that crews did not get into a Mosquito with the engines running, and he also had to borrow a pair of flying boots because, apparently, he did not look the part of an intrepid aviator without them! (via Les Bulmer)

We left the scene of the crime a bit sharpish and pondered, on the return journey, how we could explain the presence of some 35 feet of cable dangling from the port wing when we got back to Thorney Island. Bert reckoned that we might be able to creep into dispersal without anyone noticing, then have a quiet word with "Chiefy" Bishop to request a quick patch-up job, and no one would be any the wiser. But it was not to be.

As we slowed to a halt after landing, the control tower called us to ask if we knew that there was something trailing from our port wing. We had to admit to them that we did. Back in dispersal we discovered that the bottom panels of both engine nacelles were dented, and there was a chunk of wood missing from the nose just in front of the cockpit. We assumed that we had hit the wire fair and square and that the props had chopped it, flung one end over the nose causing the flash we saw, then throwing the whole lot into the port wing. I never discovered whether Bert Willers got a rocket for this episode, nor if the RAF ever got a bill from an irate French farmer for the unexpected removal of part of his property by a Mosquito. When 2 Group ordered low flying it was really low.'

By this stage of the war the Panzers and other German troops deployed in the invasion area and beyond were given no respite in the daylight raids by Mitchells and Bostons and the nightly visits by Mosquitos, all of 2nd TAF. F/L Eric Atkins DFC* KW* (Krzyz Walecznych, the Polish Cross of Valour), a Mosquito pilot in 305 (Polish) Squadron at this time, recalls:

'Prisoners captured complained, "We are attacked all day and then the Mosquitos harass and bomb us at night. We cannot 'ein Schläfchen machen' (take a nap) or 'eine Scheiesse machen' (have a crap) – we are caught with our pants down!' Nowhere was this more apparent than when we attacked the Panzer billets on the night of 6/7 December 1944 in the village of Wassenberg, just south of München-Gladbach, on the edge of the Ruhr itself. The attack on the billets would be my 78th operation, the 26th in my third tour. My navigator was F/L Jurek Majer, a Pole who spoke little English. There was talk that I would be stood down after this operation, and this made the raid even more significant. As all aircrew know, it can be a superstitious moment when you wonder whether you will "get the chop" on the last one.

However, there was no time to worry about the consequences to me of the operation – there was much to do! The Met officer warned us that although the weather was set fair for the night, snow was on the way. (December's weather was the worst of an already

Mosquitos of 605 (Polish) Squadron in flight. (via Philip Birtles)

F/L Eric Atkins DFC* KW* (centre) of 305 Squadron in 1945. (Eric Atkins collection)

something had gone wrong with our aircraft, the electrics and hydraulics were amiss, and I had to "belly-flop" at night at our new base at Epinoy, near Cambrai, France, a grass aerodrome on a slight hill. Without flaps we floated almost off the top of the hill before I forced it down. I hoped nothing like that would happen to us tonight!

Jurek said that we were approaching the German border and now we saw much more activity – searchlights and tracer fire. We were flying at about 3,000 feet.

"Look out for flares and a river," said Jurek. We had HE and incendiary loads, flares, cannons and machine guns. We were not the only ones attacking this target, and it should have been well lit up. However, we were among the first in. I came down much lower, soon picked up the Roer River and then saw the target. There were no flares at the time, but there was a glow and Jurek confirmed that it was Wassenberg. We could see the fires starting as we did our first run. In the light of the flares we dropped we came round again and bombed and strafed the target. All hell seemed to be let loose below and heavy flak was coming up just south of us. There was some rain about and I remember thinking that it might put the fires out!

We did another run strafing with cannon fire. "That's enough," said Jurek. "Save some for the others!"

bad three months. On some nights we operated when visibility at the base was less than 800 yards.) Our route to the target took us near Brussels. It was a very dark night, but the radar kept us on the track. There seemed to be a lot of activity about. I was probably more "finely tuned" than normal on this trip and thought I saw enemy aircraft on our beam, but Jurek just grunted and got on with his navigation. There was not normally a lot of conversation in our Mosquito – we both had our jobs to do and we reserved speech for when action was needed – no idle chatter!

My thoughts drifted to three operations ago, 29 November, when we had attacked Hamm, in the east Ruhr area. The weather had been appalling, and the flak over the target was heavy. After bombing,

A black shape zoomed up and passed our nose. "What the hell's that?" I cried, then realised that it was probably another Mosquito going in to attack.

We had overstayed our welcome. Flying straight and level in the darkness, heading for base, we checked our instruments, oil pressure and engine temperatures. I had flung the Mossie around rather a lot, and sometimes engines overheat, then you have to shut one down. However, everything seemed all right and Jurek grunted the course back to base. It had been a very successful operation. The Panzers had been caught with their "pants down"!

After we had landed and been de-briefed, the station commander told me that it had been my last operation. They were standing me down on my 78th – "enough was enough"! I was very disappointed, however, to lose Jurek – he had to carry on with another pilot to finish his second tour.'

'Dinty' Moore's first four operations for December had been intended to be attacks on German troop concentrations in support of the Army, but on each occasion the target area was covered with cloud and as none of the aircraft were fitted with *Gee H* they were unable to bomb.

'With the approach of Christmas I was pleasantly surprised to be given a 14-day pass. On 22 December I was flown over to Hartford Bridge in a Mitchell, where I simply walked off the aerodrome on the main London to Southampton road and hitched a lift into London. There were no Customs & Excise officers or passport controls to trouble me. I spent a very pleasant Christmas in Norwich with my wife Norma, and an equally good New Year in Hawes on a leave that neither of us had expected.'

On Christmas Eve 1944 18 German aircraft were shot down, five of them by four Mosquito crews of 100 Group. The rest were shot down by Mosquitos of 2nd TAF, which dispatched 139 Mosquitos on that night to targets in south-west Germany. 613 Squadron dispatched some 30 Mosquitos; LR374, crewed by W/O Baird, pilot, and Sgt Whateley-Knight, navigator, failed to return from a sortie to harass German movement behind the enemy thrust in the Ardennes. Also, 37 Mosquitos of 2nd TAF patrolled the areas of Aachen, Arnhem and the Dutch Frisian Islands, and flew close support sorties over the front

lines. None of these Mosquitos were lost, and they destroyed 50 vehicles and six trains. 410 RCAF Squadron dispatched nine Mosquitos on front-line patrols between 1750 hours on Christmas Eve and 0530 hours on Christmas Day, and three crews claimed two Ju 87s and a Ju 88 destroyed.

The Luftwaffe night-fighters, deprived of fuel and experienced pilots, were none the less far from finished, and in January 1945 the Luftwaffe attempted one last major air offensive against the Allied air forces on the Continent. Since 20 December 1944 many Jagdgeschwader had been transferred to airfields in the west for Operation *Bodenplatte*. About 850 fighters took off at 0745 hours on Sunday morning, 1 January, and attacked 27 airfields in northern France, Belgium and southern Holland. The 4-hour operation succeeded in destroying about 100 Allied aircraft, but it cost the Luftwaffe 300 aircraft, most of which were shot down by Allied anti-aircraft guns.

'Dinty' Moore, returning from Christmas and New Year leave, recalls:

'All good things come to an end, so on 9 January I presented myself at the Group Support Unit, which had moved from Swanton Morley to Fersfield, near the market town of Diss in Norfolk. I was flown back to the squadron in a Boston, carrying with me not only my luggage but also an extremely painful carbuncle on the back of my neck. I was admitted to the station sick quarters for a few days, but missed no flying due to weather, which grounded all the aircraft. My incarceration coincided with the historic Battle of the Bulge when the Germans, in a desperate attack, broke out though the Allied lines in the Ardennes.

My next three operations were with F/O Conchie, flying as a beam gunner, on each occasion 36 aircraft from our wing being involved. On the 21st the target was a wood at Wassenberg, in which units of the German Army were concealed. The enemy threw up a heavy barrage although the gunners had an off day, for it was inaccurate. The following day our target was the same, as was the barrage, though the gunners this time, having had some practice, punished the box flying behind us, but without shooting any of them down.'

Sgt Colin Walsh, a Liverpudlian, and a navigator in 487 Squadron, and his pilot, F/O John

Patterson, flew their first operation, a 3-hour round trip from Thorney Island to Arsbeck, on 21 January 1945. Walsh had trained at Greenwood, Nova Scotia, and training losses had been high, many of the Canadian-built Mosquitos ending up in the Bay of Fundis. However, the 21-year-old 'Scouser' was 'desperately keen' to fly the 'fast weapon'. Losses climaxed near the end of his training and he had been one of only four to volunteer for Mosquitos. Leeds-born 'Pat' Patterson had been an instructor in Canada, where he had met and married a delightful Canadian girl. Both men had teamed up at High Ercall.

'Ginger' Walsh recalls:

'North-west Germany was divided into three, one for each Mossie wing, then into three again, one for each squadron. 2nd TAF Spitfires and Mustangs, which attacked the German Army on the ground during the day, returned with details of troop concentrations and targets, which we then bombed by night. Our main target was anything that moved, especially trains and transport, but you were bloody lucky to find a moving target at night! Trains were a high priority, but they were blacked out and we were lucky to see them.

On the Arsbeck op we flew at about 1,000 feet

Sgt Colin 'Ginger' Walsh (left) and F/O John Patterson of 487 RNZAF Squadron, 140 Wing, pictured at Rosières-en-Santerre, who flew their first operation on 23 January 1945 from Thorney Island. (Colin Walsh)

through low cloud to the target. I navigated all the way using maps "illuminated" by a tiny pin-prick of

Mosquito NF XIII MM466 of 409 RCAF Squadron at a bombed-out dispersal at Lille-Vendeville (B.51), France, on 31 January 1945. (RCAF via Philip Birtles)

light from my torch filled with three layers of paper in the bottom to retain our night vision and prevent us from being seen from the air or the ground. (*Gee* could not be used too far into Germany before it got interfered with, and "railings" confused the two-three "spikes". I had to take the best signal, the best "cut".) Moonlight was a bastard. You could count the rivets. Over Germany on moonlit nights I felt that I had no clothes on. Our mates in the squadron had been to Arsbeck earlier and had started fires. We would bomb on the *Gee*-set co-ordinates. I selected the four bombs, fused them and "Pat" pressed the "tit" on his spectacle control column.

On the way home "Pat" saw a train for what was the only time. The first I knew was that the Mosquito was suddenly standing on one wing! We had been told that if we saw a train we were to go straight in – no messing! "Pat" circled (he was following his instincts) for the best position, then adopted a shallow dive and went in, all four .303 and four cannons blazing. By now I was "climbing out of the roof". The sky filled with 40 mm flak. I soon learned that German ack-ack gunners were mustard! In the cockpit cordite fumes and dust filled the air. "Pat" broke off immediately and on my advice flew to the west! On reflection it had done us good. It was thought-provoking.

It was a terrible night. Ron Batch, a fellow navigator I'd been with at navigational school and had known for 18 months, who had already flown two ops, failed to return. He and his pilot had "got the chop". Forty-eight hours later Ron's father, a Metropolitan Police Inspector, came to see me. He wanted to know what area of Germany Ron had been flying over and any other details; Ron was his only child. I could tell him nothing. It really carved me up.

We got shot up ourselves one night. We got back and landed and the props had barely stopped when our two faithful ground crew opened the door (we never bothered with the ladder). They asked if we'd hit anything. They were always so thrilled, so keen, that we should be successful. They asked, "Were we fired at?"

I said, "Yes, I think it was the British Army!"

"Were we hit?"

I said, "No."

Then they pointed to a hole beneath the wing! I looked and was thrilled. It was strangely exciting! However, next day they could see that the hole had been caused by oil dripping from the guns – our Mossie was a clapped-out machine and had flown many ops.'

On 29 January Les Bulmer and his pilot, Bert Willers, were one of the crews in 21 Squadron who flew from Thorney Island to Fersfield, Suffolk, for a secret briefing on what they discovered was to be an attack on the Gestapo HQ in Copenhagen to destroy their records of the Danish Resistance movement. Les Bulmer recalls:

'We knew that some Resistance members were held prisoner in the building and would probably die in the attack, but the Danes feared that if the records were not destroyed the whole Danish Resistance network would be at risk. We were presented with the usual model of the target area, together with photographs of the building and the approach path to be used in the attack. Some of the photographs had been taken by the Danes themselves and smuggled out. A Danish naval officer was also present. He had been brought out of Denmark to give us up-to-date information and had left his wife and family behind in Copenhagen.

The next morning we arrived at the briefing room for final instructions and found that the weather had deteriorated and was unsuitable for low flying over the sea, so the operation was postponed for 24 hours. That evening some crews went into Norwich for a few jars and finished up in the local theatre where "Jane" of *Daily Mirror* fame was performing.

On 31 January the raid was again postponed for a further 24 hours, and next morning, 1 February, Embry announced that he could not afford to have his aircraft hanging around doing nothing for any longer. The operation would have take place at a later date and we were to return to Thorney Island that day. He warned us not to breathe a word to anyone, and that when the raid did take place all the crews present would be on it. He also added that he had arranged for extra copies of the *Daily Mirror* to be delivered to the Mess at Thorney Island! On 2 February 'Daddy' Dale and Hackett, his navigator, went missing on a night patrol. Four days later, on 6 February, the squadron transferred to Rosières-en-Santerre and shortly afterwards W/C V. R. Oates took over command (he later failed to return from a sortie on 12 March).'

On 2 February 'Dinty' Moore attended a briefing with S/L Kyle.

'We found that our target was not, as was our usual practice, in immediate support of the Army, but an oil target, at Emmerich. We crossed the battle front and found the target, in spite of the usual flak. The aircraft in the second box scored direct hits on the target, which made quite an impressive sight even from our height. I flew a further seven operations during February, when having one of the leading aircraft fitted with *Gee H* proved to be invaluable. This electronic marvel was being used by the Lancasters of the Bomber Command Pathfinder Force. In our case, where cloud covered the target, the aircraft fitted with this equipment took over the lead, the observer transmitting to the rest of the formation, who dropped their bombs on his instructions. The recipients of our bombs were all German troop concentrations, the 8th at Kallenberg, the 9th at Rheinberg, the 10th at Xanton and the 11th at Sonsbeck. The German anti-aircraft gunners did their best, though their efforts were not helped by the presence of the cloud, with the result that they were not accurate. The next operation, on the 14th, was identical, other than the target being at Udem, which was notable in that our progress was not disturbed by any anti-aircraft fire at all.

I flew my last two operations on the same day, 14 February, first taking off at 0830 hours with S/L Lyle, and at 1430 hours with S/L Edmondes. The morning attack was on German troop reinforcements at Udem, and in the afternoon on Straaelen; we found no cloud on either occasion other than the threatening little black clouds of heavy flak that came up as an impressive barrage. All of these eight operations flown during February, ending on the 14th, lasted between 2 and 2½ hours without any damage to the aircraft in which I was flying.

Thus, my operational career came to an end, leaving me with the satisfaction of making my final contribution, unlike the end of my second tour with Johnny Reeve. I had taken part in 23 missions on this tour, our aircraft being hit on three occasions, nearly being decapitated in one of them, yet had survived. The role of the wireless operators and air gunners on the heavy bombers of Bomber Command was still essential, but with the sophisticated radio equipment fitted in our aircraft and the Allied air forces having complete control of the skies over the battle front, our role in medium bombers was becoming almost unnecessary. We had been an essential part of the crew, using our skill as wireless operators to maintain a link with our base and to obtain bearings and fixes for the observer. Similarly, we had been our only real defence against attacks by enemy fighters. I felt, therefore, no sense of guilt when I was told that it was time to quit, being in a position to claim to have flown

on operations in every year of the war, except 1939, with a total of 92 missions spread over, in effect four operational tours. I had been extremely fortunate to survive, my only regret being that the same degree of luck had not been extended to Peter, so we could have been together to fulfil our plans after the war.'

On 6 February 1945 21, 464 and 487 Squadrons of 140 Wing left southern England and moved to Amiens and Rosières-en-Santerre. Les Bulmer in 21 Squadron recalls:

'Personnel were scattered around the airfield in villages. The admin types naturally picked the best chateau for themselves. 21 Squadron aircrew were billeted in a chateau in Warvillers. It served as the Mess, and sleeping quarters were in an orchard at the rear. These were wooden huts thoughtfully provided by the Germans. There was even a small dance hall suitably decorated with Luftwaffe murals. It wasn't the Ritz, but at least it was better than the tents we'd had at Gravesend and Thorney Island, and which we were led to believe we would have to use in France. Actually, we did cheat a little at Thorney Island. As winter developed, so came the gales, and one night one of the senior officers lost his tent. Since there was a large empty Mess on the other side of the airfield it seemed only logical to fill it. So we did, still sleeping on our camp beds so that we could continue to qualify for the "hard living" allowance.'

The arrival of the Mosquito squadrons at Amiens and Rosières-en-Santerre coincided with the first anniversary of the Amiens raid by 140 Wing Mosquitos on 18 February 1944, when the walls of *Jericho* had come tumbling down. Pickard's widow was flown out specially from England to visit her husband's grave and for the mass in Amiens Cathedral. "Ginger" Walsh was among the personnel who attended, and afterwards he visited the wall, now patched, through which the French Resistance had escaped.

'The bulk of our squadron was billeted in Amiens. At first I slept at Meharicourt, near the bomb dump, in what had been the Luftwaffe hospital site at the airfield. Wehrmacht and Luftwaffe personnel, too badly wounded to be evacuated, were still there. Later, the local village butcher adopted me and a friend, Bob Belcher, and we were billeted at his elderly mother's small chateau. Near our base was a huge First World

War cemetery filled with thousands of white crosses. We buried F/O Joe Coe and his fellow New Zealander S/L pilot there after they crashed on take-off one day, and their bombs and fuel load exploded. Joe had already lost his fingers and been badly burned in a Wellington crash earlier in the war. At their funeral a group of French schoolchildren sang "God Save the King".'

One of the crews in 305 Squadron at Epinoy at this time was pilot F/L Reg Everson, an ex-railway policeman, and his navigator F/L Tony Rudd, a university graduate; they had crewed up at 2 Group GSU at Swanton Morley in September 1944. Everson recalls:

'At Epinoy our enthusiasm was somewhat dampened when we found the airfield covered with some 6 feet of snow, and we spent most of the daylight hours using shovels to help clear the runways. Eventually flying was possible, taking off along runways with snow piled high on either side. It did, however, concentrate the mind and made the pilots even more careful than ever to avoid a swing on take-off.

Night patrols were carried out most nights, incurring a number of casualties, attacking enemy road and rail transport when possible, and bombing rail junctions on *Gee* when bad weather prevented visual sightings. One night we returned from patrol to find 10/10 cloud at 200 feet over the base. As our *Gee* set had gone "on the blink" I declined the offer of a diversion to Brussels (I learned better later), and received permission to land at base. This proved somewhat "hairy", but landing was completed without damage. No operations were carried out for the next few nights, diverted aircraft having to return to base, and the weather remained such that even the birds were walking.

Normal service was resumed until 13 February, when the squadron had a break from operations to practise for a daylight formation operation – Operation *Clarion*. As it was to be a 12-aircraft formation some crews (including us) were not involved. However, on the day of the operation, 22 February, it was decided to increase it to maximum effort, and all crews and serviceable aircraft were to be involved. Without the benefit of practice we had an unenviable position, 18th in an 18-plane formation.'

305 Squadron was led by W/C S. Grodzicki DFC, and S/L P. Hanburg led the British Flight. For half an hour the Mosquitos of 305 Squadron

320 Squadron personnel clear snow off the wings and fuselage of a Mitchell at Melsbroek, Brussels, on 8 January 1945. (via Jan P. Kloos)

wreaked havoc in the Bremen–Hamburg–Kiel region. The German ground defences were strong. Ten aircraft suffered damage and one with a British crew was lost; the pilot was killed and the navigator taken prisoner.

Clarion was intended to be the 'coup de grace' for the German transport system. It started at 1300 hours, and in total 9,000 Allied aircraft took part in attacking German communications, railways stations, crossroads, bridges, ships and barges on canals and rivers, railway trucks and engines, stores and other targets. 2 Group put up every available aircraft, flying 215 sorties, 176 from the Continent and the remainder by 136 Wing in England. It was to be the last time that the Mosquitos operated in daylight in such numbers.

Les Bulmer of 21 Squadron recalls:

'We fielded 16 aircraft, eight from each flight. The squadron was allocated an area between Bremen and Hannover in which any form of transport was to be attacked. This area was sub-divided between "A" and "B" Flights and these two areas, in turn, were divided again so that groups of four aircraft each had their own particular patch to cover. As by now we were one of the more experienced crews on the squadron, we were to lead four aircraft to the farthest areas, just to the north of Hannover.

The whole squadron took off at 1130 and formed up in two sections of eight, "A" Flight leading. We flew north-east to the Zuider Zee, then turned east. Over the Dummer Zee "A" Flight left us to fly north-east to their area. "B" Flight continued east and shortly afterwards four aircraft turned away northwards, leaving us and our brood of three to carry on eastwards to our patch, which covered the area bounded by Nienburg, Schwarmstedt, Hannover and Wünsdorf.

Over Schwarmstedt we found two engines and a freight train in the station, so we dived on them with cannons and bombs, followed by our No 2, P/O Bolton. The other two aircraft left us to find a train of their own to play with. We got cannon strikes on the engines and Bolton reported large clouds of steam as we pulled away. We continued around our area but saw nothing worth attacking, so set off westwards for home. Just south of the Dummer Zee we found another train at Lemforde, and turned to attack it, but they'd already seen us and sent up a hail of 20 mm flak, so we decided to give it a miss. Soon afterwards, a single-engined aircraft appeared heading in the opposite direction and above us. He apparently didn't see us and we didn't stop to identify.'

Reg Everson and Tony Rudd, meanwhile, also braved flak. Reg Everson recalls:

'We flew in close formation at 4,000 feet until we crossed the enemy lines, when we encountered some light flak bursting at that height. We took evasive action and rejoined the formation as soon as we were clear of danger. When we arrived at the area Stade, River Elbe, we broke into "pairs". I was No 2 to W/O Smith. Our main targets were barges and shipping, secondary targets being warehouses, trains and road transport. During our patrol we attacked railway trucks. Considerable damage was done by the 18 aircraft, and eight of them were damaged by ground fire.

We then set course for base, formating on W/O Smith at low level. Shortly after leaving the patrol area we passed over a machine gun post and Smith's aircraft was hit and caught fire; we saw it make a crash-landing. Not being sure of our exact position, and as we had used up all our machine gun ammunition and cannon shells, I climbed to a safer height of 4,000 feet, at which we could get an accurate Gee fix.

We soon found out where we were! The guns of Bremerhaven opened up and the air was filled with black puffs of exploding shells. A sharp diving turn to

port down to nought feet followed, for a re-assessment of the situation. Bremen was to our south, so a course was set for Zwoller on the River Yssel, which was the "Bomb Line" for the day. Once we felt safer from immediate danger we made a tentative climb to 4,000 feet to enable us to use Gee to keep away from further "hot spots". Shortly after reaching this height an American Mustang formated on our starboard wing. A cigar-chewing pilot waved a friendly greeting before peeling off to go about his own business. As we approached Zwoller I opened the throttles to maximum boost, put the nose down to get maximum speed, and crossed the River Yssel as quickly as possible. The rest of the trip was uneventful.'

Les Bulmer, returning to base, noticed that all the way back to the Zuider Zee P/O Bolton was staying well back behind them.

'We couldn't figure out why he didn't stay close. (At the de-briefing he explained that we were being shot at at several points on the way out and he didn't really want to get involved. Fortunately for our peace of mind, Bert and I were totally unaware of this.) Just short of the Zuider Zee we spotted two trucks on the road north of Elspeet. We were almost over the top of them before we noticed them and did an imitation of a Stuka, with an almost vertical dive, to give them a blast of cannon. Several characters left them a bit sharpish. I only hope that they were Germans and not Dutch. From there we had an uneventful trip back to base, where we landed at 1450.

21 Squadron was one of the lucky ones that day. We lost only one aircraft, Fielding-Johnson and Harbord; 464 lost two and 487 took a hammering and lost five. I believe that this was principally because they chose to take the long route around the coast and got caught by flak and fighters as a result. 2 Group lost a total of 21 Mosquitos on Clarion, with 40 damaged. I think it taught the "powers that be" a salutary lesson that the Mosquito was not, after all, invulnerable.

Thankfully, we returned to night patrols and did our 23rd and last op together on 10 March. I had been on the squadron for 13 months and had completed 75 ops. After acting as "officers under instruction" at a court-martial in Lille, we returned to the squadron to find that we were posted to No 1 Ferry Unit at Pershore and that Peter Kleboe had arrived to take over the squadron, W/C V. R. Oats having failed to return from an op on 12 March.

We left 21 Squadron on 18 March. As we climbed

aboard the Anson to take us back to the UK the adjutant came out to see us off and whispered that the Shellhaus raid was on again and was due in the next few days. My feelings were mixed when I heard this. I'd missed out on all the much-vaunted 2 Group pin-point raids except the attack on the barracks in Nijmegen at the beginning of *Market Garden*, and that had ended in a complete fiasco. On the other hand, I would probably be pushing my luck to do just one more op. It was with sadness that I heard of Peter Kleboe's death three days later. I'd only known him for a few days but I liked him and reckoned he would be good for the squadron. With three COs lost in just over six weeks, 21 Squadron was going through a bad patch. But such is war.'

Reg Everson in 305 Squadron, meanwhile, still had a tour to finish:

'After all the excitement of *Clarion*, night operations resumed and on 5 March, on return from patrol, we found the base covered with 10/10 cloud. This time we took the offered diversion to Brussels, a wise move; owing to the adverse weather conditions we had to stay in Brussels, enjoying an enforced 48-hour "leave". By this time our patrol areas were moving further into Germany, making a longer trip there and back, which cut down the time we could spend in the patrol areas, due to fuel capacity. On these operations we used "drop tanks" and carried flares in the bomb bay instead of bombs. On sighting anything suspicious we would climb to 4,000 feet, drop a flare and circle below it to give Tony a chance to inspect the ground more thoroughly. We then attacked using machine guns and cannon.

On 8 April, for operation No 436 (the squadron's, not mine), 12 aircraft were briefed to patrol and attack enemy movements on railways and roads in the Leipzig–Berlin–Magdeburg–Braunsweig region. My aircraft was u/s so I borrowed Duke Earle's. The

On 21 March 1945 20 Mosquito FB VIs of 140 Wing, led by G/C Bob Bateson with navigator S/L Ted Sismore and escorted by 31 Mustang IIIs, attacked the Shellhaus Gestapo HQ building in Copenhagen, where 26 resistance and political prisoners were held captive on the sixth floor. This rear-facing F.24 camera shot from YH-H HR162 of 21 Squadron, flown by F/L Mac Hetherington RCAF, shows the Shellhaus in the lower right-hand corner. (via Derek Carter)

F/O Reginald Hall (left) and W/C Peter Kleboe, 21 Squadron CO, pictured at Fersfield just before take-off on 21 March. Kleboe hit a 130-foot-high floodlight pylon and crashed near the Jeanne d'Arc School; he and his navigator died instantly. One Mosquito subsequently bombed the school in error; 86 of the 482 children and 16 adults were killed, with 102 wounded. Several others died around the target. (via Derek Carter)

This second rear-facing F.24 camera shot from YH-H HR162 shows DZ414 'O-Orange', one of two Film Photographic Unit Mosquitos used on the Shellhaus raid and flown by F/L K. L. Greenwood, clearing the rooftops near the Botanical Gardens. Operation 'Carthage' freed 18 prisoners, the remainder being killed in the building. Four Mosquitos and two Mustangs were lost for the loss of nine aircrew. The Gestapo records were destroyed and 26 Nazis and 30 Danish collaborators killed. (via Derek Carter)

weather was cloudless, visibility good. All aircraft completed sorties except 'U', which returned with a defect. We completed the patrol on the Berlin–Magdeburg road and made an attack under flares on enemy transport. Lights on the transport were extinguished and movement stopped, but the flares went out so we could not assess fully the extent of the damage.

On the return flight, while flying at 4,000 feet indicated at about 0200, we were attacked by a night-fighter. He fired a long burst of machine gun fire and I immediately took violent evasive action. However, the port engine caught fire. Tony operated the fire extinguisher and I feathered the engine. A further burst of machine gun fire and the starboard engine caught fire. I throttled back and operated the fire extinguisher, but the fire did not go out so I ordered Tony to abandon the aircraft. He clipped on his parachute, jettisoned the door and successfully jumped clear. During this manoeuvre the aircraft was losing height rapidly. I struggled out of the seat, at the same time trying to keep the aircraft on an even keel. With some difficulty I reached the doorway and dived head first through the opening.'

Reg Everson was captured and taken for interrogation later, at Gestapo Headquarters in Gummerbach, where his interrogator, a former insurance agent in the Purley area before the war, questioned him at length before having him sent to Stalag VIG, a PoW camp near Olpe. After a short stay the prisoners were marched under armed guard to another camp, at Enbach. During the forced march the prisoners were quite often attacked by American fighter-bombers, who, thinking they were German troop columns, opened fire, but fortunately there were no casualties among the prisoners. Finally, on 12 April at 1400 hours, the camp was liberated by the 78th US Infantry Division. Reg was reunited with Tony Rudd and later they discovered that the aircraft that had shot them down on 8 April had been a P-61 Black Widow whose pilot had claimed a Ju 88 destroyed!' (Black Widows of the 422nd NFS were by this time based at Strassfeldt, Germany, and P-61s of the 425th NFS were stationed at Etain, France.)

When on 21 April 'Ginger' Walsh and 'Pat' Patterson in 487 Squadron in France flew an op to Emden, everything that could go wrong, went wrong. Walsh remembers the event:

'We took off and landed at Melsbroek first before going to the Rhine. We had a funnel only about 2 miles wide. A Mossie that had aborted flew back past us at a closing speed of more than 600 mph and narrowly missed us! Crossing the Rhine we almost hit a barrage balloon that our boys were flying from a barge. We ended up at 1,000–1,500 feet in the middle of a German airfield. I compressed myself into a small space but nothing happened. We turned west and came back towards Hamburg. Finally, we dropped our bombs on a German town. "Pat" threw the aircraft around but nothing happened. Back at Amiens our NZ S/L who was acting CO berated "Pat" for bringing his ammo back.

"Pat" must have taken it to heart because four days later, on 25 April, when we were coming back from Emden, he lowered the nose and began firing. I told him three times that we were nearing our lines! His target could have been a haystack or it could have been Hitler. "Pat" continued firing off our ammo. We got light flak; the tracer was utterly fascinating and missed us, but I had to do something. I reached up and

F/L Johnny Evans and F/O Ifor Jenkins of 487 RNZAF Squadron who were lost on 25 April during an operation to Emden. Evans had lost two pilot brothers killed in the war. (Colin 'Ginger' Walsh)

VE Day, 8 May 1945. Phillip Beck (on the nose of Mosquito FB VI 'U') and fellow ground crew of 613 Squadron at Epinoy celebrate. (Phillip Beck)

fired off the red and yellow colours of the day from the Verey Pistol mounted in the roof of the cockpit. It did the trick! The cockpit filled with cordite and there was a big flash.

"Pat" said, "What the . . . was that?"

I giggled and told him that I'd fired the Verey Pistol. You never gave away the colours of the day, but it was of no consequence to me! The firing stopped. I had visions of a German down below looking at his flimsy [his 'colours of the day', which could be easily destroyed when no longer needed].

It was on this operation that F/L Johnny Evans and his navigator, F/O Ifor Jenkins, were lost. Johnny had lost two pilot brothers killed in the war. I'd spent time in Montreal with Ifor. They put out a Mayday call: "I'm on fire and losing height!" They'd got him.

Another voice said, "You'll be all right". Evans replied caustically, "It's all right for you." That was it – they were dead.'

During April the retreat by the Wehrmacht had left medium bombers far to the rear of the battle front, so at the end of the month 138 Wing advanced to Achmer. Right up until the German surrender, Mosquitos, Mitchells and Bostons of 2 Group continued operations against rail and road targets. On the night of 2 May, for instance, 42 aircraft attacked troop transports with 500 lb bombs, flares and cannon and machine gun fire, leaving nine trains burning furiously. At 0800 hours on 8 May the cease-fire came into effect and VE Day was declared.

Index